A PRIEST'S TALE:

AUTOBIOGRAPHY OF A GAY PRIEST

The Rev. Father Donald A. Dodman

Neil:
All good wishes,

Don

✠

Copyright © 2008 by Fr. Donald Andrew Dodman
All rights reserved.
For information visit:
www.donalddodman.com

Manufactured by Creatspace.com

ISBN 978-0-9810750-0-6

Dedicated to the Memory of my dear friend,
BARRIE FRYETT,
who taught me that gay folk can live with dignity,
integrity and nobility.
'Quiescat in Pace'.

Acknowledgments:

*Devan Alexander Burnett, the love of my life,
for his enthusiastic encouragement and editing.*

*Bruce, for his patience, love and support during some
extremely trying times.*

Kim O'Leary, for encouraging me to write this chronicle.

*René Marcoux, mon cher ami, pour son aide avec les
textes français.*

My Family, for their acceptance, love and understanding.

*Many thanks to those who read the manuscript and
offered encouragement and sage advice:*

*Gail Kent, Dr. John Lancaster, Miriam Lancaster,
Teilhard Paradela, Daniel Wood, and
James W. Wright.*

·

"It is through the flesh that salvation comes. And yet so much in Christian spirituality and Christian life is flesh-denying, flesh-despising, flesh-devaluing. It is head-centered, ponderous, life-extinguishing, devoid of passion..."

—Father Kenneth Leech, *"The True God"*—

Preface

The initial promptings to write about my life came from a friend who on a number of occasions urged me to keep a record of some of the amusing tales and incidents that seemed to characterize my personality and perception of the world. I finally began the process by jotting down notes as ideas occurred to me; whether humorous incidents or revealing anecdotes and ideas with the intention that I might eventually flesh them out. At first I had no inkling that these incidents would ever evolve into a book with a rationale and purpose even though I instinctively arranged them in chronological order. Initially, the collecting of reminiscences served to be a pleasant diversion in my retirement and was a gratifying exercise in its own right.

As the stories began to accumulate on my computer I was surprised to discover that if I persisted with it there would eventually be a substantial amount of material. The notion of fashioning these into a memoir began to emerge somewhere at the back of my mind, because as things stood, all I had was an assortment of isolated incidents—tiny snapshots which had little connection one to another. It became apparent to me at some point that if these recollections were going to be readable or in any way useful, I must fashion some sort of framework upon which to suspended them.

In the beginning I was recording only incidents that occurred in the course of my work as a priest or which were related to my hobbies and personal interests. They were the kind of stories that I would feel comfortable sharing with almost anyone. The time came, however, when it occurred to me that if I were actually to attempt to write a memoir I would have to take the risk and be willing to reveal the whole of my life's story. Ultimately, I knew it would mean that I would not be able to avoid reference to my sexuality. To omit that facet of my life would be to deny a significant component and at the same time would tend to eliminate a vast number of the more amusing episodes.

In contemplating the dynamics of sexuality and faith I realized I inhabited a somewhat unique space; especially in these polarized days. Throughout my life I have wrestled and agonized with the alleged conflict between the realms of the spirit and the flesh. This tension, while not the dominant theme in the incidents I record, seemed to be an appropriate frame on which to stretch the canvas of my memoir. Who better to probe the entangled elements of the carnal and the spiritual but a gay priest? Through the events of my life I will attempt to argue that these two ostensibly contradictory concepts—*the flesh and the spirit*—are in reality complementary to one another and, in fact, balance the scales on the human condition.

My purpose in this memoir is to set out life as I have lived it replete with the joys, complications, and contradictions; a life I continue to find fascinating and stimulating. My intention in the following pages is to give flesh to some of the questions we all face in living spiritually, accepting that we are made in the image of God, and in embracing all that is good in the existential world. I confidently believe that the spirit and the flesh are inextricably intertwined—that this is God's intention and that it is undeniably good.

I pray that my experience might prove helpful to anyone who might feel alone in wrestling with the issue of sexuality and how it relates to faith.

One

When I look back I find myself amazed at what an early age I experienced my first sexual stirrings. Perhaps I was unusual in this respect, I cannot say; but such an early sexual awareness is perhaps more common than I would have imagined. From about age four my mother and I would often go for lunch at the home of one of her school girlfriends. The younger brother of my mother's friend lived in an attic room of their rambling family home. I never actually met 'Uncle Alex' but did hear a lot of wonderful things about him during the lunch conversations. He sounded to me like an intriguing and thoughtful young man. 'Twas a pity he was always off at work when we visited. I assumed he must be in his late teens or early twenties and in my imagination I pictured him as a handsome fellow with sandy hair and blue eyes. I recall that my mental picture of what he might be like had a decidedly sexual implication for me. As Mother and her friend prepared lunch and chatted in the kitchen, I was left to my own devices to wander off throughout the house. Invariably, I would explore the staircase that led to the attic where Uncle Alex lived. In the stairway I discovered a collection of his clothing hanging on pegs. I never dared to go very far up the stairs or to try to enter Uncle Alex's room but was content to sit there amongst his coats and jackets savouring his scent. I was entirely conscious I was experiencing something exciting and erotic—something for which, had I been discovered, I would surely have been chastised. His rubber raincoat did not in itself arouse these feelings in me; rather it was the fantasy of the mysterious man to whom it belonged. The sensation of being close to him simply by being near his possessions—things that held his essence—absorbed me. Fortunately, no one ever stumbled upon my noontime reveries.

As I grew older, my infatuation with older boys became less nebulous and one such crush is burned into my memory—a boy named Wayne. He lived in a nearby neighbourhood and I saw him often, from a distance, each day at school. I was perhaps ten years old at the time. Wayne was a few years older and very striking in a manly sort of way. He was one of those boys who seemed to be a natural leader and had a troop of followers—other boys who looked up to him and enjoyed his friendship. They actually referred to their group as "The Wayne King Gang". I was drawn to him from the start but my attraction turned into full-blown infatuation after Wayne stood up for me one day to some schoolyard bullies who were hectoring me. I cannot now remember what it was all about, except that for some reason a few of the boys were name-calling, pushing and harassing me. I was always slight and a bit of a peculiar child which seemed for some reason to attract bullying. Wayne stepped into the fray that afternoon. There was no fight. He simply told them to leave me alone. Such was Wayne's stature and charisma the others quit their taunting immediately and never bothered me again.

I had been attracted to Wayne long before the schoolyard altercation, but because of it I became much more aware of my feelings. I was fascinated by his way of talking and walking, his masculine demeanour, and by the striking figure he cut in his leather jacket. I often fantasized about being near him; touching him; being together in some secret place; affectionate and tender. The idea of being intimate with someone I liked so much was enormously exciting and I had no awareness whatever that it might be thought unusual or wrong.

I did not consider myself an unusual child at that time and only in retrospect do I recognize that I was different from most other boys my age. Although I was involved in the usual boyhood games of tag and kick-the-can, sledding and hockey, I was really a loner with interests somewhat different from my peers.

I was content to be solitary and enjoy quiet times, comfortable with my own company. Our neighbours across the street, the Wilbees, had a beautiful garden, which was Mr. Wilbee's pride and joy. He also had a large aviary in which he bred and raised canaries. I would pass hours sitting in their garden painting watercolours and doing sketches of flowers and birds. I was friendly with both the Wilbee children, Barry and Valerie, but it was with Mr. Wilbee I felt a particular kinship. He was a gentle, intelligent man and seemed to understand my eccentricities as he spent considerable time explaining to me the names of the many flowers in his garden and even becoming philosophical at times. Unlike my own father, who probably despaired at his son wasting time with watercolours and India ink drawings, Mr. Wilbee would often stop in the midst of tending his garden and take an interest in what I was attempting to sketch or paint. Frequently I would go across the street and into the Wilbee's garden simply because I knew I might have the chance to chat with Mr. Wilbee.

I felt much more at ease talking with this adult than I did with children my own age. He and I seemed to share a similar perspective on life. With him, I sensed my first experience of connecting with someone on a purely intellectual level. I am quite grateful for having known him; having had those afternoon conversations and the occasional game of Scrabble, which I much preferred to any board games, perhaps because it required some thought and knowledge.

When I was eleven years old music entered my life providing another interest that further distanced me from the other boys of the working class neighbourhood in which I lived.

While I was off at school one day, a door-to-door salesman came to our house offering group lessons on the Hawaiian guitar and other instruments. My mother thought this would be a good thing for me and signed me up. When I returned from school that afternoon she enthusiastically told me all about her plan. I was rather intrigued by the idea of learning music. When she mentioned they also taught *other* instruments, I perked up even more and asked, "Do they teach the violin?" I had been to a Vancouver Symphony school concert with my grade three class and had been mesmerized by all the violin bows—forty or so—rising and falling in unison. Mother gave me a wary look and answered with a hesitant, "Yes". She then quickly added that I might have to practise in the garage at the back of the property. She obviously anticipated that I would be making some horrible sounds. That didn't concern me—although it never did actually come to that.

A Priest's Tale

I began the violin lessons with a group of ten or twelve youngsters in a church basement. The teacher was Mrs. Brown, a middle-aged woman who wore her hair in a bun and chain-smoked her way through the day. The church basement was dingy and ripe with the intermingled scents of Mrs. Brown's tobacco and the pungent odour of the rosin we rubbed on our bow hairs. In those inauspicious surroundings I began my relationship with music—a relationship that has been central and continuous throughout my life.

We did make rather appalling screeching and scraping sounds as we started on our exploration of this noble instrument. Once we mastered the art of making ear-splitting sounds on the open strings we began to learn finger patterns. Soon enough, we were able to scratch out simple tunes—scratch perhaps being the operative word. As it was approaching Christmas, we learned such standards as *Silent Night* and the current Bing Crosby song, *I'm Dreaming of a White Christmas*.

With its graceful curves and rich, melancholy voice, the violin appealed to me in and of itself. But I think I was also drawn to it because it was such a different thing to do—unlike an interest in sports or skating. I certainly never encountered anyone else in my neighbourhood carrying a violin case.

There were times when I took my violin to school because the lesson was soon after the last bell and the meeting place nearer to school than home. This raised the bar on my being a pariah. Not only was there the occasional horror I felt when the teacher asked me to play something for the class, but being seen carrying a violin case naturally led to considerable taunting. The teasing didn't actually bother me oddly, because I somehow felt a certain gratification in being different.

After about six months, Mrs. Brown spoke with Mother about placing me with a private teacher. She explained she herself had attained only a Grade 2 level in violin and felt she would not be able to take me further. A friend of my aunt's, who was a singer, recommended a prominent Vancouver teacher and an appointment was made for an interview.

My parents took me to the studio of Douglas Stewart, which was in the penthouse of the Vancouver Block on Granville Street right under the huge clock. His protégé, Kenneth Yunke, was present as well, and I was assigned to Kenneth's tutelage. He was a brilliant violinist and was only about twenty-four years old. He had begun teaching along with Douglas Stewart when he was perhaps in his early twenties. My violin lessons with Kenneth began when I was twelve years old and lasted until age seventeen.

A Priest's Tale

On Monday evenings during the school year, the students of both Mr. Stewart and Kenneth Yunke would practise together as an orchestra in Barney's Studios—a dilapidated old building, which was situated on Richards Street just opposite Holy Rosary Cathedral. It was an opportunity for us to become acquainted with orchestral playing. The orchestra encompassed a wide range of experience, from those with minimal training to those who were of near-professional stature. During my time in the orchestra, Kenneth was the concertmaster. Rehearsals were quite a workout for us. Mr. Stewart was a rather demanding man. He would sit at an upright piano on the stage of the rehearsal room, pounding away with his left hand as he shouted out directions and conducted with his right hand. Occasionally Mr. Stewart would take a fiddle from one of the students and demonstrate a technique. I never actually heard him perform aside from these tiny snippets.

The weekly orchestral sessions were geared toward preparing us for the annual gala concert, which took place each June in the ballroom of the Vancouver Hotel. This concert was always well attended and if my memory serves me, the ballroom held almost a thousand people. The orchestra was called *The Vancouver Junior Philharmonic Orchestra*. The first portion of the concert was orchestral, followed by a solo recital by promising students beginning with the most junior players and always concluded with a masterful performance by Kenneth. Vividly impressed in my mind is the occasion when Kenneth performed Paganini's spectacular *'La Campanella'*.

For all of the aptitude I later displayed in my music lessons I got off to a somewhat poor start as far as public school was concerned. Having been born at the end of November, I was actually a little young to be enrolled in September, as I was a few months shy of six when I entered grade one. My parents and the teacher discussed the question and thought it might be worth giving it a try.

The little two-room schoolhouse was near where we lived, just off Rupert Street near 29th Avenue in East Vancouver. It was an annex of Norquay School, which was about a mile away. My grade one teacher, Miss MacPherson, was probably in her 40's and always dressed in a severe fashion and wore her hair up in a tight bun. This was the day of the single schoolmarm when lady teachers seemed almost like nuns and when there did not appear to be any male teachers in the elementary schools. Each day Miss MacPherson would do very clever colour chalk drawings in the corner of the blackboard depicting the current weather—large, orange suns with faces, grey clouds and large droplets of rain and bright yellow lightning bolts.

A Priest's Tale

We were kept busy with projects such as making fruit and vegetables out of clay, which we painted with poster paints, for our pretend store. We would label our goods with paper tags reading 5 cents or 8 cents in order to help us understand counting and money. The smell of the paint and the paste, which seemed to be used for everything imaginable, including the odd student who would eat a little, lingers in these memories.

    The wooden floors of the little schoolhouse would be swept by the janitor each evening with a sawdust compound and then oiled. The odour it left remains graven in my mind. Recess was a mêlée of activity. First there would be the distribution of iodine tablets—nasty little bitter tasting pills that seemed to be all the rage in the 40s. They were for goitre or swelling of the thyroid gland. Following that was the distribution of half pints of milk or Vi-Co, a chocolate milk drink. The boys would vie for the use of hobbyhorses, which were broomsticks with cardboard horse's heads attached. There were never enough of them for everyone at one time and it made for an administrative nightmare for the teachers. I lived only a few blocks from this little school and at noon, I would go home for my lunch. This adventure in my first year at school was short-lived because I had difficulties paying attention and kept falling asleep in the afternoons. It was finally decided I should drop out for that year and give it another try the following September.

When I restarted school the next year, things were not much improved. I was staying awake through the afternoon, but I was't doing well in my studies. Arithmetic was my major stumbling block. My Dad was concerned enough to spend hours drilling me on the times-tables. 6 x 7 is 42, 9 x 8 is 72, etc. The nine times-table was my worst horror. I came to hate arithmetic with a passion. I simply could not see why one needed to have this vast amount of information committed to memory. Of course, the more I hated it, the worse the problem became. My other studies suffered as well. Report card time was discouraging and even frightening. The marks were bad enough—D's and C-minuses and sometimes E's—but the teacher's remarks were even more unsettling. *"Don does not apply himself; Don must work much harder; Don is a disruption in class"* the report cards would say.

I didn't mean to be disruptive. Somewhere along the way I concluded I was simply a poor student. Moreover, as often happens with young boys who don't feel they are up to par in their studies, I tended to be easily distracted in class, which usually resulted in the distraction of others. My small stature was also a part of the problem.

A Priest's Tale

I was always having difficulties with bullies. Of course, my big mouth undoubtedly got me into even more trouble than I would have found otherwise. I am convinced there is a correlation between size and verbosity. My father suffered an agony having to watch as these situations unfolded. Of course, I thought he was mad at me. He would get so worked up about it, telling me to stand up for myself and fight back.

I remember Dad was so proud of me on one occasion because for some reason, while I was being threatened by a bigger boy, Dad's words came to mind…"just sock them in the nose." For some inexplicable reason, I did just that. The boy fell to the ground holding his bloody nose and looked up at me in astonishment. I stood rooted to the spot certain he would get up and pound me into oblivion. To my utter amazement, he rose to his feet with a startled look on his face and just wandered away. He left me alone from that time forward.

I had conflicting feelings over this situation. I can be quite outspoken and even a little pushy when I feel it is necessary, but real conflict, verbal or physical, turns my stomach. I would rather settle an argument by agreeing to disagree if no compromise is possible. But, at that time I think I was more impressed that my father's advice had actually worked, as was he.

The trouble with my studies, however, continued through primary school. I was even held back a grade due to my lack of progress. I had rather given up on being good in school when I reached grade eight, but then I encountered algebra.

It is ironic the subject that is often an obstacle for many students proved to be the gateway to a whole new venture in my studies. Algebra seemed to be an epiphany for me, which initiated a chain of events that ultimately altered my attitude towards school and study.

Here I was presented with the mysterious X—an unknown quantity. It might be anything—the possibilities would seem to be infinite. However, if the correct equation is constructed and other factors are considered one is able to resolve X and discover the unknown value. The wonder of this fundamental element of algebra captivated me. The unknown—the infinite—could be revealed. Here was a facet of arithmetic for which I could see a commonsense purpose. The endless chanting of the times-tables by rote had seemed the most useless waste of time and energy. With algebra I began to see the valuable and practical implications of mathematical formulae—rather a Helen Keller moment for me. I found myself drawn to the challenges presented as some people are fascinated by crossword puzzles. I delighted in the process of applying a formula; working through the various steps and almost always being able to resolve the mystery of X. I surprised myself even by dabbling with equations in my spare time, as it became more and more something of an obsession. The difference this breakthrough in mathematical confidence had on my self-perception was remarkable.

My new aptitude was probably even more surprising to my algebra teacher. Initially, I believe he thought I might be cheating on tests. During those high school years I continued to improve in algebra and even in the more advanced trigonometry and calculus. It became my favourite subject and I moved toward the top of my class. One January, when the Christmas exam results were handed out, my whole class was shocked because they had known me for years and were well acquainted with my mediocre performance. The math teacher distributed the papers in the order of the marks—from the top down. A gasp went up as the third paper bore my name. The boy sitting across the aisle from me glanced at me in disbelief and said, "Dodman, I didn't know you were a brain." His remark tickled me immensely especially as I had not realized it either.

My new talent in mathematics and the confidence I gained from actually being able to do it somehow spilled over into other subjects. Of course, I didn't realize at the time where this fascination with the unknown would ultimately lead; nor that my epiphany with algebra was but the precursor of an even more momentous discovery—one that would influence the direction of my life. Only in hindsight did I comprehend that my fascination with algebra was an early foray into other existential matters. At the time, it was more about the wonder of being good at math after so many years of feeling like it was a waste of time and feeling stupid because I was not interested in it. I didn't really stop to ponder about why the infinite possibilities of X captivated me, nor why I was so delighted when I could use a formulaic process to define X. These questions would appear later though in a different guise.

Family life during early adolescence was rather ordinary. My sister, Gail and I, being four and a half years apart, were close enough to get into occasional scraps over nonsense but we more or less led independent lives. Communication with my parents had deteriorated into the half-speak so common with teenagers. We seemed settled into a familiar and monotonous domestic routine. Then…a huge surprise!

I was fifteen when my mother announced that Gail and I would soon have a new baby brother or sister. Things changed radically in our little family over the next several

A Priest's Tale

years. There were to be two new additions to our family, not just one. First Cindy arrived, and then two years later my youngest sister, Susan, was born. Suddenly we all had new responsibilities thrust upon us. Gail and I became built in baby-sitters. Somehow, one of my particular jobs became the washing and hanging out of diapers. It never did occur to me this was an unusual job for a 16 year-old boy. It was simply a matter of each family member sharing in the responsibilities of having babies in the family.

My own birth was apparently a bit of a surprise to my parents; a fact I didn't discover until I was sixteen and sitting at the kitchen table one afternoon chatting with Mother and leafing through a box of old family photos. At the bottom of the jumbled mess of pictures I came across my parent's marriage certificate. As I glanced over it I was unusually aware of Mother watching me. I noted they were married in May of 1937. My birthday is in November. I puzzled over the arithmetic for a moment then turned to Mother and said, "Oh, they've made a mistake in the date." Mother astonished me by bursting into tears. In an instant I realized she had been pregnant when they got married. This did not bother me at all and I told her it made no difference to anything. I was struck more by how sensitive she was about this secret. Her demeanor was usually rather blunt, confrontational even—a trait I never found appealing but which I have inherited to some extent. For her to display such emotion over what seemed a little thing to me was surprising.

My father, Harold, had followed in his father's profession as an automobile refinisher, which in Grandpa's case meant he began his career in England painting and detailing horse drawn coaches. My parents, Harold Dodman and Betty Buckingham, married in 1937 and soon thereafter bought an empty lot on 28th Avenue in East Vancouver near to where my father's parents lived. My father built a tiny, temporary dwelling at the back of the property. "The Shack" as my parents called this one-room structure—which later became our garage—was the family home for a few years during the building of a house at the front of the property. Mum and Dad dug the foundation for the house by hand, using a wheelbarrow and the assistance of a few friends. Mother's father, Grandpa Buckingham, was a carpenter and he supervised the construction of the new house.

Having been born just before the Second World War, many of my childhood memories consist of my family's involvement in the war effort. My father and aunt worked in munitions works and with aircraft production. After 1939, my father's brother, George, was somewhere in Belgium with the Canadian Army. The war seemed a normal part of life in those years. As a child I was fascinated with the little books of brightly coloured ration stamps required to purchase sugar, butter, meat and other scarce commodities. During air raid practices, sirens would wail throughout Vancouver and my mother would quickly turn out all the lights until we had the cardboard window covers in place.

Living on the West Coast, even though it was a considerable distance from Japan, there was concern of a possible attack from the West. I must have been taken to the cinema in those early years as I distinctly recall Pathe newsreels, hearing the voice of Winston Churchill and seeing the tanks and troops entering Paris. It was a moving experience for me years later when I visited Normandy and saw the beaches and countryside where the initial invasion had taken place. When the War ended, I recall being with my family and throngs of people waiting at the CPR station at the foot of Granville Street for the arrival of troop trains from Montreal. My uncle George was returning home after four years in Belgium and France. I took delight in being hoisted up onto his shoulders as we moved through the crowd. His duffel bag was loaded with Belgian chocolate, foreign coins and an inordinate number of wristwatches. I shudder now to contemplate just where all the watches came from.

During and after the war times were difficult economically. I had no sense we were poor or deprived—things seemed perfectly normal to me in spite of the rationing stamps. In later years during the summers we would often take a cabin at Crescent Beach, about 20 miles east of Vancouver, for a couple of weeks. When the tide is out the sandbars and tidal pools stretch out for miles. The sand was warm to our bare feet and the water in the pools was deliciously tepid for wading. Small flatfish would scurry from one hiding place to the next in the sea grasses often tickling our feet as they attempted to hide under them. These memories of sunny, relaxed days at the beach with family members are rich with the pungent odours of the sage-like grasses that grew along the beach front; the salt air and the sounds of sea birds and wind.

At other times during the summer, we would make day-trips down to Crescent Beach. If my father was working, Mum, Gail and I would take the train and Dad would drive down after work for dinner and then drive us home. The trains left Vancouver from the Great Northern station and the trip seemed to take hours. Often while staying at Crescent Beach, we would wander up to the train station in the mornings to meet friends or simply for the excitement of seeing the train arriving. The mid morning train could be heard for miles as it chugged through the

A Priest's Tale

valley and across the trestle over the mud flats and the Nicomekl River. Presently, it would come puffing and snorting into the station spewing hot clouds of hissing steam and whiffs of carbon and oil. Boys would sometimes put pennies on the track for the train to pass over and transform them into flat, elliptical shapes. We were always a little nervous when we did this having heard apocryphal tales of a boy having derailed a train with such antics.

On other occasions there would be summer excursions to the Sunshine Coast by steamer. In those days the Princess Marguerite, SS Cardena, Princess Charlotte and other classic coastal steamers departed from Vancouver's inner harbour and stopped at Horseshoe Bay, Bowen Island, Gibson's Landing, Davis Bay, Sechelt and Pender Harbour. Those were the golden days of Union Steamships. Whenever I happen to visit the cafeteria of the modern ferries I have flashbacks to the elegant dining rooms on those old ships; oak panelling; brass railings; tables set with silver and linen napkins—the last days of an era.

I was an only child until my sister Gail was born in April of 1942. I was taken off to Grandma Dodman's house while Mum was in the hospital. Children were not allowed to visit patients in those days so when Dad took me to visit Mum after Gail had been born I was only allowed as far as the lobby. Dad showed me Gail's picture on a notice board where they posted photographs of recent newborns. The photos were cut out in the shape of raindrops for the month of April. As we were leaving I was able to wave to Mother from the parking lot when she appeared at the window of her ward.

When it came time for Mum to come home, Dad went and collected her then came to Grandma's to pick me up. It was an awkward moment for me meeting for the first time this very small bundle with her red face and shock of black hair. I vividly recall my discomfort. I had been the only child and now there was competition. Mum and Dad laughed good-naturedly at me as I tried to divert the conversation away from the baby and recapture their attention by launching into a long explanation about how I thought there might be a rat under the back seat. Oh, how protective we are of our space and sense of importance.

During high school, I lived in a basement room, which Dad and Grandpa Buckingham had constructed of wallboard. It gave me some small measure of independence though home life was still a bit difficult at times. Mother was a confrontational person who never hesitated to speak her mind. I have inherited a measure of this trait through association or genetics and am often aware I am acting just like Mother and kick myself for it. Mother could also be rather oblivious to what was coming out of her mouth.

A Priest's Tale

On one occasion we got into a loud shouting match in the kitchen as she stood at the stove preparing dinner. I cannot recall what provoked the incident or what I had said to her, but Mother looked up at me with eyes blazing and shouted, "You Son of a Bitch." I collapsed on the kitchen floor in uncontrollable laughter because poor Mother didn't get it.

Father was generally quiet and reserved, but he did have a keen sense of humour and loved to play. Dad would laugh until his sides ached at the slapstick antics of Abbot and Costello and Laurel and Hardy. I am certain it was from Dad that I inherited my own quirky sense of humour. We certainly shared a similar perspective.

One Easter, Mother made two small peach shortcakes rather than one large one. We must have had extra company to warrant the two cakes. After the main course Mother asked, "Don, will you get the first cake for Dad to serve up?" I went to the counter and carefully picked up one of the cakes balancing it on my left hand. As I walked toward the table, a devilish idea flashed through my mind. In the few steps between the counter and the table, I pondered the question, "Should I? Or shouldn't I?" I came up beside Dad and made as if to put the cake down in front of him, then the mad impulse won and instead of setting the cake on the table I slopped it in his face.

Gasps rose from all around. For a moment, my heart stopped, and I thought, Oh, he's going to kill me. After a moment two holes appeared in the whipped cream as Dad blinked—exactly like in the slapstick movies. Another breathless moment passed then he dissolved in fits of laughter and licking at the cream. Our guests were stunned, Mother was furious, but Dad thought it was hilarious. Of course, I would never have done it if there had not been that second cake.

Although things had improved with regard to my studies, high school was a difficult time for me socially when adolescent hormones began to turn on and boys and girls became acutely aware of each other. Everyone seemed to be pairing up and dating. I knew I was expected to be making similar motions but my hormones were giving me very different signals. I felt an overwhelming attraction to Todd, the boy who sat in front of me in geography class. Doubtless, because we were only a foot or two apart I was unusually aware of the scent of his hair cream, his crisp, clean shirts and noticed his every adorable mannerism. In the 50s homosexuality was still the 'love that dare not speak its name' unless it was in vulgar jokes, so I had no basis for comparison for the feelings I was experiencing. I felt the powerful emotions that sexuality creates and in reading

A Priest's Tale

'Romeo & Juliet' I identified strongly with the all-consuming passion of the doomed lovers—especially Juliet's, if I am to be honest.

Todd was one of the most popular and gorgeous boys in the entire school. I don't remember what sport he played, if any, just his sandy-blonde hair, fine chiselled features, and startlingly blue eyes. I was inches away from him that entire year and often in an agony of longing. I had no idea what to do about such feelings; there seemed no language to contain them. 'Romeo & Juliet' was the nearest reference point. And like my infatuation with Wayne when I was ten, the longings I felt for Todd were as much emotional as sexual. I wanted as much to be close to him, be held by him, to feel his kisses and sharing secret thoughts and feelings, as to fall into passionate lovemaking. I wanted the Shakespearian fantasy of true love complete with poetic whisperings of tender affection.

I worshipped Todd from a distance of a foot and a half. But I knew the distance was much greater than that. He was popular, stunningly good looking, while I was bookish—one might even say nerdy—and nobody. I may have recognized the distance in terms of sexuality as well. Here I was a boy with a crush on another boy. The feelings I had were beyond my ability to categorize at the time but I certainly knew I was different. That I was short and rather scrawny certainly didn't help matters in terms of social acceptance. In the locker room after gym class there were often taunts about 'fairies' and such things. But my worst memory from gym class concerns a common practice, which I hope, has long gone by the boards.

The gym teacher would choose two of the more athletic boys to head two teams for soccer or whatever sport we might be playing. They would then alternately choose their teams from the remaining students. Naturally, they wanted to win the game and chose the best and strongest players first. It never failed—I would be the very last one chosen. I say chosen, but the truth of it is that the last player would simply go to the losers by default. This practice was enormously cruel and does horrific things to one's self-esteem.

During high school, my friends tended to be others like myself—people who didn't easily fit into the mould. We were not sports minded and were not a part of the socializing crowd who seemed perpetually to be organizing the next dance. While others were involved in track and field or playing soccer and baseball we would be helping the science teacher with the school weather reporting station, measuring rainfall or finding pond algae and things to feed the tadpoles in the science room aquarium. I was also

A Priest's Tale

involved in the Macmillan Club, which encouraged the arts and, of course, I continued to participate in musical events.

My own formal violin lessons ended when I was 17 years old; however, my interest in classical music continued and has ever since been a recurring theme in my life. I became quite interested in chamber music and because of that I took up the cello since it was easy to find violinists and pianists but not so easy to find cellists.

For a few years, I played in the Vancouver Junior Symphony Orchestra. That was quite exciting and somewhat different for me as it was a full symphony orchestra with brass, woodwinds and percussion whereas my previous experience had been with strings only. Our conductor was Jean de Rimanoczy, who was then the concertmaster of the Vancouver Symphony. As a young man he had studied in Budapest under Bartok and Zoltan Kodály—a fact that escaped my notice then, but now impresses me enormously.

We were rehearsing Beethoven's First Symphony when I was still quite new to the orchestra. The first movement ends with a series of six or seven crashing chords firmly and unequivocally establishing the tonic as Beethoven so typically does. For the violins, these were double stopped chords where all four strings are strafed vigorously with the bow. Horror of horrors, a musician's worst fear was realized. I somehow lost count and played one extra chord—all by myself, and much to the amusement of the rest of the orchestra. The conductor, however, was not amused. He broke his baton in half and hurled part of it at me. Luckily, this was a rehearsal. As a precaution, I decided in the future to play one chord less to prevent the same thing happening during a concert. I have always wondered what would have happened if everyone had done the same thing.

✠

When I was about fifteen years of age I became fascinated with the sea. We read "Treasure Island" by Robert Louis Stevenson in English class, and there was something about exotic ports and details of life at sea that intrigued me. I had soon read my way through every book in the school library dealing with sailing and shipping. "Moby Dick", Joseph Conrad's many sea stories, and countless other books of little note about tramp steamers and sailing. I felt a kind of kinship with the outlaws and misfits who made the high seas their home. I suspect my daydreams about seafaring adventure and the freedom associated with it were probably subliminally rooted in the belief that by running away I might possibly escape some of

A Priest's Tale

life's complications, including the eventuality of having to deal with dating and marriage. But I was also fascinated by the technicalities of sailing, especially navigation—the idea that one could, with sextant and log tables, calculate from the Sun and the stars one's position on the earth's surface. Having grown up in Vancouver, a city girded by the sea, it seemed quite natural that I might pursue a career on the water. At one point in my sailing obsession, I burned with an absolute certainty that I wanted a career as a navigator or perhaps a ship's captain.

It was this fascination with the sea that led me to join the Royal Canadian Navy Reserve unit at HMCS Discovery in Stanley Park with several of my friends. I had attended a lecture given by an Officer from Discovery, the Navel Reserve base, during one of the 'Career Days' at school. It sounded interesting and would be an opportunity to learn something of navigation and seamanship. To join the Reserve Division one had to be over 16 years of age, without any legal impediments, have a willingness to commit to weekly '*divisions*' and classes at the reserve base, and a five-year term of activity.

Divisions were held on Tuesday evenings and involved parade training and classes in seamanship and navigation. I was never particularly interested in the military aspects but was there principally for the training in seamanship. There were a number of departments at the Reserve base: engineering, carpentry, electrical motors, stores, medical services, marching band and food preparation. I chose Navigation and Direction. Our classes in navigation involved reading charts, basic astronomy, course plotting and navigation techniques, including 'rules of the road', boat handling, rowing, sailing and knot tying; the essential crafts of a sailor.

One Tuesday evening at divisions, the Captain announced there would be two vacant billets on a ship about to go on a six-month training cruise. I was in grade twelve at North Burnaby High at the time and in no position to be thinking of such things. But a friend and I, thinking there would be many applicants, submitted our names as a lark. In the following weeks, the whole thing slipped from my mind. Then, just before Christmas, I received a telephone call from an officer at Discovery.

The basics of the message were; "Come and pick-up your tropical gear and be on-board HMCS Ontario in Esquimalt harbour in two weeks."

I didn't have the courage to admit that my mother probably wouldn't let me go. I just said, "Yes, sir."

Then I had to explain to my parents what the phone call was all about. It was a long night of debate—and screaming on my mother's part. Part of the difficulty in convincing my parents to let me go was that I had no idea where the ship was actually going. That had not yet been revealed. I was also one of the only people in the family who had ever finished high school—or was about to. My parents had serious concerns as to whether I would go back to school when I returned. I tried to justify the trip by arguing it would be educational and promised I would return to school to complete my courses the following year. In the end, my parents agreed to let me go.

Because all of this happened during the Christmas break, we completely forgot about informing the school. About two weeks into the new term the vice-principal called Mother and asked, "Mrs. Dodman, we haven't seen Don for a few weeks, is he alright?" By this time I had written home informing my parents of the ship's itinerary, which had just been posted aboard the *Ontario*. Mother was taken aback at having forgotten about the school, and said, "Oh, I'm so sorry we didn't tell you, but Don has gone to China." Apparently, he took some convincing that this was not a joke!

We sailed on January 7th 1957. The *Ontario* was a light cruiser, and on this voyage two frigates, HMCS Jonquière and HMCS Stettler, accompanied us. The cruise was a training exercise for the Officer Cadets from the naval school at Esquimalt. My rating onboard was Ordinary Seaman. My work was the usual thing for lower deck ratings; cleaning toilets, endless painting of everything and standing bridge watches.

    I was quite excited on the day we put out to sea. I had dreamed of a life at sea so often the idea had achieved the stature of a romantic legend in my mind. Having imagined myself walking the tilting and bucking decks, I thought myself a sailor already. As we slipped out of the harbour at Esquimalt and passed the craggy promontories of Race Rocks and Cape Flattery, I felt my dream was coming true. Then the ship began to rise and fall gently with the undulating ground swell as we entered the open sea. I had been on a few smaller ships in the waters protected by the island chains along the coast during my time with the Naval Reserve, but never in the open ocean. The thought of seasickness crossed my mind fleetingly but I thought to myself, You won't get sick. You love the sea. You have a bent for this life. This thought seemed to buoy me up for some time. Gradually the action of the sea became increasingly more vigorous as we headed into a low-pressure system. The *Ontario* was ten thousand tonnes—a fairly large ship. From my lookout post on the bridge I watched the much smaller frigates rising and diving as they ploughed through the swells, their prows frequently lifting completely out of the surging torrents. Soon, in spite of my mantra about being born to this life, I began to feel rather queasy. By then my stomach was churning and by the middle of the watch I was very nauseous.

The philosophy of the navy is to keep you busy doing things to keep your mind off the seasickness. I was doing bridge watches off and on all that first night of the heavy weather. By this time, I believe the swells were reaching at least forty to fifty feet high. The working bridge on the *Ontario* was a 'flying bridge'—open to the sky and weather—which was fortunate for me as I was able to conceal my sickness somewhat although Every so often I would be overwhelmed by nausea and would throw up over the side. I am sure the officer of the watch knew exactly what was going on but the thunderous noise of the sea and wind was so loud I doubt anyone heard me.

The next evening, I was feeling even worse. This time I was sent below to the steering position. The wheelhouse was housed some seven decks below the bridge in order to be less vulnerable to enemy fire. All of a sudden, I found myself as steersman trying desperately to keep the ship on a compass course. The compass repeater figures ticked back and forth, north to south, as the ship wallowed to and fro in the heavy seas. The trick apparently, was to steer a mean course within the sweep of the readings. The wheel was a huge wooden thing as tall as I was then, and took enormous strength to move although hydraulics did the actual work to move the huge rudder. I had only been steering for about five minutes when I was overcome with nausea and threw-up on the wheel, which did not amuse the others in the wheelhouse. I was of course immediately removed and strangely, never invited to steer again.

Many people seem to think that seasickness is no more than an upset stomach, but it is considerably more complicated than that. Coupled with the stomach upset is a profound psychological depression—at least this was true for me. At the end of the first day of my ordeal I was so ill I thought I would die. The second day, I wanted to die and thought that was as bad as it could get. How naive I was. By the third day I was afraid I wasn't going to die. Then, on the fourth day, I began to take an upward turn. Although the seas were still rough, the sun had come out and with its return I felt a ray of hope. It was perhaps another twenty-four hours before I was feeling reasonably well again. After surviving this horrible ordeal, I never became seasick again despite frequent storms and heavy weather. I was beginning to think of myself, truly, as a sailor.

A Priest's Tale

Our first port of call was Hilo on the Big Island of Hawaii where we were anchored in the outer roads of the harbour. A welcoming party of some town officials and hula dancers came out to greet us. We then went on to Pearl Harbour; a solemn moment as we sailed past the sunken American battleship *Arizona*. Our ship's company assembled along the port side and a 21-gun salute was given as we slowly sailed past. This was 1957, only 16 years after the attack on Pearl Harbour, and the memory was still relatively recent history.

The passage from the Hawaiian Islands to Guam was the longest stretch of sea time for us—two weeks. Most of this leg of our journey was in heavy weather. The turbulence of the sea and the enormity of the waves astonished me. The ship, in spite of her 10,000 tonne mass, was tossed about like a cork. One minute, we would be riding high on a mountain of water and the next; we would be deep in a trough, looking up at 60-foot high walls of water on either side.

On a Saturday afternoon during our haul between Hawaii and Guam, where we would stop for refuelling, it was decided we would engage in a jackstay transfer with one of the frigates so the Padre could go over for Sunday Mass. In my opinion, the seas were far too rough to attempt this. I can only imagine the Padre, perhaps in a rush of religious fervour, talked the Captain into this transfer so he might be with his flock on Sunday. Jackstay transfers are tricky even under the best conditions. In rough seas, the danger in bringing two ships so close together is ten-fold. However, the order was given, and we set about preparations.

The frigate, Jonquière, came alongside the Ontario at a reasonable distance to allow for manoeuvrability. Then someone on the foredeck of the Jonquière shot a light line across our foredeck with a rifle while we all hid behind machinery so as not to be accidentally hit by the bolt. A heavier line was run across using the lighter one. Then the heavy jackstay cable was sent across. This line was fastened securely to Jonquière and then ran back to the Ontario through a wooden block and along our starboard rail where about 30 of us played tug-of-war to keep the line between the two ships taut. A few canvas bags of supplies and movie films were sent over and one was returned to us. That was the test run. Now it was Padre's turn.

The Padre was secured in a boatswain's chair and began his crossing. The poor dear Padre. When he was about halfway across a rogue wave caused the two ships to lurch toward one another rendering the cable slack and causing those of us in the tug-of-war line to fall down on our backsides. The Padre plunged into the churning sea. As the wave passed by the two ships surged away from each

A Priest's Tale

other drawing the line taut again and causing the Padre to shoot into the air and over the top of the jackstay cable like a rag doll. Those of us holding the line were dragged along the deck but managed to hold on. We completed the transfer without further incident and the Padre was pulled aboard the Jonquière, soaking wet but otherwise unharmed. I would have given anything to overhear the conversation in the wardroom over hot rums after that episode or to hear the Padre's homily on Sunday morning. There must have been ample grist for a good sermon that day.

Evenings at sea were often tedious. So many of the things one does for recreation were simply not possible at sea. Even simple diversions like ping-pong were out of the question in rough weather. Movies were the main source of entertainment. Of course, only a certain number of 16mm films were carried on the ship, and these soon entered into double-digit repeats. *Casablanca* and *High Noon* were particular favourites. But just when it seemed the re-running would surely drive us mad, there began a new twist to movie viewings. We had become so familiar with the dialogue, the movie would be run without sound, and spontaneous dialogue would emerge from the group. Initially, it was an accurate facsimile of the film. But as the films were repeated again and again, we became more creative and the dialogue, while fitting the action on the screen, departed completely from the original. It was quite hilarious to watch as Humphrey Bogart propositioned Ingrid Bergman in the most vulgar language. With this new twist, there was no end to the number of times the movies could be run.

Other nights would find me bundled in my duffel coat, the strap on my cap fastened securely under my chin, standing in the port lookout niche on the bridge. The bridge was open to the elements and the sky. During night watches I was supposed to be scanning the horizon for the lights of other ships—the usual caution against accidental collision. The weather at the beginning of the cruise was generally overcast, making the night a vast, featureless blackness beyond the lights of the ship. Alone in my perch I had much time to think on a night watch.

These watches are taken in one-hour rotations. I recall one evening in particular, as my first hour was about half over the heavy clouds seemed to be breaking. A few small gaps appeared, offering a peek at the stars. The Officer of the Watch disappeared for a few minutes. He must have gone down to the chartroom for he returned with a sextant. I couldn't help but wonder what on earth he thought he was going to accomplish in this weather, a few breaks in the clouds or no. He waited for some time peering intently towards one particular patch of sky. I watched him, expectantly. The clouds broke again. A single star was visible, at least to my eyes. The Officer of the Watch took a sight on it and disappeared back down into the chartroom leaving me shaking my head in astonishment. How could he possibly know which star that was without the other stars to place it? He must have known the heavens incredibly well to be able to anticipate just where to look for that particular star. I was impressed and filled with a reassurance that the seaman's life was indeed for me.

After my hour on lookout, I went down to the Rec. Room and stretched out on one of the canvas cots put there for the night watch crew and slept fitfully. Then it was time for another hour on the bridge.

As I climbed up to the bridge and took my place in the lookout niche I was astounded by the brilliance of the heavens. The clouds had vanished and there was no moon. The stars literally went on forever. As a city boy I had never seen such a sky. I knew I was supposed to be scanning the horizon for the lights of passing ships but my eyes were drawn time and again upward—awestruck by the billions of dazzling stars. Intuitively I sensed that this was my first genuine connection with the sacred. I had a rudimentary intellectual concept of how far I was looking in terms of distance yet at the same time was aware that I was looking back in time. I understood from my studies in basic navigation that Mizar, in the constellation Ursa Major was some 78 light years away from our Sun while other stars are thousands, some millions of light years away. In all probability many of the stars I was looking at had expired aeons ago. The immensity of the universe seemed at that moment to bear down on me and expose my insignificance, yet curiously, in the same instant there was a sensation of elation; of being mystically connected and drawn into it.

Contemplating the splendour of the endless heavens, I found my thoughts drifting toward other questions: of creation, existence and infinity. This surely must be that unknown 'X' on a scale I had never imagined; an unknown so vast it seemed it would devour me. Thoughts about creation and 'being' flooded my head and I felt simultaneously sensations of comfort and anxiety leading to a host of other questions—and the ache to reach out to that Unknown.

My only real notion of religion at that time came from my childhood when my sister, Gail, and I would go for overnight visits with Grandma Buckingham. After Grandma and Grandpa separated, Grandma lived alone in a little house she rented from a friend in the suburbs of Vancouver. At the time of our visits Gail would have been four or five and I seven years old. Part of the charm of visiting Grandma was that the house had no electricity, which was unusual at that time for a house within the city limits of Vancouver. As dusk fell, the ritual of lighting the coal oil lamps began. The smell of the kerosene, the pools of light surrounded by shifting shadows made the house feel cosy and warm.

At bedtime Gail and I would put on our pyjamas, get into Grandma's bed and she would read us Bible stories from a large illustrated volume which contained engravings of the Ark of the Covenant, Old Testament scenes of David and Goliath, and soft, dreamy pictures of gentle Jesus. Although Grandma seemed to be aligned with some kind of evangelical expression of Christianity she never exhibited any pressure or indoctrination that was noticeable. She was gentle and extremely loving allowing the stories to stand on their own for us to absorb on their own merit. These were particularly memorable and pleasant moments, which undoubtedly etched themselves upon my mind. My first initiation into things Christian was during those bedtime trysts. My parents were not spiritually inclined themselves, and we never attended church while I was growing up. What I took away from these evenings snuggled in bed with Gail and Grandma was little more than a Sunday school sketch of Christianity.

Cognizant of the sense of infinity in the starry sky from the bridge of a ship steaming its way across the Pacific Ocean I felt very small indeed; but not at all lost. I was overwhelmed with a profound sense of God—God as an idea beyond comprehension, but still, that which can be known in some vague sense. It was all a rather hazy blur at the time but was perhaps the primal stirrings of an inquisitive mind. In retrospect, I see it as my first juvenile approach to life in relationship to creation and the Creator.

The cruise continued with a marvellous potpourri of visits to Guam, Manila, Singapore, Hong Kong, Okinawa and Tokyo. At 19, I was impressionable and in awe of the enormity of the sea and the scope of cultural diversity I witnessed in the exotic ports of call. I had argued that this experience would be educational when I was pleading the case to my parents. And that certainly proved true. But oddly, although the time at sea was fascinating and enjoyable, it proved to be the turning point in my desire to make a career of it. Perhaps it was something I simply needed to get out of my system so I could proceed into the next phase of my life.

A Priest's Tale

✠

When I returned to high school to complete Grade 12, I discovered a thirst for knowledge had been awakened within me. When my guidance counsellor suggested I should upgrade my courses so that I could enter university if I chose, I did so. I had previously given no thought to continuing on to university. But now that actually seemed to be a possibility. I delved into my studies with a renewed vigour.

More mathematics, more science, more of an understanding of astronomy and cosmology—the list was never-ending. In a strange way, it seemed science and spirituality had become linked together in my mind. Perhaps that was the thing I needed to process in order to go the next step. At sea, the stars in the night sky had impressed upon me the vastness of the universe, and yet, at the same time they had stirred the realization that all of this began somewhere—that there was a Principle behind it all.

One thing spilled over into the other. I began to see a link between the world and the holy. English class, which had been a subject to suffer through, became the source of much joy and interest. Everywhere I looked I seemed to be seeing connections and fascinating signs.

When I saw we would be reading Coleridge's *Rime of the Ancient Mariner* I became enthused because of my interest in the sea, but had not the slightest idea that I was about to delve into spiritual waters. I felt very like the young Wedding Guest who became spellbound by the tale told by the Mariner. The Mariner's situation became worse when he committed the offensive act of killing the albatross. His offence is an affront to God and all of Creation. Tragedy strikes the ship and all goes horribly wrong until, in the midst of death and agony, the Mariner changes his attitude and is able to bless the water serpents in his heart and is thus absolved.

My reading of portions of Chaucer's *Canterbury Tales* impressed me as being another variation on the 'spirit versus the flesh' theme. It drew me into its vortex and struck me not simply as history—some other person's life—but in a mystical way, as part of my own experience. The pilgrims on their way to the Shrine of Thomas Becket in Canterbury Cathedral were people of faith. They wanted to pray, do penance, be healed of their infirmities. They were seeking God and Truth, and yet were human and frail. They had failings—illness, anger, lust. They were on a quest to reconcile the two facets of their lives—body and spirit—entertaining and enlightening each other with tales of their passions, loves, sins, and moral quandaries. I felt a kinship with these characters caught between the pull of the flesh, the push of the divine.

My experiences at sea had aroused in me a curiosity about God, spirituality, religion, the church, and faith…so many things about which I had only the fuzziest of notions. I wanted to know more. As I was raised in a vaguely Christian milieu, it was within the Christian faith that I began my search for God and a pathway—a style of spirituality—that would put me in communion with God.

I don't specifically recall how it came about, but my sister Gail and I began to visit churches in our neighbourhood. I had no specific idea of what I was searching for and found many of the churches we visited disappointing. They were either dull as dust, overly emotional, or full of obvious phoney posturing. Eventually, however, our circuit brought us to the tiny St. Andrew's Anglican Church in our neighbourhood. Here Gail and I found worship not only orderly and rational but also reverently done. The people were pleasant and welcomed us in a sincere and natural manner. The priest was friendly, dignified, and didn't exhibit any of the stereotypical attributes one sometimes associates with clergy—no supercilious, saccharine way of speaking and no pretence to holiness. His name was Norman Tanner and I quickly came to feel that his ordinary, matter of fact, sincere manner was truly a holy approach to God and to those with whom he came into contact. It did not take me very long to conclude that St. Andrew's was where I should be.

In the simple elegance of the worship I felt my musings on the infinite, the unknown, were being undergirded and strengthened with a framework of understanding and empathy. St. Andrew's at that time was a very tiny mission parish about half a mile from our home. It was a typical Anglican Church, an early 1900s, wooden structure with a small congregation struggling to remain afloat. During the first few years of my association, the rector had recognized my interest and enthusiasm and involved me as a volunteer in a fund raising programme for the building of a new church. Before long, I found myself visiting people as a member of the fundraising team—a rather rapid and novel change of direction for me. Property had been obtained only one block from our house and the building was realized during the following year.

At sea, I had stared up into those billions of stars and thought, There is more to this than can be explained. Simple chance cannot be the sum of this magnificent universe. Feeble as my idea of God was at the time, looking up into that infinity, I felt I could see His hand in it. Now here in this small, plain Anglican Church, I felt I had found the first conduit and took the first step on my pilgrimage to

A Priest's Tale

Canterbury. My thoughts and intuitions about spirituality, which had begun and were set into play by the sea and stars, were now being connected to the wider human experience of the Divine. Here, the scriptures and Bible stories that Grandma had told us were developed and joined to the broader experience of humanity. I sensed a great depth to the tradition of the Church and the techniques of spirituality. My craving to explore further was truly compelling. I began the long process of learning about the intricacies of Christianity, and the Anglican Church in particular.

The liturgy and rational approach to worship of Anglicanism that attracted me from the beginning were the result of a very long and complex history. Many years of experience have shown me that when the subject of the Anglican Church arises, the most common response is a simplistic one. "Oh, yes, the Church that was started by Henry VIII who wanted a divorce". Although this observation does hold a few grains of truth, like all generalizations, it is far too simplistic. It brings to mind the rather clever philosophical axiom; "All generalizations are false".

The Church in England—rather than *of* England—existed from the earliest centuries of the

Christian era. The Church was present in England at the time of the Roman occupation of Britain, which was soon after Jesus' lifetime. Legend has it that Joseph of Arimathea went to Britain soon after Jesus' Ascension, although this would be very difficult to verify. Alban, who shielded a fleeing priest, and who was converted in the process, was martyred in the year 304—perhaps the first English martyr. So often, we read that Pope Gregory the Great had commissioned Augustine to take Christianity to England in the sixth century. The Catholic Encyclopaedia still claims that Augustine was the "Apostle to the English". To give Augustine his due, he did manage to unify the liturgical and ecclesial nature of the independent Celtic Churches with Rome. However, the Celtic Church in England existed centuries before St. Augustine arrived.

Now, if we jump forward to the 1500's we come to Henry VIII. This is where it becomes extremely complicated and space only permits me to touch on a few of the more salient points. During my ministry I discovered that the most frequently asked question about the Anglican Church by non-Anglicans is the one concerning Henry VIII. I have to confess that over the years, when asked this question, I always felt awkwardness and embarrassment because I was never personally convinced that Henry did anything of much importance. In fact, on the contrary, I think that his action was an appalling and selfish blunder rather like the behaviour of a spoiled child angry because he could not have his way.

The problem centred on Henry's numerous marriages and his determination to produce a male heir. The Pope refused to grant an annulment and Henry rebelled and declared himself head of the English Church. He was not seeking a divorce as people routinely insist on saying. He divorced none of his wives because divorce did not even exist in England or Europe at that time. He was seeking an annulment—a declaration that the marriage was void—which was the way he dispatched two of his previous wives. Annulments in the Church of Rome were and still are common. It is a way of circumventing the biblical condemnation of divorce by declaring that there never really was a valid marriage in the first place.

Henry's request to the Holy See placed the Vatican in an extremely uncomfortable position. Firstly, the Pope had already granted Henry one or two annulments. Secondly, the Pope had conferred upon him the title, "*Defender of the Faith*" in recognition of his book "*Assertio Septem Sacramentorum*", a defence of the seven sacraments. No amateur theologian was Henry. In his eagerness to have a male heir, however, Henry went through a number of wives dispatching some in ways far worse than annulment.

Henry's latest request for the annulment of his marriage with Catherine of Aragon placed the Holy See in an impossible situation. The Pope had granted Henry special permission to marry Catherine in the first place, because Catherine was the widow of Henry's brother, which according to the Church's theology of marriage would make Catherine and Henry of the 'same flesh'. Of course, Rome has a penchant for finding loopholes to get around legalities such as this. However, there was more. Pope Clement VII was beholden to Catherine's nephew, Charles V, Holy Roman Emperor, who did not feel the marriage of his aunt to Henry was a good idea, and thus added to the unlikelihood of Rome acceding to Henry's request for an annulment. In the end, Henry simply said 'to hell with them all' and made himself the head of the English Church. All ties with the Church of Rome were severed and the English Church became autonomous.

Henry was in the mood to satisfy even more of his ambitions since it seemed he now had control over the English Church. Although his wealth was already immense, he sought to add to it by confiscating church lands and especially the monasteries.

I am not naive enough to believe that there were no problems associated with the monastic system, but correcting such problems hardly ever requires throwing out the baby with the bathwater.

Contrary to popular belief, Henry's actions had little if anything to do with the Reformation, which had only recently begun in Europe, in fact Henry's book was in essence an attack upon the novel views of Martin Luther. After the break with Rome, for a period of perhaps 15 years, the Mass in England continued to be celebrated in Latin and the average person in the pew would scarcely have noticed any change at all except perhaps for places where the monastic houses had been confiscated.

The significant changes in the English Church came under the rule of Elizabeth I rather than with Henry. They were set forward in two Acts of the Parliament of England. The Act of Supremacy of 1559 re-established the English church's independence from Rome and The Act of Uniformity of 1559 set out the form the English church would now take. These events established the course of the Church of England.

During the next few centuries, different streams of emphasis began to emerge in the Anglican Church. The 17th Century was truly the Golden Age of Anglicanism when the Caroline Divines—men like Laud, Sparrow, Ken, Andrewes and Hooker—shone brightest. In this period, we see theologians recognizing development and revelation as important in the life of the Church and the basis of faith being rooted in Scripture, Tradition and Reason. Many of the problems we are experiencing in the Church of the 21st Century have come about because the concepts of development and revelation have been largely abandoned.

The development of teaching and tradition in the Church is no recent innovation. The Council of Jerusalem, chronicled in the Acts of the Apostles, attests to several of the adjustments the Christian community needed to make including attitudes about circumcision and how the Church would deal with Gentiles. The Church over the centuries has adjusted its thinking concerning numerous issues about which scripture has always held definite opinions, such as usury (money lending), slavery and divorce, to name a few.

Movements and trends in the Church unfold in a way similar to those in the secular sphere. When one view gains sway, there is typically a swing of the pendulum and an opposite reaction is stimulated. The Age of Enlightenment, in which the Rationalists of the 18th Century stressed moral philosophy and reason, was eventually countered by an evangelical revival, led by people like John Wesley, a priest of the Anglican Church. Anglicanism seemed able to embrace it all, which was certainly its crowning virtue. When people tired of the evangelical approach, which tended to undervalue intellectual pursuits and overvalue emotion, another movement sprang up. This was the Tractarian or Oxford Movement, which emphasized the sacramental, catholic and intellectual heritage of the English Church. The term "Tractarian" came from small publications the group produced which dealt with the nature of the Anglican Church. Newman's "Tract 90" on the Thirty Nine Articles of Religion raised a horrendous firestorm and seems to have curtailed the series. Men like Pusey, Newman and Froude established a renewed interest in the historic and catholic tradition of the Church. It was in this era that the terms 'High Church' and 'Low Church' came into use.

A common misconception about this terminology is that 'high' implies fancy ritual and ceremony and 'low' the lack thereof. The original concept had much more to do with opinions about the nature of the Church. Early Anglo-Catholics in the 1830s and 40s were actually rather moderate in their ceremonial, but had a very strong position on the authority and tradition of the Church.

People sometimes have odd ideas of what churchmanship actually is with regard to high and low. I recall my Grandmother telling me about an incident that happened in her parish church in 1912, not long after they emigrated from England to Canada. At the time, they were living in Sapperton near New Westminster. The vicar of St.

Mary's decided to introduce the surplice—a simple white linen vestment—to wear over his cassock instead of the black academic gown that had apparently been common in some places at that time. This was thought to be moving the parish in a decidedly 'high church' direction. Today it would be considered quite protestant. On one occasion, I encountered a man who, in the course of a discussion about churchmanship, told me he thought High Church meant that the clergy spoke with British accents! I presume he must have concluded that I was not very 'High Church'.

Over time, the High Church movement did move more and more toward expressing Anglican 'catholicity' in Roman forms. There is a wonderful story (perhaps apocryphal) about a Rector of the Church of St. Mary Magdalene in Toronto. St. Mary's is in a middle class, Italian neighbourhood of Toronto. One morning, the priest noticed a woman draped in a black mantilla saying her rosary in the Lady Chapel. Her Marian devotion was nothing unusual at St. Mary's, but she was so obviously Italian the rector worried she might have mistakenly come into the wrong church. He respectfully approached her and whispered:

"Signora, do you know this is an Anglican Church?"
"Si!"

"Perhaps you don't understand. This is the Church of England."

"Si!"

"Church of England! ... No Pope!"

"Good!"

Gradually, the Church of England began to see itself as not only for the English, but as a Church with an important function in the wider world and today Anglicanism is found in most countries and numbers some 77 million people.

The genius of the Anglican Communion was that such diversity was able to hold together for over 400 years without legislation or vigorous definition. In the years to come, my attraction to this inclusiveness would evolve into great sadness as division and intolerance emerged, and lines were drawn in the sand between supposedly opposing factions.

✠

Soon after my introduction to St. Andrew's I took on a number of volunteer jobs within the parish; singing in the choir; teaching Sunday school; being a volunteer janitor and generally immersing myself in the workings of the church. During this period, a friend from high school had also become involved with an Anglican parish. Knowing I had recently been baptized and confirmed, he asked me if I wanted to come to his confirmation service. It would be at St. James' Church in East Vancouver, and I could get a ride with his family. His father was Anglican and his mother, Baptist. On the appointed day, they came by, picked me up, and off we went to St. James'.

At this point in my spiritual growth, I knew that the liturgy in the Anglican Church had a 'catholic' feel, which appealed to me. However, all I knew of the Anglican Church service was from St. Andrews, which was really a small country parish, very simple and even a little stark. Imagine then my wonder as I stepped into St. James' where I was met with the fragrant, sweet odour of incense, rich and mystical pipe organ music, and all within a magnificent church building. It was rather like Dorothy stepping out of her black and white house and into the Technicolor land of OZ.

As the liturgy unfolded I experienced a sensation of being transported into heaven—not unlike the heaven described by St. John the Evangelist in the book of Revelation—crystal, gold and dazzling light. My friend's Baptist mother, seated next to me, also appeared to be stirred by the grandeur of the ceremonial. The rite began

A Priest's Tale

with the entrance of the Bishop from the north sanctuary aisle; Bishop Gower vested in festal cope and mitre, accompanied by a stately organ fanfare and preceded by the sanctuary party of clergy, crucifer, thurifer and torches. It proved to be a defining moment for me—one of a number of significant occasions in my spiritual journey.

At sea the infinite arch of stars over the dark sea had elicited thoughts and queries about existence and a deep yearning for its Creator. There was an irresistible beckoning to reach upward and outward-to draw together the ostensibly conflicting notions of the spiritual and fleshly realms and to find my dwelling place in the overwhelming scheme of God's design. Worship at St. James' at that confirmation service offered yet another glimpse into the dimension of the transcendent and spurred me on to seek out communion with the Divine.

As I muse upon it now, the feelings and emotions that I experienced at the time were undoubtedly the validation of my senses. Catholic worship is so full of sounds and smells and sensations, the very essence of all that is 'body affirming' and existential.

At coffee time after the confirmation service I was talking to Jack Cochrane, one of the alter servers who in the course of our conversation, said, "Well, if you liked this, you should come back on a Sunday for High Mass". Over the course of the next year when I could, I did so and it was exquisitely enriching.

Sometime before I graduated from high school, or just after, I spoke with the Rector at St. Andrew's regarding ministry. On my first approach, I asked him what one had to do to prepare for the ministry. He said one had to go to university for seven years. Well, so much for that, I thought! I couldn't see myself managing seven years of university. However, in a few months I broached the subject with him again. This time I asked him what one had to study in preparation for ordination. He answered with a list of things: liturgy, Church history, New Testament, Old Testament, Apologetics, and…Greek. That did it. Greek? I didn't think so. And yet, after another interval, I found myself opening the subject once again.

Oddly, I thought, the Rector never appeared excited or eager when I asked my questions, always maintaining a very matter-of-fact attitude. I expected him to beam, or at least show some encouragement. In retrospect, I think he was wise not to promote anything, but rather to let me come to my own decision. However, the third time I started asking my questions, he just looked at me and said, "I think we should make an appointment with Father Peake at the college, and go for a visit."

A Priest's Tale

A week or so later we drove out to the college and we had an interview with Fr. Peake. I was shown around the College, the library, the chapel and refectory. I found it all quite intriguing. Over the course of the next few months, and a few more interviews, it was decided I would enter into the liberal arts program at UBC with the expectation of moving on to the Theological programme afterward.

As my family did not have the financial means to assist in this academic endeavour, I worked for a year as a bank teller at the Bank of Nova Scotia after graduating from North Burnaby High School and saved money. In September 1959, I enrolled in First Year Arts at U.B.C. and moved into residence at the Anglican Theological College.

Life at the Anglican Theological College (ATC) was a very broadening experience for me. The College, on the University of British Columbia campus, was the result of the joining of St. Mark's College and Latimer Hall in the 1920s. The former had a Tractarian, High Church leaning and the latter, a Low Church tradition. When I first lived at ATC the college had about 30 rooms for residents, half of which were occupied by theologs, and the other half by arts and science students. It was very like an Oxford college in many respects. The daily chapel services of Matins and

Evensong and the Wednesday, Friday and Sunday celebrations of the Holy Eucharist were mandatory for the theologs and pre-theology students. Academic gowns, jackets and ties were the norm for chapel, lectures and meals.

The discipline of the daily office was a marvellous preparation for priestly life and has shaped my daily routine over these past 50 years. The atmosphere in the college was somewhat monastic. Meals in the refectory were formal; the faculty dined at the head table and white-jacketed student waiters served. I began waiting on tables in my second year, and did so each year after as it brought in a modest stipend, which assisted my finances for board and tuition.

Looking back on those first months, I blush to recall my naiveté. Before entering this life, I had often wondered if I was good enough to live in such hallowed halls with people preparing for the priesthood. It didn't take long for me to realize they were no different than I.

There was a rule in the college that after 8:00 pm there would be quiet throughout the building—this was an institution of learning. I found it exciting to be living in this 'holy' environment. My small room was adorned with crucifixes and votive lights, as were the rooms of my other 'catholic' friends. One particular evening after I had been in residence for a couple of weeks I was saying my evening

A Priest's Tale

devotions around ten PM and heard raucous voices just outside my door. I waited for a few minutes to see if the noise would subside. It didn't. Finally I opened my door. The four students engaged in boisterous conversation fell silent and looked at me. With the most hurt expression and tone of voice I could muster, I said, "Some people are trying to pray." There was a few seconds of silent tableau, then one of the group said, "Oh Dodman, fuck-off." I was so astonished I retreated into my room and quickly closed the door.

I had been advised that taking classical Greek would stand me in good stead for later studies in New Testament Greek. Thus began an interesting association with Dr. Malcolm McGregor who taught Greek and Classics at UBC. He was a tremendously colourful character. He was the last member of the academic staff at UBC to retain the academic gown and he was easily identified as he strode about the campus, gown flowing in his wake. He was a very tall and striking man with a wonderful mane of grey hair. Initially, I thought he must be a Presbyterian or something of that stripe because he took great delight in teasing and heckling the Anglican theologs in his classes. I discovered, however, he too was an Anglican. One of Dr. McGregor's eccentricities was his insistence that his students have the spring-coil type of exercise book with cardboard covers, because when he returned our corrected lessons he did so by air, and he thought these had the best aerodynamic design. He would shout our surnames and fling the books toward us. The beginning of each class was always a frantic scramble to catch our corrected work without being struck in the face.

My studies in Greek with Dr. McGregor were instrumental in instilling in me a love for the Greek language and history. Dr. McGregor spoke glowingly of the ideal society and achievements of Greece—the legacy of people like Solon and Pericles. Many years later, when I visited Athens, I walked around in the Agora, the Acropolis and Mars Hill. It was thrilling to stand on the very spot where St. Paul had addressed the Athenians. It was here that Paul noted an altar to an *unknown god* and spoke of it to them, insisting that he knew who that god was. Floods of associations ran through my mind in those few moments that afternoon. That evening I think someone tried to pick me up. I had dined near the Acropolis and was strolling through the trendy Plaka area, which is at the foot of the Acropolis. I had made an attempt to learn some Modern Greek for this visit and was able to get by just a little. At this moment, a distinguished looking gentleman about my own age stopped by me as I looked in a shop window. He was very pleasant and said "Good evening". I was able to

A Priest's Tale

fake it for a few moments, but when it came out that I was visiting from Canada, he immediately switched to English—mercifully. He said he was surprised and that I looked Greek. I thought, "Oh you're just trying to make conversation—or more than likely it is because of my nose—I've heard that one before." Nothing came of this chance encounter; thankfully, as I am not attracted to men my own age and he did not try to steer the conversation in any particular direction. He was very discreet. We finally wandered on our respective ways after saying good-byes.

One frustration with my Greek studies in college was that the first year Greek course was designed to prepare one to read Herodotus, Xenophon, and some of the other historians. The vocabulary was militaristic; spears, soldiers, chariots and battles. The reading for the second year course, however, consisted of philosophy—quite a shock to the system. Plato's *Euthyphro*, a dialogue between Euthyphro and Socrates, uses a completely different kind of vocabulary. I found Plato difficult enough to grasp in English translation. However, I muddled through.

My other studies at UBC were a mixture of the humanities: English Literature, Greek and Roman history, psychology, sociology, geography, and mathematics. Although I had done exceptionally well in the advanced mathematics courses in high school, I found Math 101 quite demanding. It consisted mostly of statistics and calculus. The professor was Dr. Ben Moyls, who I came to know later as he was also the organist at the university parish. Our section was very large, about 250 of us, and the class was taught in one of the largest lecture halls. At the first lecture, Dr. Moyls asked us if we would be kind enough to keep the same seats throughout the semester. He began the first day to memorize about a dozen names. Next class he memorized another dozen. This continued until he got right to the back rows and had mastered all of our names, which amazed me.

I spent the summers of these first three years working in the north at the asbestos mine in Cassiar, B.C., which has long been closed since asbestos was discovered to have such health risks. As I had some experience in banking, I was assigned to work in the payroll office. During these summers I also did some lay leadership of worship in the local Anglican Church, as there was no incumbent priest at that time. The money I earned in the summers went toward the following year's tuition and board.

My infatuation with Wayne when I was ten had raised no questions in my mind. As children, boys and girls typically eschew each other so my early feelings did not stand out as anything unusual. I assumed everyone was experiencing the same feelings. And it felt natural and wonderful to me. It was not until adolescence, and the onslaught of puberty, that I became aware the boys and girls around me were beginning to interact and take a new interest in each other. It was then that I began to realize my lack of interest in girls and my growing interest in other boys made me different. But that was how I perceived it—as being different. Homosexuality was not spoken of in those days, and therefore could not be a topic of conversation. However, I could see I was not like the other boys, and it went quite beyond my somewhat unusual interests. But at that time I relegated the whole issue to the back of my mind. I don't recall that being a conscious decision—I simply didn't think about it nor deal with it. Perhaps I simply considered it another one of my many quirks.

During my first years at university, however, this compartmentalization was probed and began to break down when I became infatuated and fell completely in love with my best friend.

I had known Bruce for some years. We were from the same general neighbourhood and attended the same schools. Until I became involved with St. Andrew's, Bruce was just another one of those handsome, popular boys I admired from a distance. Through our association at St. Andrew's, where we both sang in the choir and taught Sunday School, Bruce and I fell rather naturally into a friendship and began chumming around together. Never before had I been friends with one of the young men to whom I was attracted and the experience proved to be, by turns, wonderful and excruciatingly stressful. Seeing Bruce almost every weekend; talking about everything and nothing; going out to dinner; movies; trips to local beaches and parks, or to church, I could no longer deny or ignore the reality of my feelings. They were constantly before me.

Over the course of my first two years at university it got to the point where my thoughts were preoccupied with Bruce. All the fantasies I had about boys seemed to be focussed in him. He was funny, charming and very handsome—all of which made the situation impossible to bear. It was an agony to be together so often—to be so close—yet never as close as I longed to be.

To make matters worse, I was completely alone with these feelings. I may have known the word homosexual but I didn't know anyone else who was one—at least, that was what I believed. As far as I knew, I was the only person in the world with such desires. All around me my friends were beginning to date and pair up and I saw no place for myself in that. I simply was not attracted to girls and it seemed like that was the only option. No matter how I looked at it, all I really desired was Bruce.

My emotions were so twisted up worrying about my sexuality and obsessing over Bruce that my studies began to deteriorate. In lectures I found myself daydreaming and even falling asleep. The drone of the lecturer's voice became a soothing narcotic and I would simply tune out, thus losing any ability to absorb the subject matter. It became more and more difficult to follow the course work. When exam times came around I was unable to deal with the questions, as I had not done sufficient reading. I was on the verge of failing in most of my courses but had not the slightest idea how to go about rectifying the situation. With Cole's notes and a very cursory skim of the novel *Pride and Prejudice* (which I found painfully boring) I was able to at least pass by a slim margin. The response to my essay question, I fear, was full of platitudinous drivel sounding much like what we frequently hear in political speeches, amounting to almost no content whatever.

✠

In 1962, during the second semester of my third year at UBC, I stumbled across an advertisement in a church magazine placed by an Anglo-Catholic theological college in Barbados. There was a photograph of the historic buildings and another showing the seminarians and clergy in procession led by a thurifer and torches on their way to the Sunday High Mass in the College Chapel. Accompanying the photograph was an article about the college, which in those days served the Province of the West Indies. My curiosity was aroused by the idea of such a 'catholic' college and something in me was drawn to the idea of missionary work in exotic places. I wondered if perhaps a change of venue would wrench me out the doldrums.

At the time it never occurred to me I was attracted to this exotic college because it would allow me to put some distance between my problems and myself. At the time I was in such a state of confusion over my studies; my feelings for Bruce; and generally so miserable that I thought—as one is wont to do—things might be different in a different location. As if I could give my problems the slip. This quaint historic college in the Caribbean was the perfect escape hatch—or so I thought—from my life and seemed to represent a future when more and more each day I was wondering if I even had one.

I entered into a lengthy correspondence with Father Anselm Genders, the Principal of Codrington College, and was eventually accepted for the fall semester. After the long flight, we finally touched down in Bridgetown. I was pleasantly startled at the blast of warm, hibiscus-scented air that rushed in when the flight attendant opened the door. A welcoming party of several white cassocked monks and seminarians awaited us in the terminal building at Seawell Airport.

At that time Codrington College was run by the Community of the Resurrection, whose motherhouse is in Mirfield, Yorkshire. Mirfield maintained a considerable presence in South Africa, and in the late 1950's the monks of Mirfield were invited to administer Codrington College as a theological seminary for the West Indies. Previously it had been a liberal arts college affiliated with Durham University. The considerable lands and wonderfully historic buildings that made up the Codrington Estate and sugar plantation had been given to the Church by Christopher Codrington, who was born there in 1668 when it was home to his family.

There were two principal buildings on the Estate. The larger was the grand Codrington mansion, which was situated at the end of a beautiful palm-lined drive. In front of the building was a huge lily pool inhabited by enormous bullfrogs and goldfish.

The monks lived in the Priory, which was a somewhat smaller house predating the main house. It sounds luxurious although it was quite rustic. There were electric lights, but no hot water. Windows were always open but had no glass or screens as is typical in tropical climates, only shutters for use in the hurricane season. One shared one's living space with all manner of bats and cockroaches and beetles. I never quite got used to being wakened in the night by something struggling to get out from underneath me to discover it was a horrid inch and a half long insect of some sort.

The monastic existence at Codrington was of another age and was a wonderful change from the world I had left behind. This was before Vatican II, and the liturgical life in Anglican religious communities was quite different then from what it is today. Strange as it may seem to some, Vatican II had a noticeable impact on the Anglican Church. Just as an example—today in communities it is customary to celebrate only one Conventual Mass each day with the whole community gathered as an act of unity. In those days, it was the custom for each priest to celebrate his own private Mass each day as his offering of the Holy Sacrifice.

I enjoyed the cycle of worship at Codrington immensely but found studying almost impossible. It was not due to my worries about my sexuality, or the subjects, but because of the atmosphere. The weather was at least 80 degrees every day; there was rarely a cloud in the sky; and the vegetation was wild and luxuriant—a most distracting setting when one is trying to lend attention to Greek and Hebrew.

The College was within the Parish of St. John on the eastern coast of the island not far from the rugged Bathsheba coast. Afternoon excursions to bathe in the surf at Conset Beach were a welcome reprieve from the heat. There was a swimming pool at the College but its waters had long ago gone murky and stagnant lacking adequate filtration. Recreation took other forms as when the seminarians played cricket against the Diocesan clergy team. In those days it seemed almost every priest and the bishop of the Diocese of Barbados was English, which is no longer the case. Cricket was a strange experience for me, who neither understood nor appreciated even the basic principles of baseball.

It was a little less than an hour's journey by car through the cane fields to Bridgetown, the capital. On occasions when someone had to be met at the airport or when one of the Fathers needed to go into town it was a special treat for anyone who might be asked to go to assist. We always wore white cassocks which were for special occasions, and it was a thrill for a 'would be priest' to be wandering around in public in clerical garb. The people of

Barbados knew the College well and we were always very respectfully and warmly greeted in Bridgetown.

At that time the population of Barbados was largely Anglican and the Church in that diocese, as well as in most of the West Indies, was decidedly 'catholic'. Despite the large Anglican population of Barbados, it was amazing how many odd splinter groups and cults were represented on the Island. This was most apparent at the bus terminal in Bridgetown where the practitioners of these churches could be encountered giving impromptu evangelical speeches. Often they wore an incongruous assortment of liturgical things including crucifixes, eucharistic vestments and even birettas. There always seemed to be religious antics going on there. Not only the exotic street preachers, but also animated discussions about the minutiae of theological thought from the theology of grace to the real meaning of the word *baptize*. Did the Greek *'baptizein'* mean just 'pouring' or was it 'immersion'? Could a child below the age of reason be baptized? It was fascinating to see these islanders getting into such intricate debates. Perhaps the strong presence of the Church had provoked this highly charged theological atmosphere. Anyone daring to appear in Bridgetown in a cassock was surely fair game for an argument. It was a novel and encouraging thing to be living in an ethos where Anglicanism was so robust.

A Priest's Tale

The College Estate was extremely large—it encompassed almost all the land within sight from the seminary. There were scores of tenant families living on the Estate and who were dependent upon it. It was rather like a large family and many of the people lived in the traditional one-room, Bajan huts and would raise yams, a few chickens and perhaps a goat or pig for sustenance. Visiting in the Parish of St. John—just to the north of the College—was my first experience with real poverty. There were many women, often grandmothers, with children to tend to but rarely did I notice many husbands. They did not seem to exist. One afternoon I was in a little house talking with a woman and there were chickens jumping up onto the table and piglets squealing at my feet, which for a Canadian boy was quite another dimension.

Sometimes Estate tenants would bring their sows to the College Farm to be inseminated by one of the 'Codrington' boars (No, not the teaching faculty). The College had, amongst other animals, two huge boars. People would bring their sows in ox-carts, then open the gate at the end of the boar pen and force them out. One needs to remember that these animals are enormous, sometimes weighing 300-400 pounds. Once the sow was into the enclosure the boar then apparently needed to be 'excited' by manipulation to get him going. The sows never seemed to like this procedure at all. Perhaps they were shy and didn't appreciate all the cassocked spectators. On one such occasion, a large group of us had come over to watch the proceedings. Rather appropriate, I thought to myself, that *seminarians* were so keenly interested in this activity. During the process this time there was some sort of miscalculation and the sow went berserk breaking through the fence and rampaging around. That was the day I discovered that I could actually climb a breadfruit tree while wearing a cassock.

Christmas was a rather odd experience for me that year. We had met a Winnipeg businessman—a friend of Codrington College—who owned a lovely beach cottage on the St. James' Coast. My friend and fellow Canadian, John, and I had met this man at a College function and he kindly encouraged us to make use of his beach house for the Christmas holidays. It was right on the beach between the sea and the St. James' Cemetery. We had also met and become friendly with a Canadian family living in Bridgetown. Mrs. Mosbaugh was an interesting woman who owned a fashion dress shop in Hastings and was a concert pianist who sometimes gave recitals around the Island. She and her family had come to Barbados because of her husband's work. When he died suddenly, she and the children had remained. John and I invited the family to join us for Christmas Dinner along with about ten of the West Indian students from the College. Somehow, we managed to find a turkey and Christmas puddings and all the trimmings including a Christmas tree, which was obviously imported. The West Indian students came bringing with them their own exotic looking Christmas pastries and candies, making it something of a cross-cultural affair. But for me, nothing was as peculiar as celebrating Christmas in eighty-degree weather in a house overlooking a white sandy beach and tropical blue ocean.

As the fall semester came to a close, I knew I could not continue at Codrington. As fascinating as the tropics and the life of a West Indian missionary were, I knew it would be too much of a shift. The heat was a constant distraction and I found myself continually longing for the changing Canadian seasons, and for my family and friends. Needless to say, it was extremely difficult in this glamorous setting to put one's mind to the study of Greek and Hebrew.

My sexuality was also continuing to puzzle and torment me. I questioned my ability to find a place in society or to have a place in the priesthood. Homosexuality was something I knew very little about, but for the feelings I harboured within me. It was never mentioned in the sermons I heard or discussed in church circles. Virtue, goodness, morality, honouring the Lord through our daily work; all of these were well-worked grist in sermons. Sexuality, however, and specifically homosexuality, was an unknown entity. I doubted my place in society because society showed me only the ideal of one man and one woman, happy or unhappy, it didn't matter so long as they were married. That was the 'norm'. And there I was, flooded with feelings, desires, and longings for men. I had no basis by which to evaluate my feelings but for the existing model of heterosexual marriage. During the era in which I grew up that was simply what one did—marry, settle down, and raise a family. There seemed no other alternative. Where did this leave me? In the Anglican Church, priests are allowed to marry, and most did. A friend once remarked that where the Roman Catholic Church has compulsory celibacy, the Anglican Church seems almost to have compulsory marriage. How could I go on into the priesthood when I still had no idea what place I had in society but as a freak that had yearnings no one else seemed to have?

I returned to Vancouver in January of 1963, uncertain about everything. I had left Codrington in the middle of the year and I didn't know if I would be going back to UBC to pursue my theological degree in the fall. I was seriously questioning whether the priesthood was where I belonged. Was it the right path for me?

Once back in Vancouver I set about looking for work. I was hoping to find something in the city, as I had missed a number of family occasions during my first few years of university as I was working summers in the north, including the wedding of my sister Gail. But at the time unemployment levels were high in urban areas so once again, I approached the Vancouver hiring offices for the northern mines.

Cassiar, the mine I had worked at for several summers had no openings at the time but there was a lead-zinc-silver mine in Elsa, in the centre of the Yukon Territory that was hiring. It wasn't until I arrived there and the personnel man was looking over my work history at Cassiar, that I discovered they didn't have any openings for clerical work. The manager informed me I would be working underground. I was somewhat concerned about this, being of slight build. I wondered if I would be physically able to handle the work required of a hard rock miner.

Outfitted with all the necessary clothing and a hardhat with the miner's battery powered lamp fixed upon it, off I went to my first shift. The batteries were charged while one was off shift and they worked well for an 8-hour work period. The light was focussed in quite a direct way, like a flashlight beam. As it is fixed on the hardhat, one must move his head in order to direct the light to whatever is to be seen. It was not at all apparent to me at the time but later on I was amazed to see how the use of these lamps had conditioned my responses. When I returned home at the end of summer, my mother was the first to notice. At the dinner table I would be looking around to locate the butter or salt and pepper and in the process moving my whole head so it pointed at the desired object. Mother looked at me and said, "What is wrong with you?" I hadn't even noticed it. It was a little while before I got back into the habit of moving my eyes rather than my head to look around.

I went to my first shift underground with a sense of trepidation. We walked into the main entrance of the mine, a long drift that went into the side of the mountain. The drifts and raises in the mine were very rough and crudely blasted out of solid rock. Finally, we reached the rickety elevator they called 'the cage'. The descent was rather fast for my taste. As we dropped our gravity became almost zero G. I was working on the 900-foot level. It didn't take long to get used to the fact we were so far underground. Ten feet or 900 feet, it didn't feel any different to me.

A Priest's Tale

Miners always work in pairs or groups depending on the task. I was paired with Erich who seemed a very affable though rather gruff German. He was welcoming, however, and we got on quite well. He had the most pronounced German accent I had ever heard—of the quintessential Second World War Hollywood variety. During our time together, I learned some of his background. In 1944 Erich had been a U-Boat crewmember and his sub had been captured off the coast of New England. He was taken to a prisoner of war camp in Texas where he learned English. His attitude about life after his capture was commendable. I never quite discovered how he ended up in Canada, but I know he loved the Queen and was very happy to be living here.

Erich was a shift boss for the 900-foot level. During lunch break he would get on the telephone with his superior in the mine office and give updates on our progress. There would be 15 or so of us in the lunch station, which was really just an enlarged part of a drift but with lights and heating. We always got a chuckle out of listening to Erich's side of the conversation. I entertained visions of being on a U-Boat. Erich never seemed to be saying—or should I say shouting—anything other than, "JA…JA…JA…JA…JA." Then he would come off the phone and start cursing the boss. And could Erich curse—in English, German, French and Yiddish. It was so extreme I found it hilarious rather than offensive.

During work whenever something went wrong, or if he hurt himself, he would let go with a string of expletives that seemed endless. It usually went something like, "Fucken, whoren, bitchen, cunten, dirty." For some odd reason the string of profanities always seemed to end with 'dirty' (which he pronounced "duhdy"). I think he believed that 'dirty' was the vilest curse of all in English and therefore should be saved for last. I delighted in his tirades—they made the cold, wet atmosphere of the mine a little more bearable.

The endless Yukon summer days played havoc with my sleep. It was constantly light, the sun only dipping below the mountains for a few hours each night. We put a heavy blanket over our bunkhouse window to try to create the illusion of night. That only solved one problem. The other thing that made it impossible to sleep was the noise in the bunkhouse from doors slamming as people came and went and the constant conversations in the hallway. The one place I found I could really sleep was in the depths of the mine where it was quiet. I would sometimes take a nap at lunch break.

My time in the north was also a time to think about my future, and whether or not I would have one as a priest.

A Priest's Tale

If the truth were told, I don't believe it ever actually crossed my mind that my attraction to men negated the possibility of my being a priest. My real concerns were rooted in how I would relate to society. Would I simply accept the fact that my life was going to be that of a bachelor? Would I ever experience the love and affection that I craved? I envied the men and women who seemed to have such happy lives together—husbands and wives, marriage and children. That certainly did not seem to be an option and to be honest; the thought of raising children was certainly never an attraction for me at all.

In the end, I decided not to return to the theological college. I was too unsure of myself, and my place in society. Instead, I enrolled in the music program at UBC and unwittingly entered into what was probably the bleakest chapter of my life.

I was still hopelessly in love with Bruce and he was undoubtedly the chief reason I went into the music programme. He was in year two of the programme, and I knew I would be able to be near him. I was also rather confused about my life and my future—I loved music and thought perhaps this was the path I should be taking. I was boarding at that time with Gail and Gordie Kent, my sister and brother-in-law, and Bruce and I travelled to the university together each day. These were precious times for me in spite of my confusion and dark moments.

It is painful and agonising for me, even to this day, to recall and write about my friendship with Bruce. Never had I adored anyone so intensely. Being with him so often was both a delight and a torment because, although I was infatuated with him, I knew I could never really possess him to the extent I wanted. My heart was swollen with desires and longings so powerful I could barely contain them. The anguish of being so close to Bruce, and yet feeling at such a distance, finally drove me to the point where I felt I had to confess my feelings and explain my situation to him. This was the first time I ever revealed my inmost secret to anyone. And when I say, 'explain my situation', I have to confess, at the time I was hardly able to adequately express what it was I was feeling, I had such a crude, imprecise notion of it myself.

Bruce was a bit dazed at first, but he didn't flee or reject me, rather he was concerned and extremely understanding. I, of course, thought this sharing would ease the agony of longing I felt, especially as Bruce responded with such compassion. I was wrong about that. After he knew the situation it actually exacerbated everything and made the misery of my longing more intense. My feelings were on the table. However, Bruce could not reciprocate. I loved him all the more because of his empathetic attitude. Yet, to be honest, part of what drove me to confide in Bruce was the secret hope that he might tell me he felt the same way. When that didn't happen, my fantasy of Bruce and me as lovers suffered a severe blow. But such intense hopes and desires do not die easily.

My outlook during this period was exceedingly grim. My thoughts seemed to be constantly focussed upon my sexuality, which was entangled with my love for Bruce, and there seemed to be no way to resolve the situation. I would watch Bruce interacting with his many friends and feel such a longing to have the seemingly carefree life he had. His social life appeared to be so vast and rich compared to mine. I ached to be *normal*. In retrospect, I know my problems were as much a difficulty for Bruce, inasmuch as they consumed a considerable amount of his time and emotional energy. But, he was always supportive in talking to me, being there for me and encouraging me.

One evening after an outing to the pub we sat in the car late into the night talking about my situation. Finally, when I went to leave Bruce smiled, kissed his fingers and touched them to my lips. It was a beautiful and tender gesture—thoughtfully acknowledging my feelings for him, yet at the same time, not allowing things to be misunderstood.

Bruce's mother was a godsend during this time. She was one person I was able to chat with easily and objectively when my own mother was simply unable to fill that role. She was also very wise and practical. I spent many hours with her at their kitchen table having coffee and conversation. After I came out to Bruce, he must have shared the news with her for she obviously knew of the situation. I think the poor boy was overwhelmed and needed to share with someone. I certainly had no problem with this, in fact, it was a relief and quite helpful. Bruce was so concerned about me and did not have the experience to grapple with such complex issues. I realize now how many people along my journey assisted in the very slow process of helping me make sense of my life.

To compound the confusion I felt during this difficult period in my life, I became involved with a girl. The music faculty at UBC was relatively small and consequently there was a high degree of social interaction between us. It didn't take long for well meaning friends to link me up with a partner for social events. She was a very nice person, short like me, and it appears the matchmakers thought we made a nice couple. I do have to admit it was pleasant to be able to go bowling—one of the few sports I liked—and be involved in other activities with someone and to be recognized and accepted as a couple.

A Priest's Tale

I quite liked Gaye—yes, the irony of her name has always amused me too—and we got along well together. However, I did not feel any attraction to her other than respect and delight in our friendship. I felt quite rotten at times, using Gaye as a sort of experiment to develop a heterosexual persona while all the time struggling with who I was and what my desires meant. The issue became even more complex when I realized Gaye was actually falling in love with me. That was certainly an experience I had never before encountered and it alarmed me.

At the time, however, I so wanted to be 'normal' I was prepared to go to any lengths. The pinnacle of this longing for supposed normalcy came one evening after Gaye and I had been to see a movie. As I was driving her home we parked by the ocean. She thought this a nice idea. It was a lovely starry night and I felt perhaps I could possibly get into the groove—in a manner of speaking—with hetero behaviour. We talked for some time and eventually began kissing and petting.

I had bought some condoms that afternoon, obviously premeditating some strategy. I was surprised to find myself actually becoming aroused, and could have certainly gone all the way—as they say. Thankfully, Gaye stopped things before they went too far. We settled down, composed ourselves, and I drove her home.

I say thankfully, because for all that I was aroused enough to fulfill the act, it would have been a gross abuse of our friendship. My heart would not have been in it. For all that I enjoyed Gaye's company, there was some deeper element lacking, some primordial connection of spirit and flesh, to which we give the name 'love'. I could never have loved Gaye in the romantic sense of the word where passion and reason come together; creating a bond that defies explanation, measure, or limit. And having had sex would likely have made the inevitable end of our relationship that much more hurtful for her.

I was frequently asked the question, usually by my parents or relatives, "When are you going to find a nice girl and settle down?" The question always irritated me. I knew it was not an option for me, nor did I want it. At least not with a girl. They meant well, of course, and I understood that. So after Gaye and I had been keeping company for a while, I thought it might be good to introduce her to my family. Gaye seemed to want that as well. I arranged with my family to bring Gaye over for dinner on a Sunday evening.

When we arrived at the house my parents and sisters were waiting in eager expectation, especially Mother. I realized how important this was for them and I was not a little uneasy. To me everyone in my family seemed unnaturally exuberant. I don't think Gaye noticed, as she didn't know them. Dinner proceeded pleasantly. No one asked any embarrassing or probing questions and Gaye seemed to be enjoying the situation. For me, however, the whole exercise felt like a ghastly charade—like I was using Gaye as a prop to placate my family's expectations.

Still, the social dynamics of dating Gaye were intriguing to me. I found it novel and somehow comfortable to be able to relax in the company of our circle of friends at the bowling alley or the occasional party and be thought of as a couple. Somehow, I had become abnormally accustomed to believing I had to justify my singleness. However, things were not to remain comfortable for long. As time progressed my relationship with Gaye seemed to require more definition. I sensed she was becoming much more attached to the relationship than I was. I knew it was heading for…Well, I didn't know what, but it seemed to be closing in on me. I came to realize it should be nipped in the bud now, before things got even more complicated.

I telephoned Gaye one Saturday afternoon and arranged to go round to her place that evening for coffee. It was one of those rainy, winter Vancouver evenings. I felt I should get right to the point when I arrived. But before I knew it, Gaye produced coffee and muffins and put on some music and the conversation was pleasant. A feeling of dread overcame me knowing what I had come to do. Choosing the right moment to do it was excruciating because there would be no right moment. We chatted about school and the dreadful weather and before I knew it the evening had been wiled away. Around eleven o'clock as I was putting on my shoes and coat, I knew I simply could not depart without having done the deed. Somehow I raised the subject and told her I could not continue with the relationship. I even told her I was gay, thinking it might help her understand it wasn't her, but me. Such a threadbare excuse! Although it happened to be true, I wondered to myself how many times that one has been proffered?

She somehow maintained her composure through all this. I said goodnight, careful to avoid any pecks on the cheek or touching. As soon as the door closed behind me, in spite of the roar of wind and rain, I could hear her anguish. The sound brought a sharp stab of guilt. As I ran the two blocks to the bus stop—umbrella inverting in the wind and tears welling in my eyes—for some odd reason I had flashes of my mother going through my mind. Perhaps some Freudian idea that I picked up somewhere, I thought, but God only knows why because I certainly do not subscribe to that particular psychological assumption. What a Vincent Price moment it was! I did feel I had done the right thing. Awkward and painful as the circumstances were, I took away from it a sense of closure. It was far more preferable to have confronted the issue then, before things went too far, got too involved, and evolved into a more convoluted and painful situation.

During that black year I was involved in the University Choir as was Bruce. Each year the Choir did one major concert. That particular year we performed a gala concert at the Queen Elizabeth Theatre—the combined University Choir and the Vancouver Bach Choir with the Vancouver Symphony Orchestra. The work was Verdi's "Requiem". Bruce and I were nowhere near each other in the risers as I sang tenor and he, bass; but I was abundantly aware of his presence. My emotions during that performance have remained vivid in my memory ever since.

I was constantly depressed at that time; overwhelmed by what I believed was a completely hopelessness situation. Thoughts of ending my life obsessed me from time to time and seemed an immediate and irrevocable way to stop the confusion and pain. I thought I was the only person on the face of the earth who had these desires. The utter loneliness was a constant burden. My life seemed worthless—would never include any dimension of love or intimacy. My attempt at 'normal' life—my brief relationship with Gaye—had of necessity been aborted.

Moreover, for all that Bruce continued to be extremely compassionate regarding my feelings for him, the knowledge that he could never return my ardour had settled like a weight in my heart.

The theatre was packed. The music was overwhelming—spiritual and lush. I was quickly caught up and remember thinking to myself, "This Requiem is for me. I am dead and have passed into God's grace". The familiar Latin texts had an uncanny affect, casting the whole experience in a surreal light. The turmoil within me collided with the music enveloping me. I felt a tangible union with the performance, and yet at the same time, a sense that I was the disembodied spirit for which the requiem was being offered. This was perhaps the most vivid experience in my life of being torn between what I perceived as two opposing forces—the spiritual and the carnal.

When I listen to the Requiem today, my mind is transported back to that performance and that moment in time although my thoughts about it are now pleasant—the old fears having been long since expunged. I love the Verdi Requiem immensely—perhaps even more so because of the passion I experienced while performing it.

The burden of my continual depression finally forced me to muster the courage to speak to my psychology professor. He was very practical and matter-of-fact about the whole thing. He was unfazed by my confession and simply gave me the name and telephone number of a psychologist at the University Hospital who specialized in counselling students with similar concerns. I made an appointment and began a series of sessions with him.

I went into these sessions with the unambiguous notion that I simply wanted to be cured. I suppose I truly believed that I had been unfortunately born with a handicap like a disease or deformity. I yearned to be like everyone else and enjoy the same things others enjoyed, however I had no presuppositions about how this might be achieved. I was prepared for anything—aversion therapy, surgery, medication—and I poured this all out to the doctor. Imagine my surprise when he bluntly stated that those things were not practical or even possible; that I would simply have to come to terms with and accept my sexuality.

In the year of my birth, 1937, Sigmund Freud had written, *"Homosexuality is assuredly no advantage, but it is nothing to be ashamed of, no vice, no degradation, it cannot be classified as an illness."* However, it was not until 1975 that the psychiatric community officially acknowledged this position. I look back now and realize how fortunate I was that the psychologist who dealt with me was far ahead of his time.

The counsellor didn't think I needed to change and explained that if I really was attracted to men nothing could be done to change that. It was not the 'norm' perhaps but it was no less a valid lifestyle. He counselled that I should accept my situation and adjust my thinking to take into account my desires. He even spoke about a Dean of Canterbury Cathedral—current at that time I believe—who was apparently known to be gay and lived with his lover. The doctor had obviously done his homework and knew exactly how best to approach me in all of this. But still, it was not that easy for him to convince me.

I was sunk deep in my depression and resisted what he was saying for many months. The counsellor encouraged me to accept myself. He may even have said in so many words that I was not alone. Homosexuality might not be the dominant persuasion, but it certainly wasn't a disorder to be treated. It was a slow process. Today, I shudder when I hear Christians talking about homosexuals as being sick, sinful, and abominations or making wrong choices. It is particularly offensive that the Catholic Church in the 21st century persists in using the term *disordered* to describe us. One assumes that would have direct implications for the One who orders all things; and that assertion begs the next and obvious question, "Why ever would He do that?"

A Priest's Tale

The sessions eventually ended although the details of how that came about are now lost to me in the mists of time. Afterward, I needed considerable time to digest all of this new information. It is a process that has been unfolding through all the years of my life as I've met more and more couples, gay and straight, and seen first hand how much they have in common; how what defines a happy relationship is not the gender of those involved, but how they treat one another.

There was something of an immediate reaction, however. During the last part of that academic year, the wise counsel of the doctor seemed to be taking an actual hold on my perception. My depression began to subside, and I was able to begin eliminating some of the debilitating ideas that had unfortunately become a part of my psyche. I started to see that life was not as dreary or as lonely as I had thought. The slowly maturing realization that I was not alone, that my life might unfold in a productive way, began to emerge from the darkness in which I had existed. Life is a process of growing and learning which never ends, or at least *should* never end.

As I began to think more about my life—or the idea that I actually had a life—my thoughts turned once again to entering seminary and moving seriously toward ordination.

What had seemed for several years the final, bleak act of my life was thankfully just a brief layover in hell.

I received a mixed response from my friends in the music faculty when I announced I would be returning to theological college and preparation for the priesthood. Some wondered why I would ever want to do such a thing. Others were supportive and happy for me. One girl in particular, Sheila, seemed to have an axe to grind with religion and began to badger me unmercifully with endless thorny questions and criticisms. They were not so much unanswerable questions as they were sharp opinions and darts thinly veiled as questions.

It was the habit of our small group to have frequent, inexpensive dinners in the cafeteria near the music building. Of an evening, ten or so of us would gather and it was in this setting that Sheila would mount her attacks. I sensed a number of the others were uncomfortable and perhaps even a little annoyed with Sheila's constant badgering. I remained silent for the most part, shrugging off the questions. I didn't wish to engage in what was obviously a senseless debate.

However, after enduring this incessant baiting for a number of weeks, one evening I finally snapped. Sheila got onto me about believing in an afterlife and heaven. It wasn't her question I found so irritating—the question is an excellent and important one—but her insinuation that because I did believe in such things I must be rather dim-witted. My hackles rose. I was quite fed up with this constant flack in front of people I liked and respected. In all probability Sheila thought this inquisition would impress them. Maintaining my composure, I finally looked across the table at her and said, "Look at it this way, Sheila. If I am wrong I will never know the difference, will I? But if you are wrong, you *will* know." That was followed by a short silence and for some reason that was the end of her harassment. The conversation turned to other things and Sheila never brought up the subject again. At the time I falsely prided myself for having come up with such a brilliant riposte only to discover in my studies some years later that Blaise Paschal had said the very thing several centuries before. There is truly nothing new under the sun as the book of Ecclesiastes affirms.

✠

It was a crisp fall evening in 1965 when my theological studies began in earnest. After a Sung Evensong in the beautiful new Chapel of the Epiphany there was a wine and cheese reception in the Principal's residence. Thirty students representing each of the three years of the programme at the Anglican Theological College of British Columbia made informal introductions to each other during conversation and began the year on a festive note—warmed by a glowing fire in the hearth and some fine sherry and snacks. I felt remarkably good having made the decision to continue toward the priesthood. I had weathered the grim storm of depression and hopelessness, and come out of it with a new determination—even a sense of optimism.

Throughout my undergraduate years, the buildings of the college were as they had been since the college opened in 1927. In the two years prior to my entering Divinity, the college had undergone significant change. A new residential wing had been added, along with offices and the new Chapel. Clever architecture and landscaping had created an open-ended quad with a lawn between the new residence, the offices, and the Chapel. I lived almost the whole of my three years of seminary on the lower floor of the new residence overlooking the quad. Formerly, the College had about 30 rooms but now had 85, with perhaps 70 arts and science students living in residence. To my mind, this afforded a very good mix. Theologs interacting with the arts and science students was to prove a healthy atmosphere where hallway and common room discussions were energetic and keen. The non-theology residents were all Anglican to one degree or another. Naturally, there were many who were testing out their first go at independence, taking on new ideas, flexing their perspective, and debating their beliefs.

As one would expect, the perennial discussion was the 'religion versus science' debate. Frequently the discussion in the dining room turned to the arguments for creation or the big bang. One of the senior theological students had been a science major and held a degree in physics. He was quite adept at discussing these issues from either the theological or scientific point of view, as he was fluent in the language of each. Scientists often take the attitude that physics is a closed discipline in which everything is always constant. Ken, to my delight, was able to point out numbers of exceptions for which science simply has no explanation. The importance of being able to cross over the divide between the disciplines and discuss issues from different approaches was gradually etched into my brain. I marvel at how much learning can occur in an atmosphere of open discussion and debate.

New and challenging ideas were not just the fodder of the dining hall. My perceptions were being tested and stretched in the classroom as well. Old Testament studies were the first arena in which I encountered some of the thorny problems that abound in the study of scripture. I, like so many people, had a simplistic view of the Bible. It was the Word of God and our task was simply to learn it and apply it to life. Quite logically, our introduction to scripture delved into the questions of textual transmission, translation, canon and technical issues, which are a part of caring for and preserving the scriptures. I assumed the Bible, with gilt edges and black leather covers, had existed from the very earliest days of the Church. I discovered the very first task in scriptural studies was to tackle the question of 'canon', or the body of writings the Church accepted as authoritative in the first formative centuries. During the years of my parish ministry I met scores of people who believe that the Church fashioned itself around the principles already contained in the Bible. This was not at all accurate. The Scriptures are truly the Church's Book—the product of an already existing community. Much deliberation was put into deciding which of the thousands of existing writings should be included. No simple matter. Should the strange Gospel of Thomas be in it? Should Revelation be included? Why not the beautiful and pastoral letters of Clement? In my opinion the inclusion of the extremely cryptic Apocalypse of St. John the Divine, which had for some time been on the dubious list, has brought more grief and false teaching to the life of Christianity than any other writing. It is, quite predictably, the favourite source of preaching by the lunatic fringe. However, the

A Priest's Tale

Church spoke with a unified voice and that decision seems to be about the only one all Christians continue to honour leaving aside the issue of the Inter-Testamental, sometimes called Apocryphal, writings.

Then began a study of the Pentateuch, the first five books of the Hebrew Scriptures. The question of authorship became our first major inquiry. The tradition of the scriptures seems to say Moses was the sole author. Thanks to the advent of biblical criticism in the last two centuries, we recognize the Pentateuch as having a number of literary threads and authors. This caused problems with some of the students in class who held a more literal view of scripture and its inerrancy. The notion of inaccuracy in the Bible was considered to be anathema—a true test of faith—and opened the way for many heated and vigorous discussions.

The whole field of higher and lower criticism fascinated me. Today, some 40 years later, I often shake my head in bemusement, and sometimes frustration, to find that so many Christians appear to be sinking into a literalistic fundamentalism that was unknown, even by the early Church and the theologians of the Patristic period, especially amongst the Alexandrian group including, Origen and Clement. I shared a certain anxiety about delving into criticism of the Bible. The very word criticism, innocent as it may be in its true meaning, seems at first glance an affront to Holy Scripture because, in our everyday parlance, criticism is viewed as a pejorative concept. I imagine this feeling arises from the unspoken fear that to show any one part of the scripture as incorrect, factually or otherwise, is to open the way for negation of the Bible as a whole; as if the Bible were as tenuous as a house of cards.

I had much the same reaction to New Testament studies initially. Father Thomas Bailey began with an introduction to texts, manuscripts and the question of the canon of scripture. This is the story of how the Bible as we know it today came to be. My greatest discomfort in this case came when he began to talk about the development of episcopacy. Were there bishops, priests and deacons right from the outset? Or, did this develop gradually over the first few centuries? For an Anglo-Catholic who had a concept of the Church firmly rooted in apostolic succession, this question was disturbing. Father Bailey knew he was distressing us. He knew many of us had never thought it all out, but had simply accepted the existing premise as gospel, and moved on from there. Over the course of many months, he cleverly dismantled our preconceived ideas and began rebuilding them in the way the Early Church had done. Other courses, like Systematic Theology, were doing much the same thing—unravelling the complex history and variant interpretations of the Bible, and then weaving them into a more solid understanding and appreciation.

My introduction to systematic theology began that first year in a course taught by a young English priest. This was a comprehensive course, which attempted to relate Biblical texts to the Church's formulation of theological teaching. It dealt with the doctrines of creation, man, the church and all the usual foundational under-girding of theological thought. Father Cooper was a bright and thoughtful man. He was with the college for the duration of that year only, so we had a rather brief time to become acquainted with him. My most vivid memory of him is associated with an examination question he posed. It must have been on the Christmas exam in my first year at the theological college. I recently found the paper as I have saved all those notes and exams. The essay question was, "*For the Bible, sex is a necessary evil. Why is this statement wrong? Discuss.*" In my answer I outlined the usual biblical teachings about creation, procreation, and the understanding that sex is a part of God's plan for the human race, which is all well and good, placing sexual activity in the context of the purpose of human existence. However, I felt it only proper to discuss some of the rather negative biblical injunctions about sex. St. Paul presents a rather bleak and prohibitive view of sexuality at times. I didn't really know

Father Cooper very well and I wondered about including in my answer a charming limerick that was a commentary on this very subject. Limericks can somehow, in a very terse way, cut to the core of an idea. I was visibly shaking as I penned the limerick into my essay question. It went as follows:

> *An old Archaeologist, Throstle*
> *Discovered an unusual fossil,*
> > *He could tell from the bend*
> > *And the knot in the end,*
> *'Twas the penis of Paul the Apostle.*

Fortunately, Father Cooper had a sense of humour and rather delighted in my having included it in my paper.

Those years at the College studying theology were three of the happiest years of my life. I was able to put aside agonizing about sexuality for the most part and apply myself to my studies. The courses were captivating and I gave myself wholeheartedly to the work. My attraction toward the Anglo-Catholic side of things was evident from my first experience with the College when I met other young, zealous 'catholics'. It was exciting being catholic—it was spiritually uplifting to embrace a sacramental system in which God is real and present—in which one could become caught up in the numinous. Thoughts of the Church Triumphant made the practise of the faith otherworldly and yet in a profound sense, tangible. Meditations, rosaries, and litanies became the core of my private prayer life along with the daily offices and Mass, all of which have continued to nourish me into my retirement years.

ATC in the '60s was styled much like an Oxford college in that studies were in classical areas such as Systematic Theology, Apologetics, Greek, Scriptural studies, Patristics and Church History. My third year was quite different. It was a tutorial year. No more classes—except for Greek. One subject only would be explored for a five or 6-week period. Topics were assigned each Friday and the necessary heap of reading material gathered from the library. From Monday to Thursday afternoon, we were immersed in reading the material and finally writing the paper. This usually took until the small hours of Friday morning to complete. I was so very thankful I had taken typing in high school as I was able to collect all my data on index cards, arrange them in the desired sequence and simply write the paper directly on my big, black Underwood. No intermediate stage seemed necessary as the paper was simply read to the tutor on Friday morning and discussed. My papers were not necessarily very literary works, as they were never actually given to the tutor. It took a few weeks to get into the swing of it, but eventually it came to me without much difficulty. During the course of that year, I must have written some hundreds of thousands of words. It made for quite intense but fulfilling study.

✠

The college chapel was chosen to be the venue for the consecration of Ted Scott in 1965. He had been elected as the Bishop of Kootenay. Ted Scott was a graduate of ATC, which was one of the determining factors in the choice of the Chapel of the Epiphany for the consecration. His old friend and classmate, Edwin Thain, then an Archdeacon in the Diocese of Edmonton, was directing a 'pre-consecration' retreat for the bishop-elect. The divinity students and the faculty spent much of the day before this grand event preparing the Chapel. Extra seating in the sanctuary was made available, brass was polished and special music prepared by the students who formed the choir. We borrowed some things from St. James' for the occasion including the Ethiopian processional cross and a set of torches. My friend and fellow divinity student, Ron Sands, and I took the liberty of introducing the pleasant odour of

A Priest's Tale

incense during the early afternoon of the day before the consecration. When things were nearing completion, Fr. Bailey and the Principal were looking things over. Someone mentioned the smell of the incense and Fr. Blewett glanced knowingly at Ron and me and said, "It could stand a little more." Ron and I looked at each other and read the same thought in each other's eyes.

Late that evening we went to the Chapel unlocked it and then locked ourselves inside. We took a metal wastepaper bin and covered the bottom with charcoals. Once those were going, we poured on a huge amount of lovely Nashdom Abbey incense. As we walked around the chapel with the wastebasket belching clouds of incense that rose to the ceiling of the A-frame chapel we noticed the bottom of the cloud gradually descending as a distinct layer. Eventually it was about six feet above the floor and the space we occupied remained clear. We continued our circuit of the chapel until the fog descended to the floor.

Standing in the murky darkness at the back of the chapel preparing to leave, we heard someone's key in the door. We looked at each other through the smoke and I thought, This is it. We'll be expelled. When the door finally opened, in came Ted Scott and Archdeacon Ed Thain for late evening prayers. Ron and I were mortified. I was literally speechless. The only thing I could think to say was, "Good Evening." They nodded, repeated the greeting, and went on their way through the smoke to the front of the chapel and Ron and I made a hasty escape.

Many years later, I recounted the incident to Ed Thain from our point of view. He told me that when he and Ted walked up to the front of the chapel and knelt down for their prayers, Ted turned to him and said quietly, "They're just like we were, aren't they."

The next morning the chapel appeared normal—the smoke of the incense had dissipated though the scent remained. Some weeks after the consecration the Principal received a thank you letter from Bishop Scott, which contained a remark similar to this: *"Many thanks to those who did so much preparation, for the catering staff and the wonderful reception, and to those two young men who made the chapel smell so holy."*

Perhaps it was because of my various jobs and offices around the College or knowing the student body, but in my senior year of Divinity, I was elected Senior Student. This meant being a liaison between the Faculty and the student body and in chairing the student body meetings.

Things were beginning to change in the 60's and many traditions were beginning to be challenged. One such was the tradition of wearing academic gowns to College dinners and chapel. While many found the gowns unique and took pride in the traditional aspect of the affectation, there were some who found the expense of the gown a burden. At least that was what they claimed. I suspect they simply didn't like the idea. The inevitable finally happened. At a student council meeting that I chaired gowns were voted out. I thought it a sad day. As chairman I had no vote. Thereafter, non-theological residents were not required to wear gowns.

Also during my last year, another crisis erupted in the old residence wing, which proved to be of great concern. A UBC professor occupied a suite of rooms in the old wing and was the 'don' for that wing. The rent was undoubtedly very reasonable but the arrangement was that he was supposed to be a mentor for the young students. As it happened this man didn't relate well to the youth, nor was he particularly interested in them as far as I could see. He resented any horseplay and noise, which are a normal part of student life in a residential setting.

On one particular weekend a drinking party was held in one of the rooms in that wing. When the professor discovered this—hearing all the noise emanating from a particular room, he reported it to the Principal—including some names of those he supposed were involved. As alcohol was forbidden on the premises, the Principal immediately expelled the three students. When word got around, all hell broke loose and we had something of a student uprising. The boys came to me as Senior Student to see if I could intervene. I was a little taken aback realizing what a mess it had become but felt that my position required that I become involved. I soon realized there had been a slip-up. The professor had made a mistake. One of the three he named happened to be in Victoria that weekend, and could easily prove it. The other two were undoubtedly there, and the drinking should not have happened. But still, there was such strong feeling among the student body about an injustice having been perpetrated I was afraid there might be damage done to the College. I went to speak with the Principal.

      He was a rather strict and disciplined man. He explained to me he had made a decision and must hold to it. He maintained that he had never gone back on a decision before and was not prepared do so now. I realized his position, but in light of this error and the extremely passionate response of the student body perhaps just this once he could rescind the decision and make some sort of compromise. To encourage him, I offered to trade rooms with one of the students in the old wing and move there myself to attempt to smooth things over. This was not really a sacrifice for me as I loved the quaint rooms of the old wing with their radiators, wood paneling and all—that

A Priest's Tale

was where I had begun at the College and I loved the old part of the building. Fr. Blewett was not immediately convinced. How would this impact upon my studies during this final tutorial year? I assured him that I would be able to deal with it. He said he would give the matter some thought overnight and I was dismissed.

    The students knew of my meeting with the Principal and were eager to know what had transpired. It was a tense time. Students were loitering in the hallways when I emerged from our meeting the next morning. To my surprise and delight, the Principal agreed with my suggestion. That evening I called a meeting of the residents of the old wing in the Senior Common Room and explained what the agreement would be. The three expelled students were to be reinstated and someone had to offer to switch rooms with me. One of the boys immediately offered to switch with me—no surprise as the New Wing was really much more comfortable and modern. Before the meeting ended I stressed once again how very crucial it was that order and discipline be maintained, and also how critical this year was for me personally. All agreed with the arrangement and were delighted with the compromise.

    A rather humorous telephone conversation took place during this episode as Father attempted to sort out the problem of the alleged drinking party. He had called the aunt of the boy in whose room the party took place as he had gone home to her house after the party. When told that her nephew had been drinking in the College she simply didn't believe it and remarked, "Oh, he couldn't have been drinking. When he got up the next morning he was *so* thirsty."

The boys of the Old Wing certainly did cooperate. I was proud of them and delighted with how well things worked out. There was only one moment when I thought there was going to be a relapse. I came home late one evening and found the entire hallway blanketed under about three inches of shredded toilet paper, which looked very much like a fresh snowfall; a common prank akin to filling a student's room to the ceiling with crumpled newspapers. Several boys were standing in the hall as I passed through the snowdrifts to my room. I said nothing, just shook my head sadly in disappointment. Not long after I closed my door I heard muted talking and the whoosh, whoosh of brooms. In the morning, there was not a trace of the unnatural snowfall.

I graduated from the Anglican Theological College of British Columbia in April of 1968. As usual, the convocation ceremony was held in Brock Hall, not far from the College. Along with the presentation of degrees and

A Priest's Tale

licentiates and the usual convocation address, various prizes were awarded. One of these was a small bursary for the "All 'Round Student" or something to that effect. It was called The Seymour Prize. And every year there were titters amongst the theologs because this was a prize for nothing in particular and was generally seen to be the 'brown-noser' award. It was a cheque for $30. As my name was announced in conjunction with this prize, my heart skipped a beat and I rose in my new clerical dignity to approach the podium amidst muted hisses, catcalls and other rude sounds from my fellow students.

Three days before the convocation, I had been ordained to the diaconate at St. Andrew's in Burnaby—my home parish. That was certainly a memorable day for me. The church was packed on that spring morning in April, the sun was shining through the clear glass east window at the front of the church, and the new leaves were just appearing on the trees. The choir I had sung with all those years ago turned out in full force and even Bruce came back to join them. Clergy from neighbouring parishes came to support me and it was an enormously thrilling day. My family was, of course, sitting in the front pews. Fr. Blewett was my presenter at the ordination and it was he who placed the stole over my left shoulder after the Laying-On-Of-Hands—the vesture of the office of a deacon. Bishop

Munn's visit to Vancouver was both to speak at the College Convocation as well as to preside at this ordination. The ordination was memorable because not only did it mark my beginning in ordained ministry but also it happened to be the commencement of Fr. William Youngman's retirement. Fr. Youngman had been Rector of St. Andrew's for a number of years. He was also a long-time friend of Bishop Munn. He had been a layman at St. James' years before when Bp. Munn was a curate there. Father Youngman preached the sermon on this occasion and in his very down to earth and practical way he spoke about ordination and the calling to service in the Church.

My father was not at all a churchman and in the beginning, he thought my idea of taking Holy Orders was crazy. When I first mentioned my intentions, he said, "You'll never make any bloody money doing that." Gradually over the years of my preparation Dad came to respect my decision and, in the end, he was honestly proud. I am sure Dad spent years planning the remark he made immediately after my ordination. It was a lovely spring day and the procession moved out of the sanctuary, down the aisle and outside to the churchyard. The Bishop, visiting clergy, and I stood greeting the congregation as they poured out of the church. Finally, my family came by—Dad shook my hand and said, "Congratulations, *Father*." He didn't know that deacons are not properly called 'Father', but the thought was delightfully funny and endearing.

A few days after graduation and ordination, I returned to the College to pick up some books and personal belongings. It was a longstanding tradition at ATC that on 'special' occasions, such as a birthday or graduation, a student would be seized and taken to the washroom to be plunged into a bathtub full of cold water. I contemplated this as I approached the second floor. I assumed it was inevitable and simply resigned myself to it. However, I did wish I had worn something other than my brand new blacks and clerical collar.

I came to the staircase and met a gang of students lurking and looking rather like vultures. I said, "Good evening, guys," and passed through them to my room. Any minute, I thought. I continued collecting my things and eventually left the room on my way back to the car. The hallway was empty as I passed through. I grinned to myself. They couldn't bring themselves to do it. They were a good lot.

It was quite a novelty walking around in a clerical collar those first few weeks. I went back to the neighbourhood where I had grown up and stopped by to visit the Wilbees. Like my father, Mr. Wilbee was not a churchman and was not familiar with the nuances of church terminology. I waited at the door filled with pride wearing my new clericals knowing he would be so happy for me. He was indeed happy, but I was quickly brought back to earth when he answered the door, took one look at me, and said, enthusiastically, "Donnie Dodman, come on in—I see you're wearing your costume."

A Priest's Tale

Two

Six months before my graduation, Bishop Munn wrote to me of his intent to appoint me to the staff of the Mission to the Lakes District, which was centred at Burns Lake, B.C. I was put in contact with the Rector, John Frame, whom I had met several times during my college years. I was impressed with him and was quite looking forward to serving a curacy under his supervision. The Mission at Burns Lake had been a testing ground for young clerics for many years as it was one of the few parishes in the Diocese of Caledonia to have a team of clergy. However, sometime during the six months before my graduation John was appointed as the bishop of the Diocese of the Yukon and moved with his family to Whitehorse. However, the plan for my move to the Mission continued. A college friend, Alan McLeod, was on staff there as well and during my time in Burns Lake he became the Priest-in-Charge.

After ordination and graduation, I was eager to begin work and anxious to set out on my adventure. I managed to pack all of my belongings into the Volkswagen Beetle, which my father had bought as a wreck and restored for me. My most important items were my old, black Underwood typewriter and my violin along with articles of

A Priest's Tale

clothing and some books. I set out early one morning for the long drive through Hope and up the Fraser Canyon. My plan was to stop for the night halfway through the journey. The best laid plans.

I didn't realize how hard I had been working and how tired I had become. That last month of school had been draining. The two-week period of intensive study and revision for the final exams, then the ordination, with its attendant celebrations and parties, and then the Convocation all added up so that early in the afternoon of the day I set out, when I was near 100 Mile House, I dozed off. I woke up with a start when my tires touched the gravel verge on the opposite side of the highway. I was travelling at about 50 miles per hour. In a split second I consciously decided not to try to correct my steering, intuitively knowing the car would roll if I did. I simply drove it straight off the road down an embankment and that was the last I remember for a time.

The car ended up on its side with the windshield knocked out and the entire undercarriage destroyed. From what I was told later, judging by the amount of blood, I was probably unconscious for ten or fifteen minutes. I was disoriented when I came to and crawled out through the windshield and then scrambled up the steep embankment to the highway. I was in shock and didn't realize how injured I was in spite of the fact that I pulled my dangling, broken front teeth out and carefully put them into my pocket thinking that they could be reinstalled. In my dazed state my main concern was how I was going to get the car back on the road.

A heavily loaded logging truck came along before too long and I hailed it. The driver wasn't going to stop initially. However, as he drew near, I imagine he saw the blood and realized there had been an accident. I heard the frantic sounds of air brakes as the truck slowly came to a stop a distance from where I was standing by the side of the road. The driver ran back to me and then hailed a passing car and asked them if they would drive me to the hospital in 100 Mile House. There, I was attended to and a telephone call was made to my family. My parents drove up the next day to take me home. Poor Dad, he was beside himself. He thought perhaps there had been some fault in his restoration of the Beetle.

Bishop and Mrs. Munn discovered what had happened during their drive back to Prince Rupert. They had apparently heard about the accident on the radio news. They visited me at the hospital not long after the accident, which I found somewhat embarrassing despite the fact that I was still in a state of shock. Bishop Munn assured me I

A Priest's Tale

would have whatever time off I needed to recuperate—with salary—which was more than generous.

My jaw was broken in three places and had to be wired back together. Thus began a period of keeping my mouth firmly shut for a change and eating food that had been put through a blender. I stayed with my parents during the recuperation period and idled away much of my time reading or talking and visiting with my friend Ron Sands.

After my two months of recuperation and the repair of my teeth—a partial, as it was too late to do anything with the actual teeth—I set out once again for Burns Lake, this time well rested and with considerably more attention to my driving. It felt awkward to be driving again, much like getting back on a horse after having been thrown. I stopped in Cache Creek for the evening, had a good night's sleep, and continued on my journey the next day without any further misadventure.

When I arrived at the parish hall in Burns Lake I was duly welcomed by my college friend, Alan McLeod. I was shown to my rooms—a suite in the attic of the parish hall. It was very spartan with a sloping A-frame ceiling that descended to two feet above the floor on the sides. Until I got accustomed to this I kept bumping my head reaching for books on the low shelves. The room was comfortable, however, and had its own plumbing. The only downside to these rooms I discovered was that whenever there was a function in the hall below the resulting noise funnelled up directly into my rooms—and the Parish Hall was used frequently as it was one of the few large meeting places in the town.

The Mission to the Lakes District comprised twelve points surrounding Burns Lake, an area that was roughly one hundred miles wide and 60 miles north to south. St John's Parish in Burns Lake was the centre of the Mission with points in Fraser Lake, Endako, Fort Fraser in the East; Houston and Topley in the West; François Lake, Takysie Lake, Ootsa Lake and Wistaria in the South and Granisle in the north.

Each Sunday Alan and I would take different routes, one going to the west the other to the east. Leaving home at about six am on Sunday mornings and arriving back around 10:30 pm, we would each have driven around 200 miles and taken three or four services—often for just a small handful of people. Once a month I would travel the 60 miles to the new village of Granisle that served the copper mines on Babine Lake. There were only a couple of Anglican families there and we worshipped in a schoolroom. The 30-mile road from Highway 16 to Granisle was excellent in the winter when it was frozen solid but in the spring thaw it was often treacherous as much of it deteriorated into a quagmire of mud and potholes.

At the end of one of my Sunday tours, I was tired and anxious to get home. I had to pass through the small hamlet of Decker Lake, which was 10 miles west of Burns Lake. It had the usual reduce speed signs but being such a tiny place people often zoomed through without altering speed and, of course, the police patrolled that part of the highway with diligence. I was pulled over by the RCMP for doing just that. The officer ticketed me and with little ado I was on my way again. Not a big deal—just a $30 ticket. However, the next morning I was having a coffee with Alan and his wife Joan. I complained about the speeding ticket, making the often-heard comment, "Oh well, they're probably just collecting money for the policeman's ball." To this Joan innocently replied, "The Police in Burns Lake don't have balls."

The first funeral I ever took posed a somewhat unusual challenge. For one thing, I was alone in the parish when the death occurred, otherwise a priest colleague would have officiated. Add to that, the funeral in question was of a relatively young man who had taken his own life. As a newly ordained deacon, I was full of all the college training and theoretical knowledge but had not the experience to go with it. I knew suicide posed certain difficulties and the

Canadian Book of Common Prayer has some specific directives as to what is to be done to accommodate such a situation. I searched the rubrics to see exactly what was required. Apparently, it was no problem to bury the man, but the Prayer Book explicitly outlined that an exception to the normal procedure was to be made. Instead of using the usual, and very beautiful, reading from Paul's dissertation on death from I Corinthians, I was to substitute a passage from St. Matthew's Gospel. It is a story from the 25th chapter, where Jesus is teaching about the Last Judgment, and it includes the phrase: "And He shall set the sheep on his right hand, but the goats on the left." I always thought of myself as a rather devoted, if not zealous, follower of the teachings of Holy Mother Church. However, reading this passage over, I knew I could not make the substitution. It seemed to me that to do so would be even worse than outright refusing to have anything to do with the funeral. It seemed to imply rather blatantly that the deceased man was not considered to be one of the sheep. I decided I would simply use the Burial Office as it was with the usual reading. No one would know the difference anyway, and as such readings are intended for the family and friends, the traditional one would be of much greater comfort. As to thoughts of the Last Judgment—that was none of my business.

A Priest's Tale

The clergy of the Diocese of Caledonia were extremely devoted to Bishop Munn who radiated pastoral love and gentleness. It was a shock for all when he died suddenly early in 1969. Many years later I was recounting this story to a friend—how the bishop had died shortly after I was ordained—and he asked, "You mean at the same service?"

After the bishop's death there was a disruption in the Diocese for a time and many things were put on hold. I remained in deacon's orders for a longer time than was customary. In the Western Church there has been a history of not quite knowing what to do with deacons other than regarding the diaconate as a sort of apprenticeship for the priesthood. Deacons wear clerical collars and are considered to be clerics; he or she may read the Gospel in the liturgy; preach; visit the sick and baptize. However, the deacon cannot bless things nor celebrate the Eucharist. Being a deacon is rather like being a teenager—you are no longer a child, yet you are not an adult. Laypeople can do all of the things deacons do.

In recent years, there has been an attempt to define more clearly what the Office of a deacon actually is; however, I am not at all convinced that it has been successful. The permanent or vocational diaconate has emerged as a solution to the dilemma. I know of so many situations where the intention was to enter into a permanent diaconate, but eventually there seems to be the need to continue to priestly ordination.

This situation does not seem to be a problem in the Greek Orthodox Church. On a visit to Greece some years ago, I engaged in a wonderful conversation with Athena—our tour guide, not the deity. When she discovered I was a priest, she was interested to know more about Anglican ways. A local parish priest happened to pass by as we talked and Athena said to me, "You see that man over there? He is a vineyard worker and also a priest. He works all week in the vineyards and olive groves and then on Sunday celebrates the Divine Liturgy. He is unschooled in theology except for his ability to read and pray the Liturgy. In the Greek Orthodox Church, deacons are typically the theologians, professors, church administrators and intellectuals." What a completely different and refreshing complexion it seemed to put on the office of a deacon. However, in the Western Church it would be a hopeless task to attempt to readjust such a deep-rooted tradition.

The year and a half I was in the Mission to the Lakes District was rather frustrating because I was doing all the work of a priest with the exception that I could not celebrate the Eucharist. This meant I carried the Blessed Sacrament around with me in a wooden box and took

A Priest's Tale

communion services without needing to consecrate the bread and wine. This has been referred to as a 'dry mass' like the mass on Good Friday when no actual celebration is permitted and communion is from the reserved Sacrament. In the present day Roman Church, this is happening frequently due to the drastic shortage of priests. The lay people who function in this capacity are undoubtedly very honoured to perform such a ministry—and rightly so. My dilemma was I had done extensive theological training in preparation for the vocation I had been called to—the priesthood—and was anxious to be exercising that calling in its fullness.

In the wake of Bishop Munn's death, an election was called and the clergy and Synod delegates set off for the see city of Prince Rupert. This election was an entirely new experience for me. I have since been involved in a number of episcopal elections, many of them quite difficult and prolonged. One even ended in a stalemate and had to be reconvened the following year. By contrast, this election was remarkably brief.

Being new in the Diocese, I knew only a few of the clergy, but there was one man who was obviously held in high esteem by everyone present. He was actually elected on the first ballot, although a second, confirming ballot had to be made according to the canons of the Diocese. It, too, proved to be unanimous. The man in question was Douglas Hambidge who at the time was the Rector of Smithers. Douglas Hambidge was a brilliant man and an eloquent preacher with a remarkable sense of humour. He, like me, is short. When Archbishop Gower, who presided over the electoral synod, asked the bishop-elect if he would accept his election Douglas was seated near the back of the cathedral. After the Archbishop asked this obligatory question, he then said, "Would you please stand?" Bishop-elect Hambidge who was already standing stepped up onto a kneeler and replied, "I am standing, Your Grace."

The consecration to the episcopate of Father Hambidge took place a few months later, again in Prince Rupert. This change of leadership would be quite a new experience for the Diocese in a number of ways, but one in particular. Whereas Bishop Munn had been very much the Tractarian, high-churchman, Douglas Hambidge was from the evangelical tradition.

He visited us in Burns Lake that summer for a confirmation service. Mrs. Munn had given him a cope and mitre that had belonged to her husband. Bishop Munn and Douglas had been close friends and highly respected each other's traditions. I noticed Bishop Hambidge had the cope and mitre in his case. He remarked that he had not yet used them. It was a blistering hot day and when it came time for us to vest and enter the church for the confirmation service, the bishop looked at Alan and me and said wryly, "Well, as it is a little chilly, I think I'll wear these." He proceeded to don the cope and mitre and looked every bit the Prelate.

Even in the smallest of communities, I have found, it is possible to find interesting diversions. Through social activities, I came to know Moira Vine, a very talented pianist who taught piano students from many regions of the Bulkley Valley, as well as teaching in the Burns Lake high school. Moira and I linked up with a friend of hers from Vanderhoof, Cynthia Davies, another pianist who also played the cello. We formed a piano trio and met together from time to time for dinner and to play. One year the Kiwanis Music Festival was held in Burns Lake for the Bulkley Valley communities. We signed up and were the only entry in the 'chamber music' category. Most of the other entries were piano soloists or singers. When we played our Mozart Piano Trio for the judges there was quite a large group of people who came out simply to hear these instruments played live—a bit of a novelty. As we were the only entry we won in our category. This meant that we would play again at the 'gala' on the following Saturday night. The three of us had become quite good friends and we did enjoy playing together.

At the concert on Saturday evening, we were slotted near the end of the programme. The curtains on the high school stage were drawn as we took our places and began to tune up. We had been on the stage that afternoon to rehearse and for Cynthia to find the necessary place for her cello endpin. We were all tuned up and ready in the dim backstage light. The man operating the curtains looked at us expectantly waiting for a signal to open them. Before Moira or I could give any sign of assent, Cynthia gasped, "Wait. Wait. I can't find my hole," as she struggled to secure her cello. The three of us burst into uncontrollable giggles. After a few tries, Cynthia finally found her place; the curtains flowed open gracefully; and the audience clapped while the three of us struggled desperately to stop laughing and pull ourselves together before the applause subsided.

Each of the various communities in the Mission had at least one unforgettable resident. Sometimes it was the person who offered leadership and stability to the community, but more often than not, it was the person who agitated situations, who was even a bit of a thorn in the collective side of the community. It is amazing how such people can often spark action and direction in others, if only in reaction to their antics.

A Priest's Tale

On the outskirts of Topley lived a woman named May. May and I fell into a friendship that was not unlike the one I had with my own irascible mother. May made herself known to me at the first Sunday service I took in Topley. Her outspoken nature and unfettered candour was often funny and refreshing. One Sunday afternoon in the middle of my sermon and in the context of formal Anglican worship, May shouted out something from the back of the church. I don't recall what it was that got under May's girdle. She took issue with something I said in my sermon. I tried to respond to her 'question', though it was more of an opinion and May and I got into a little private skirmish. The rest of the congregation let us go on for a bit, but finally someone interjected, "Maybe you two could finish this later." I welcomed the second interruption and soon got the service back on track.

May lived on the main highway and I frequently drove past on my rounds, often stopping in for a coffee. On one occasion May offered me a glass of her beet wine, which sounded intriguing even though I had already been cautioned by another parishioner to avoid it at all costs. I politely accepted. To my surprise, she returned from the kitchen with a huge tumbler full of the stuff. I thanked her and took a drink. I tried not to wince visibly, but it was truly dreadful. I sipped slowly. Eventually, May went to the kitchen for something. As soon as she was out of sight, I looked around in desperation for somewhere to tip the wine. A Christmas cactus in a large pot stood nearby. I offered up a private little prayer of thanks, and deposited it there. My plan was foiled, however. When May returned and noticed my empty glass, she quickly refilled it. This time I choked down a bit more of the vile brew. Some of the second glass also went the way of the first. On my next visit, I noticed the cactus was gone from its spot. I didn't think I needed to ask what happened to it. Sometime later, another friend who knew May well told me that the subject of the cactus had come up and May remarked, "I just don't understand it—I had that cactus for 20 years".

On Christmas Eve of my first year in the Mission, I was scheduled to go to Topley for Midnight Mass. However, someone had forgotten to light the stove in the little church and the temperature inside was about thirty below zero. It actually felt colder inside the church than outside. When the small congregation eventually gathered we discussed the dilemma. May made the suggestion we go back to her house and have the service there. We all agreed and left a note tacked to the door explaining where we would be. Our tiny band of a dozen got into several cars and made for May's place. It was a memorable Christmas Eve, gathered in May's homey kitchen with long johns hanging on a line behind us and the oil stove giving off merry warmth.

Christmas Eve the following year proved to be quite a different occasion. I had become used to the long distances between the various points in the parish as well as the rather tiny groups of people who came to worship. Often it was only five or six people. I realized even then—the late 60's, early 70's—that the mainline churches were dwindling. Perhaps I should have been more astute in noticing the phenomenon. However, I was new to the ministry, full of enthusiasm and believed things could be restored with effort and attentive pastoral work.

One of the churches in our Mission was a beautiful, early 1900's frame building, which was still in quite remarkable repair. St. Mary's Church in Fort Fraser had been basically closed down because the congregation had diminished to practically nothing. I understood that someone there had made a request to the Rector that there be a service at St. Mary's on Christmas Eve of 1969. I was thus scheduled to travel to Fort Fraser—a distance of about 50 miles from Burns Lake—for a service early that evening.

This was my second Christmas in the Mission. As I was still a deacon, I took with me my wooden sacrament case to celebrate yet another dry Mass. Christmas Eve had always been very special for me—I had wonderful memories of High Masses at St. James', of Christmas carols, robust singing and the rich thunder of the pipe organ. I arrived at St. Mary's early in order to compose myself and unpack all my hardware. As the service time approached I was happy and quite looking forward to the service.

Eventually, a woman arrived and we chatted for a few moments. The service had been set for seven thirty, which came and passed and no one else had arrived so we decided to wait a bit. I busied myself with books and equipment and the woman took a pew near the front of the church. Time dragged on and still no one else came. By ten to eight it began to weigh upon me that I had a commitment for the midnight service in Burns Lake.

I have always enjoyed the worship and preaching, but taking a service for such a small number of people, one, proves an uncomfortable task. We began straight away, not attempting to sing anything, and it went fairly well until it came to the sermon. I foolishly attempted to preach a sermon and it was a disaster. The poor woman was feeling the discomfort as much as I. Eventually, I simply went and sat beside her and we talked.

She had been a long-time resident in Fort Fraser and remembered the days when the church was active and the centre of the community. She was grieved that it had faded away. As we talked it flashed through my mind that she

A Priest's Tale

must have been the person requesting the service. She revealed that she had been giving some thought to becoming Roman Catholic. They had a parish in Fort Fraser that was quite busy and alive—as was the case in most communities. I felt I should try to encourage her to remain with the Anglican Communion and talked about the nature of things Anglican and the possible disadvantages of going to Rome.

Alas, it was a difficult case to make when even then I had experienced feelings similar to those the woman was expressing and wondered where things in the Anglican Church were going. And yet, I could hardly be so irresponsible as to simply say, "Yes, I understand. Why don't you just join the Roman Church?"

It amazes me now to think how early in my career I had a sense of things collapsing and how sad it still makes me. That was definitely my most depressing and discouraging Christmas. We finally finished the service and she went on her way into the crisp winter evening. I packed up my things and began the drive back to Burns Lake pondering what had just happened. Back in Burns Lake the Midnight Mass was very well attended and my spirits were raised, although I could not easily expunge the thoughts of Fort Fraser. I felt an ache for the poor woman. I later learned that she was indeed received into the Roman

Church, which I could see was the most sensible thing for her.

✠

While at Burns Lake my attention was very much on my work and becoming involved in the community and parish. I was finally doing the job I felt I was called to do and for which I had been trained. Despite the frustration of remaining in deacon's orders the whole time I was there, the daily ministry was wonderfully fulfilling. However, the question of my sexuality eventually began manifest itself again. I longed to meet someone special, to have intimacy, and to have someone with whom to share the little things of life. But in a small community like Burns Lake one must be circumspect. Everyone knows everything and any blunder could unleash havoc.

These were the days before the Internet and the quick, easy access to communication we have today. However, at one point I somehow came into possession of an alternate newspaper, which I found had some gay personal ads. I was young, naive, and feeling lonely. I spotted an ad from a fellow who was going to be staying over for a couple of nights in Prince George while on business. After a great deal of agonizing I wrote him a letter

A Priest's Tale

to a post office box number, telling him a bit about myself, and included a photo. He responded with a letter and photograph, which I would later discover, didn't resemble him very much. We agreed to meet.

I drove the two hours into Prince George in a state of both trepidation and excitement. I had booked a room in the same hotel where he would be staying. Once I settled in I worked up the courage to go around to his door and knock. He must have been out to dinner. We hadn't made any specific arrangement about times. I went out for a quick sandwich and returned to my room an hour later. Getting my nerve back, I again tried his room and this time he was in.

After our introductions and a period of chitchat he was quite forward about a little recreation. I was completely inexperienced and, as is so often the case with one's 'first time', things did not really go, shall we say, swimmingly. I suspect it was also coloured by the fact that he was not quite what I expected judging by the photograph. He was quite a large man. This of course was not detectable in the picture and even his facial features did not look much the same. However, he was very gentlemanly and considerate. We eventually undressed and things began to happen—sort of! If I had been physically attracted to him it would probably have worked much better. Eventually, he wanted to have anal sex and I just knew that this was not about to happen. He was very big! I felt a certain embarrassment about not being able to be more accommodating, but I sensed that he understood. Perhaps my reluctance was even in itself a veiled compliment to him. Afterward, I took a bath to get cleaned up for the night as I stayed over in his room. He came into the bathroom and seeing me sitting in the tub said, with mock derision, "Oh, washing the sin away, I see!" He did not mean it in a nasty way, but knew what my work was and perhaps he was half right in his assumption about my mental state.

The next morning we breakfasted together, then parted ways afterward in a very civil manner both of us recognizing this had been something of a non-event. We didn't exchange phone numbers or make any foolish talk about seeing each other again. I drove the two hours back to Burns Lake feeling somewhat silly and not a little disillusioned by 'gay' life, however, that is not to say I had doubts about my sexuality. More than anything that first awkward, unfulfilling attempt clarified for me the importance of having a meaningful relationship before anything else. I had just had a one-night stand and knew it was not at all what I yearned for.

A Priest's Tale

✠

I remained in deacon's orders much longer than was usual because of the circumstances in the diocese. As time went on, I did not foresee any change in this state of affairs. After giving my situation much thought over several months, deliberating with God and myself about whether or not I should simply remain a lifelong deacon, I came to the conclusion that my vocation was to the priesthood and decided it would be prudent to seek a position in another diocese.

A college friend had written to me and put out a 'feeler' about a position as parish priest on the Blood Reserve; the position he currently held. He had recently taken a government position as Administrator of St. Paul's School on the same reserve and was handling the school and the parish as he cast about for a suitable person to fill his old position.

The process moved forward swiftly. I flew out to Calgary to meet with Bishop Goodman and we spent a day or two talking and attending a Deanery meeting in the region, which includes the Blood Reserve. After breakfast on the second day of my visit to Calgary the bishop and I headed out in his car for southern Alberta to attend the Deanery Chapter meeting. We stopped at the rectory in

Claresholm to have a coffee and meet the two priests working there. We then headed off south along the main highway. During the Deanery meeting we all had a chance to get to know each other somewhat and the group seemed very friendly and welcoming. By this time I must have known that the bishop was indeed going to appoint me to the Reserve. I was impressed with the group and everything that I had seen. And I quite liked Bishop Goodman. We shared many common thoughts about ministry and the priesthood.

The bishop was eager to ordain me to the priesthood as soon as possible after my arrival. This news, of course, thrilled me. It was arranged that I would live in a suite of rooms at St. Paul's School and function as Chaplain there as well as being appointed the Priest-in-Charge of St. Paul's at Moses Lake.

I moved to Alberta in early January of 1970. The drive through eastern British Columbia toward Crow's Nest Pass was beautiful in a mantle of fresh snow. As night fell, the moon rose full and silvery and highlighted the snow on the trees. The prairie landscape was a vivid contrast with its intersecting coulees and seemingly endless straight highways lined with telephone poles and fences. Driving through this land, seeing only the occasional light of a house, gave one a sense of the vastness of the prairies.

A Priest's Tale

The School was a large, red brick building sitting majestically in the middle of this stark prairie. In the eastern region of the reserve, the flat plain is broken only where coolies and dry streambeds dissect the parched plains. Foothills characterize the western region with the stately Rocky Mountains rising above them making a jagged horizon. From St. Paul's School one can see the square outline of Ninastako, the holy mountain, which is in Montana, just south of the border. Ninastako is 'Chief Mountain', revered by the Blackfoot as a holy place.

The Blood Reserve is the largest reserve in all of Canada running in a northeasterly direction for some fifty miles between Cardston and Lethbridge in a swath bordered by the St. Mary's and Belly Rivers. The population of the Reserve was approximately half Roman Catholic and half Anglican.

Before I went to work with the Kainai People of the Blood Reserve, I had no experience with Native Canadians. It was by turns exciting and romantic to explore the history and customs of the noble Blackfoot People and to attempt to learn a little of the Blackfoot language.

The People of the Blood Reserve are part of the Blackfoot Confederacy, which consists of four different tribes. The name Blood had been coined by white traders who identified the Kainai with the red ochre they used on their faces and ceremonial objects. The Blackfoot word, Kainai, by which they identify themselves, literally means "Many Chiefs". The story goes; a Blackfoot who visited a Kainai'wa camp asked, "Who is the Chief here?" All the Kainai'wa men who heard the question answered, "I am." The Blackfoot then stated, "I will call you the Tribe of Many Chiefs." The other tribes in the Blackfoot Confederacy are the Siksika, Pikuni, and the Blackfoot—in Montana the name is always *Blackfeet*, for some reason always the plural—perhaps an Anglicization. They were a powerful bison hunting society of the northern plains who were initially pleased when Europeans arrived because the introduction of horses became invaluable in the buffalo hunt. Unfortunately, some features of contact with the visitors proved to be catastrophic as when smallpox epidemics ravaged the Blackfoot population in the mid 1800s.

✠

My ordination to the priesthood took place in January of 1970 at St. Augustine's, Church, in Lethbridge. It was a magnificent occasion with many of the people from St. Paul's on the reserve in attendance; the choir out in full; and quite a large number of Diocesan clergy as well as clergy

A Priest's Tale

from other Lethbridge churches. Bishop Goodman had a fine catholic sense of things and made the ordination a memorable occasion for me. I was vested in an ornate red chasuble, which had belonged to Bishop Munn; a gift to me from Mrs. Munn after the bishop's passing. During the ordination rite Bishop Goodman included the presentation of the *instruments*—a chalice and paten—symbols of priestly ministry. Anglo-Catholics have always regarded this act as significant in that it symbolizes the sacrificial nature of priesthood and identifies priestly ordination with catholic Christianity throughout the centuries. It was a special touch for which I was truly grateful considering that it is not actually an element of the Canadian rite in the Book of Common Prayer.

The clergy of my new Deanery were enormously supportive. I spent a couple of 'quiet days' beforehand with Fr. Bob Cowan at St. Mary's Rectory in Lethbridge, which was a wonderful preparation. In the Vestry immediately after the Ordination I was caught a little off guard when Fr. John Prince, whom I had met years before, knelt down in front of me and said "Bless me Father". That is another little custom in catholic circles—being blessed by a brand new priest. I always thought it was in some way analogous to catching the bride's bouquet at a wedding.

On the evening of the ordination day there was a Pontifical Mass in St. Paul's Church at Moses Lake. We all drove the fifty miles back to the Reserve so that I could celebrate my First Mass with the Blood People. Although I was the celebrant, the Bishop gave the Absolution and the Blessing at the end of Mass, which is the usual practice when he is present, but it meant in a sense, that my next Mass was really my first proper Mass.

I had received the sad news that Mr. Wilbee had died the day before my first mass and was able to remember him in the intercessions for the departed at that first celebration.

✠

Photography had been a hobby from the days of my navy experience when I took 8 mm movie pictures with a very cheap Kodak camera. In the early years after ordination to the diaconate, I had taken up black and white photography. I bought a modest set of developing trays and a simple enlarger quite enjoying the process. It is truly an art form. In the weeks following my ordination to the priesthood, I decided to take a few ordination pictures. I set my camera on a tripod and did them on my own using a timer device. When I had taken all the shots I wanted I

A Priest's Tale

discovered there were three or four frames still unexposed, so I decided to take a few whimsical shots. One of these showed me still wearing my collar and cotta and posed in a very dignified way but for the fact that I was crossing my eyes. The picture turned out quite well and looked like a professional portrait. A college friend, Bill, then a priest in the Diocese of Oregon, was visiting me about that time and thought the picture amusing. He asked if I might do him a copy.

Little did I know the picture would be framed and grace his desk where his parishioners came to know me. Furthermore, it somehow got into the hands of a charming lady I had met in Portland who was the bishop's secretary. The photo by some means appeared on her desk as well. Presumably, the bishop of Oregon and visitors to the office saw the photo but apparently no one ever had the audacity to enquire about the poor, cross-eyed priest.

Some years later I visited Bill in Portland and he asked if I would preach at the Sunday Mass. I was honoured and so, agreed. Bill's parish was small, very welcoming and close-knit. As he introduced me just before the sermon I was quite startled when he announced, "This morning we welcome Father Don Dodman, a college friend from Canada. As you can see, all the money we collected for his eye operation has been very well spent." It seems everyone in the parish was familiar with the ridiculous picture; and furthermore knew the truth of the situation.

Bill had an outrageous sense of humour and there were not very many times when he was at a loss for words. However, there was one occasion when he was completely deflated. He recounted this incident to me with glee. He had been attending an Episcopal national convention in Texas. He ran into another very campy priest who had long ago worked in Portland. They started catching up on news and gossip. During the conversation, Bill's friend asked him about a mutual friend from Portland.

"Do you ever see Elmer?"

Bill responded enthusiastically, "Well, yes; as a matter of fact, we're going to Bangkok together next month." His colleague, without a hesitation, wryly retorted, "Ooooh, your place or his?"

✠

Early in my time on the Blood Reserve I met a very old man, Willie Scraping White, who was more commonly known by the Blackfoot name, *Napi*. The affectionate name Napi can mean a number of things from 'Creator' to 'Medicine Man', or even 'Santa Claus'. Unfortunately, the term 'medicine man' has a pejorative ring to it for English

A Priest's Tale

speakers. Perhaps a better translation of the word would be *Holy Man*.

Willie was about 95 years old when I first met him. I learned that in 1887, when he was about 15 years old, he had been chosen to accompany a group from the Reserve to Queen Victoria's Jubilee as representatives of the Blackfoot People. My reaction to Willie was initially one of some hesitation as in those days I naively thought native religion and its practice was pagan and outside the bounds of faith as I could acknowledge it even though Willie was a faithful communicant in our parish. He would often preach a sermon in Blackfoot at funerals in St. Paul's Church. During the years I served on the reserve, my feelings and thoughts about native spirituality underwent quite a development. In time I came to recognize it as a valid and noble form of spiritual tradition. I came to regard Blackfoot spirituality and Christianity as being entirely compatible.

On one occasion I went to Willie's house to deliver a large print Bible I had purchased for him because of his failing eyesight. I parked my car and as I approached the door of his little house, I could hear chanting. I knocked and Willie called out something in Blackfoot, which I assumed was, "come in". (They don't really do door knocking, but I never could quite get used to just walking into someone's house). I entered and found Willie sitting cross-legged on the floor with a shallow wooden box in front of him filled with sand and some other objects. His face was smeared with red ochre. It was an enlightening moment as I realized Willie was saying his morning devotions to the Creator—just as I had done that morning at Matins. It was another step in my deepening respect for the rich spirituality of the Blackfoot people, which maintains a splendid sense of reverence for the earth, the heavens, and all life.

One morning I received a phone call at the school informing me that Willie had been admitted to the Band Hospital in rather critical condition. He had felt a severe pain in his abdomen, walked to the main highway from his little house, and then hitchhiked into town. It was his appendix. They operated immediately. After the surgery, because of Willie's advanced age, there were complications. He didn't regain consciousness after the anaesthetic wore off.

When I arrived at his room, one of Willie's old friends was at the bedside. This friend, Yellow Bull, was probably in his 70's and he often assisted Willie with shopping and other tasks. Recognizing the gravity of the situation, I told Willie's friend I would return in just a short while.

A Priest's Tale

I rushed over to the Church to get my oil stock and stole so I could anoint Willie. When I returned, I placed the little velvet bag containing my oil stock on the bedside table and put on my stole. Old Yellow Bull, I think, made a connection between my sacramental tools and the little medicine bundles that are common among the Blackfoot, which are usually cloth or skin bags and contain objects held to be sacred. I asked him if he would go around to the other side of the bed and hold Willie's hand while we said prayers. After the Laying-on-of-Hands and anointing, I talked with Yellow Bull and some others who had arrived. News of what had just taken place quickly spread. I knew Willie's condition was very serious and even as I walked out of the hospital, I thought I would not see him alive again.

The next morning I went to do my rounds at the hospital. To my great surprise, Willie was sitting up and talking with visitors. He no longer had need of the I.V. However, for some inexplicable reason, he didn't seem to speak English any more. I could understand enough of his Blackfoot to know what was happening.

Willie motioned for me to come to his bedside. They normally called me Buka'tuyapikuan, which means the "Little Holy White Man". My colleague, Allan McCuaig, who was much bigger than I, was called N'tuyapikuan, the 'Holy White Man'—my name had evolved as a way of distinguishing between us. Willie's friends were gathered around the bed and were cheerful and delighted he had recovered. Willie began some sort of oration and ended with a gesture I had seen before—he thumped me on the shoulder with his fist and declared me *Pitah-Otocan*—'Eagle Head'. I was rather startled but honoured to be given a Blackfoot name. Names from the past are often passed on to others in an honorary sense.

Pitah-Otocan was a minor chief and one of the signers of Treaty No. 7 along with Crowfoot at the Blackfoot Crossing of the Bow River in 1877. My only concern in the aftermath of Willie's miraculous recovery was that the people might attribute it to my having anointing him. Although I firmly believe in the possibility of healing, one cannot guarantee to be able to repeat such a thing. As it happened, the next time I anointed someone it was a young woman who had been in a terrible car crash and she died soon afterward. Willie was actually the first person I had ever anointed. After his brush with death, he continued his colourful life and ministry until he was almost 100. I came to regard him as a colleague in ministry.

My attempt to learn a little of the Blackfoot language was assisted mostly by students at St. Paul's School during our times in the dining room. They delighted in teaching me new words and enjoyed hearing this white man trying to get his tongue around some of those difficult Blackfoot sounds. Also eager to assist me in learning the language were Senator James Gladstone and his wife Janie. Senator Gladstone was the first Canadian Indian to have been appointed to the senate in Ottawa. He and Janie were faithful members of St. Paul's parish. We would sometimes take a day trip together into Lethbridge for shopping and lunch—and to further delve into the intricacies of Blackfoot. The whole effort was aural because at that time there was no written work to support the language.

During the summer months, there were a number of celebrations of native culture on the Blood Reserve; the first to be observed was *Indian Days*, which was held at Standoff during July. It centred upon a rodeo, dancing competitions, and plenty of local food. Tourists were most welcome and encouraged to come and experience the traditions of these proud people. In the parking lot one could spot many out of province Canadian license plates, as well as those of Idaho, Montana, and Utah. Indian Days had the atmosphere of a fair and all were invited to take part in the festivities and witness the events.

Later in the summer came the Sundance. Whereas the Indian Days celebration at Standoff was open and somewhat commercial, the Sundance was a restricted celebration. It was a sacred and spiritual ritual which took place at an ancient site in the Belly Buttes. This celebration was important for the renewal of personal spirituality and also for the regeneration of the living earth. It is an occasion when both the social and natural realms are reaffirmed. Tipis would be set up in a huge circle on a mesa at the top of the bluffs. The Belly Buttes are off the beaten path and non-Band visitors are normally not encouraged to intrude on these events. In Blackfoot mythology, *Apistotoki*—the Creator God—gave many gifts to the people, the principal and most precious one being the buffalo. For aeons the buffalo had sustained the Kainai and the plains lifestyle. The Sundance ceremonies last for almost a week and are a religious observation in honour of the Creator. Originally, the central ceremony involved young males offering a sacrifice of the flesh. This somewhat harsh ceremony was documented in the film, "*A Man Called Horse*" with Richard Harris. Piercing was the most sacred part of the Sundance ceremony. It represented the tribe's awareness of the balance of nature, and was an attempt to offer back something in return for the buffalo.

Formerly, the Sundancers who had pledged to be pierced would lie next to a pole on buffalo robes. The Medicine Man would cut two incisions in the man's chest. Pegs carved from wood or buffalo bone was inserted through the slits. Leather ties were attached to both ends of

A Priest's Tale

the protruding lances and joined by a cord to the centre pole. The dancer begins by dancing toward the pole and then lurching back with all of his might trying to cause the pegs to tear through the flesh. The torn skin is then cut off and placed at the base of the tree—the blood sacrifice is made. A variation was for the dancer to hang from the pole by the pegs in his chest until the skin gave way. The government eventually banned this ceremony as being too brutal and dangerous to health. Several of the older Blackfoot men I knew had scars from the Sundance ceremonies of their youth, almost a century ago.

    One summer during the Sun Dance ceremonies, a colleague in a nearby parish had relatives visiting him from England. They expressed an interest in visiting with and learning something about the *Red Indians*, as the English often refer to them. I assumed this was their way of distinguishing the native North American people and the Indians of India. We arranged to meet in Standoff one afternoon. As we stood in the street chatting along came Willie Scraping White. I introduced Willie to the visitors who were duly impressed by this venerable old man. I mentioned to Willie that these visitors were from England. This jogged Willie's recollections of his youthful visit to London for the Jubilee and he whispered, "Ooooh, Queen Victoria" and ambled off. Afterward, I filled the visitors in on the details of Willie's youth and they appeared to be caught up in a delicious time warp.

We drove up to the Sun Dance site hoping to have just a glimpse of the encircled tipis. I didn't believe we had any chance of actually entering the site. As we approached, I stopped the car and talked with someone at the entranceway. As they knew me, we were invited to proceed into the camp, a remarkable departure for these quiet and reserved people. We parked and began a walk around the camp. The guests were fascinated. I wondered to myself if we might even have a peek inside a tipi. Before long, I found the tipi of a family I knew from the Parish. I knocked…well, how does one knock on the door of a tipi? Somehow, I hailed someone inside. It was Mrs. Many Grey Horses. I explained our interest. She was a little flustered and said the tipi was in a mess—a typical housewife—and could we come back in half an hour? I said that would be wonderful and we carried on with our walk around the camp.

We returned after the agreed interval and were welcomed into the tipi of the Many Grey Horses family. Many Grey Horses was also there now and he and his wife settled us on furs and blankets and he began a dissertation on tipi living. Many Grey Horses did the speaking in Blackfoot and his wife gave a running translation. I was amazed at how much of the Blackfoot I actually understood. This language is very beautiful and melodic. The English visitors sat in awe as Many Grey Horses explained how every element of tipi design had meaning; from the artwork on the outside buffalo hides, to the importance of the fire in the centre; the smoke flap in the upper regions of the tipi; and the many customs observed by these People. I felt an overwhelming pride as our English guests drank in this remarkable slice of life on the plains; things which tourists would normally never see. Incidentally, a Blackfoot tipi is much larger than most people would imagine. On one occasion, at such a camp we celebrated a Sunday Eucharist in a tipi and there were almost 50 people present.

High profile visitors frequently visited the Blood Reserve, as it was one of the especially progressive native communities. One year, Prince Charles, on a visit to the Blood Reserve, was initiated into the Kainai Chieftainship—a considerable honour. He attended the Indian Days celebrations at Standoff and was duly decorated with paint, smudged and adorned with an eagle plume bonnet. At a banquet in his honour, Prince Charles seemed quite comfortable with the people and table conversation flowed easily. In turn, the Blood people, while displaying all due respect, were not at all overwhelmed by the prestige of their visitor. During the collecting of the plates after the main course one of the young women who was serving paused as she picked up the Prince's plate with its knife and fork. Extending the plate toward him, she remarked, "You might want to keep your fork, Prince, there's pie."

✠

I was fortunate to be able to take my second European holiday during my time on the Blood Reserve. Upon hearing I planned to take Holy Orders, my father had said, "You'll never make any bloody money doing that." He was not entirely wrong in the sense that I have not become rich in the worldly sense, but rather have discovered that with a little prudence and budgeting I have done many of the things I longed to do. On this second trip, I travelled with a colleague, Ted, and took along my 17-year-old sister, Susan. Susan is also seventeen years my junior. I left home for work and university when she was quite young, so this trip afforded us a wonderful opportunity to spend some time together.

We travelled in England, France and Italy and Susan was wonderful fun. This was all new to her which made it all the more exciting for me. In England, we went to Wantage and visited a second cousin who was a nun with the Community of St. Mary the Virgin. I was duly

A Priest's Tale

impressed with the size of the Community and the extent of its property and adjacent extended care facility. We arrived around 11 am and had a chance to chat and to meet with a number of the Sisters. At noon, we went to the large and beautiful, Victorian chapel for the office of Sext. The Office was sung by perhaps eighty or so sisters—a commendable tribute to the Anglo-Catholic tradition. We then proceeded to the refectory where Ted, Susan, and I ate at a 'guests table'. The meal was quite sparse and silent but for a priest reading from St. Augustine's *'The City of God'*. We passed a few hours after lunch chatting and wandering the Convent grounds with Ella before saying our farewells and going back to London.

Susan and I left Ted in Bristol to visit with his cousin and continued on our own adventure. We took the ferry from Southampton to Cherbourg where we rented a Renault 500 and began a tour through Normandy on our way to Paris. We stopped at some of the beaches along the coast where rusting hulks of WWII landing craft still litter the shallows—sobering reminders of the not so distant past.

We continued on our way through country villages and cities like Caan and Rouen. As we approached Paris, we found the traffic extremely heavy and wondered what was happening. There were decorative national flags and armoured vehicles everywhere. All of a sudden, I realized it was July 14th—Bastille Day. We were fortunate to find a hotel in the Rive Gauche area of Paris near the Sorbonne. As Susan and I approached the lobby, I could see a couple of tourists negotiating with the clerk, in English, about accommodation. They seemed undecided and were perhaps haggling about the price. This was at a very busy time in the summer and finding any lodging at all would be lucky, I thought. As soon as there was a lull in their conversation, I moved forward, spoke to the woman at the desk in French, and asked if there were any double rooms available. She said, yes, there was one, but on the fourth floor and added that there was no elevator. She quoted what I thought was a very reasonable price for that time of year and I accepted it immediately. We gave her our passports in exchange for the room key and proceeded up the narrow, winding staircase.

We began our exploration of Paris comfortably settled in our room in the *Hôtel Des Deux Continents* in Rue Jacob. We preferred to wander around willy-nilly and stumble onto important places at random. That was more relaxing than trying to follow guidebook tours and we enjoyed our time there, stopping when hungry or thirsty for refreshment.

The return trip through Normandy was pleasant, stopping to explore some of the beautiful and austere abbeys and churches, which abound in that region.

A Priest's Tale

The flight back to Canada was rather a disaster. The departure was from Gatwick on the outskirts of London. We were less than an hour in the air when we noticed the faint odour of something burning. It had that pungent ozone smell which I always associate with overheated electrical wiring. No one was saying anything, but the cabin crew began furtively inspecting cupboards and overhead bins. Eventually the captain came on the intercom and announced, very calmly, that we should fasten our seat belts, as we would be returning to Gatwick—click! That was it. No further explanation was offered.

Susan, Ted, and I were seated near a door. There was a jump seat on the wall in front of us, which a young flight steward pulled down and buckled into. A few moments later, the plane banked sharply to the left and nosed straight down. Sandwiches and apple juice went scattering everywhere. The oxygen masks popped out from overhead and we were instructed to use them. Mine didn't seem to be working; I could sense nothing coming out of it. Ted noticed the hose for my mask had fallen away from its connection and was dangling in the aisle and was able to put it aright.

Glancing out my window I noticed that, although the orientation on the plane appeared usual aside from the commotion, the horizon was vertical with the earth directly ahead. We were going straight down—and under power. People began to panic—screaming, moaning and praying aloud which was, I suppose, to be expected on an Anglican charter flight. Susan became panicked and joined in the general pandemonium. The steward seated in front of us eventually came over and slapped her on the face. That stopped her instantly.

She turned to me and asked, "Don, are we going to live?" I said, "Of course we are," even though I was thinking to myself, *But we are not...this is it! We have about two minutes before it's all over.* Strangely, it flashed through my mind that Mother would be so annoyed at me for having taken Susan on this trip to Europe.

Another tense minute passed before we felt the plane slowly struggling out of its dive and levelling off with the accompanying sensation of heavy G force. Everyone was now very quiet. I could hear the motors of the undercarriage being activated what seemed many times over. I wondered if perhaps this was part of the problem and whether the wheels were actually coming down. Finally, we made a very hard landing at Gatwick and I could see the runway was lined with red emergency vehicles. The plane rolled to a stop and instead of the usual applause that was then common on trans-continental flights there was just an eerie silence.

A Priest's Tale

We were deplaned and led into an airport lounge where we were briefed on the situation. Apparently, a motor that pumps oxygen throughout the cabin had burned a bearing—that explained the ozone smell. The dive manoeuvre was to get the plane down from 33,000 feet to an altitude where there was enough natural oxygen. The steward explained that flight crews practise such procedures from time to time. I was praying they would put us on a nice Lufthansa plane to get us back home although I had my doubts about getting Susan onto any aircraft at that point. A replacement plane was apparently not to be. We waited seven hours at Gatwick as they replaced the faulty motor. We consumed quite a few martinis. They didn't even seem to be at all concerned about providing drinks to Susan who was underage; but then, they are much more relaxed about such things in Europe.

Once we were back onboard and in the air again the steward came by to speak to Susan. He wanted to apologize to her for the slap. He explained they have to do everything possible to avert panic. Susan understood and did not seem to harbour any malice toward him. After his explanation he stayed to chat for a bit. He asked Susan what she wanted to do after finishing high school. Without hesitation, she said, "Well, two things I never want to be are a nun or a stewardess." The flight was without incident except that we were now about eight hours late arriving in Calgary.

✠

A month in Europe seemed quite a long time. Living out of a suitcase can become a little tiresome and I delighted in being back at home amongst my own things and in familiar surroundings. September soon arrived and the students came back again to St. Paul's for another term. It was pleasant to be back in my routine at the School and my parish work.

Community activities were an important element in our parish and the church basement was often the centre of social life. There were few facilities at the southern end of the Reserve where St. Paul's church was located. The southern boundary of the Reserve lies immediately across the street from the town of Cardston, which is Mormon and consequently, there are no bars or beer parlours, and only one renegade coffee shop. If people wanted to go for a drink, they had to drive quite a distance—either to Fort McLeod or to Lethbridge. As a result, there were frequently nasty road accidents.

The parish ran bingos on most Saturday evenings to try and provide an alternative to the drives to bars in neighbouring towns. This was an opportunity for families to be together and socialize in a non-drinking atmosphere. If lucky enough to win, they would go home with a large hamper of groceries. Unfortunately, on one summer afternoon the bishop drove past the church on his way to Waterton Park where the Diocese of Calgary had a cottage and saw our large Bingo sign. The next week he was on the phone to us protesting. Like many Anglican Dioceses, a prohibition existed in the canons about gambling. The bishop didn't seem at all impressed with our concern that there was little recreational space available for the people of that community, nor about the drinking and driving question. I could never quite understand how Anglican women's organizations got around this gambling restriction in order to have their cherished raffles. We felt we were a very far-flung parish—light years away from life of Calgary—and simply continued as we had before, convinced that the bingos were serving a good purpose. We did, however, find a less conspicuous location for the bingo sign.

When I first went to work on the Blood Reserve my friend, Fr. John Prince had been working at the sister Blackfoot Reserve at Gleichen for several years. Sometime during my first two years at St. Paul's, John left to take another appointment. Bishop Goodman contacted me about doing some work at Gleichen. He proposed I go there one week of each month. It was nearly a two hundred mile drive from Cardston to Gleichen, and I asked if perhaps a priest from Calgary or somewhere closer might not be a better, more efficient alternative. The bishop was aware I had been making an effort to learn some Blackfoot and used that as his reasoning for why he thought I would be the best person to do pastoral work there. I had to admit, my limited knowledge of the language did create an immediate bond and opening for me when I visited the people on the Blackfoot Reserve. But I did think the bishop had a rather exaggerated notion of how much Blackfoot I could speak. In the end, however, I began my monthly trips to Gleichen.

During the weeklong visits at Gleichen, I stayed in a very tiny, stiflingly hot room in the Old Sun School. Old steam heated buildings could be very difficult to regulate; the only recourse seemed to be to open the window a little bit and tolerate the freezing but refreshing air. The size of the accommodation was not really a problem to me as it was basically a place to sleep for six days each month.

The Blackfoot People were very appreciative of the time I was able to spend there. I drove up on Monday and visited around during the week with a parishioner, Arthur Ayoungman, who was extremely helpful in guiding me around and acting as interpreter. Arthur later took Holy Orders and served there as a priest himself.

On Sunday, we celebrated the Liturgy in the Old Sun School Chapel and the people turned out in large numbers. Arthur would assist me in the Mass, which was a mixture of English and Blackfoot—particularly the readings from Scripture in Blackfoot. In those days, there were no written biblical texts in Blackfoot. I found Arthur was absolutely amazing in that he could translate the readings into Blackfoot directly from the English of the Prayer Book. I was always in awe of his wonderful gifts. My comprehension of spoken Blackfoot was such that I could vaguely follow what was being said, of course, having the English in my hand helped considerably.

On one particular visit, it was the week of Pentecost Sunday, which I thought would be a wonderful opportunity to introduce, or at least emphasize, the wonderful diversity of language and culture that God has called us to share. I looked over the readings as I prepared my sermon. I was completely stalled when I looked at the reading from Acts. It was, of course, the account of the Day of Pentecost where the author—undoubtedly Luke—describes the scene. People of many heritages and cultures gathered together to share in the wonderful experience of receiving the Holy Spirit. I read the words over and over:

"And how hear we every man in our own tongue, Elamites, and the dwellers in Mesopotamia, and in Judea, and Cappadocia, in Pontus, and Asia, Phrygia, and Pamphylia, in Egypt, and in the parts of Libya about Cyrene, and strangers of Rome, Jews and Proselytes, Cretans, and Arabians, we do hear them speak in our tongues the wonderful works of God."

I thought to myself, My God, whatever will a Blackfoot Indian in the middle of the Alberta plains ever make of that? Phrygians and Cretans! As I contemplated the dilemma, I thought, Somehow I must try to make this a little more understandable. I am not, and never have been, any sort of revolutionary, nor have I ever thought of myself as being on the cutting edge of innovation in liturgy, but it seemed important that this be clarified if possible. I sat down at my portable typewriter and tried to come up with a translation that would convey the real meaning of this text. Eventually, I came up with something like this:

"And how hear we every man in our own tongue, Sarcee, and the dwellers in Brockett, and in Siksikai, and Calgary, in Gleichen, and Montana, and we do hear them speak in our tongues the wonderful works of God."

A Priest's Tale

I met Arthur for coffee on the Saturday morning and showed him my typescript suggestion for use as the Acts reading, which he would translate into Blackfoot for our liturgy on Sunday. In his stoic Blackfoot way, he looked it over but made absolutely no comment. I presumed that he was comfortable with the idea and all was well. On Sunday morning, I was to receive a revelation with regard to the ingenuity and tactfulness of the Blackfoot people. As Arthur rose to read the Epistle, I sat in my seat in the sanctuary and listened with pride. He opened his maroon copy of the Prayer Book, in which I could see my little typescript page, and he began the Epistle reading. I was able to follow the gist of the Blackfoot, and my mind went into overdrive as I heard him recounting the beautiful Pentecost story:

> "....we hear every man in our own tongue wherein we were born; Sarcee, and the dwellers in Brockett, and in Siksikai, and Calgary, in Gleichen, and Montana, and Cappadocia. Parthians and Medes and Elamites, those from Pontus, and Asia, Phrygia, and Pamphylia, in Egypt, and in the parts of Libya about Cyrene, and strangers from Rome, Jews and Proselytes, Cretes, and Arabians, we do hear them speak in our tongues the wonderful works of God."

He did the entire thing. Instead of challenging me about tampering with Holy Scripture or engaging in an argument, he had simply done what I asked, but also remained faithful to the Church's appointed reading. I learned a little lesson that day about diplomacy, respect and Native wisdom.

During another of my visits to Gleichen, Arthur and I stopped into the local coffee shop which was a wonderful place to meet people. A woman approached and spoke to Arthur. After a lengthy conversation, almost all of which I didn't understand, Arthur turned to me and said that she would like me to bless her house. I sensed there was more to this than a simple blessing. I asked if there was a problem. Arthur spoke to her again in Blackfoot and it was revealed there had been some sort of strange *activity* in her house. I asked Arthur to explain to her that I understood. I am open to the possibility of disagreeable spiritual entities and wanted to assure the woman I was comfortable with that and would be happy to bless her house. We arranged to visit her after the parish Mass on the Sunday morning.

I arrived at the appointed time to find a typical, tiny, one room house full of people. There were about twenty of them—all sitting on the floor leaning against the walls. A wood-stove crackled in the kitchen area. I knew from

A Priest's Tale

Arthur the problem was some sort of a presence that rattled pots and pans in the night. They assured Arthur it was definitely not the wind or prairie dogs causing this. The woman and her children were frightened to death by the noises.

I realized what she was really asking for was an exorcism. While recognized and practised by the Church, exorcism is done only after great care and preparation, and never by one priest alone, or without the bishop's authorization. My intention was simply to bless the house and say some prayers for the repose of departed souls. The people assembled in the house were all silent. I vested myself in surplice and stole, and then prepared the holy water. I tried to explain what we were going to do. We would invoke the name of the Holy Trinity, then read an appropriate psalm during which I would *asperge*, or sprinkle, the room with Holy Water, and then say prayers asking God to grant rest to the departed.

Everyone stood, and I began the rite. As we began reciting a psalm, I moved around the room sprinkling Holy Water. I had forgotten about the hot wood stove and as I passed it and some water hit it, a cloud of hissing steam rose up. Everyone gasped. Rather a dramatic touch which even startled me. There were a few giggles but this was only a momentary distraction. We continued with our psalm, read from Holy Scripture, and said prayers for the departed and for those who lived in the house.

Several months later I learned from some of the people who had been involved that the pot rattling had stopped. *Laus Deo!* One does wonder whether the blessings and prayers were responsible or if the minds of those affected were freed by the ritual to let go of their 'ghosts'.

After eight months of these once-monthly visits to Gleichen, the bishop must have realized he needed to do something permanent for the people there. I received a phone call from his secretary telling me the bishop wanted to meet with me. An appointment was arranged. I drove into Calgary on the agreed day and waited in the outer office until the bishop was free. I had not the slightest idea what the purpose of this meeting was. Finally, Bishop Goodman came to the door and invited me in. The secretary brought us coffees and we chatted about the work on the Blood Reserve and made conversation for a short while. Then, out of the blue, he changed the subject and asked, "Would you consider moving to Gleichen to work there?"

I thought to myself how brief a time I had been at St. Paul's and of all the unfinished work there. Naturally, I realized that this kind of work is never really finished. I also felt the bishop had a somewhat limited perception of the

A Priest's Tale

day-to-day difficulties of living in this very depressed community where there was no adequate accommodation for a priest. Father Prince had lived in a tiny trailer when he was there but it had long since been removed. The bishop had framed this as a question, and I naturally assumed he wanted an honest reply.

"I don't think so, Bishop," I said. I did not realize how much this was going to ruffle his feathers. He went rigid and a little red in the face and said with a flustered tone, "Well, Father...What do you think about your obedience to your bishop?"

I was somewhat startled by his reaction. Just at that moment the secretary knocked, poked her head in and told the bishop there was an important long distance phone call for him. As he took the call, I left the office to give him privacy, motioning that I would wait in the outer office. I was extremely flustered and a flood of questions ricocheted around in my head after this surprise ambush. What *did* I think about my obedience to the bishop?

After about four agonizing minutes his door opened and he ushered me back in. He looked at me from behind his big desk and picking up the conversation—and with the same tone of voice—he repeated, "*Well*, what do you think about your obedience to your Bishop?"

I have not the faintest idea what prompted me to respond as I did, but I said, "Well, Bishop, I do take my obedience to you very seriously. However, if this office were on the tenth floor of a high-rise building and you told me to jump, I wouldn't."

Now it was his turn to be startled. The interview ended and I cannot remember the exact details of how it actually concluded, except to say, very abruptly. I was quite upset about it all happening as it did as a bolt out of the blue. Leaving his office, I drove down to the Four Seasons Hotel and had several double Scotches: something I never do at eleven o'clock in the morning.

Musing on these events after the fact I thought that if only the bishop had said to me, "Donald, I'm reassigning you to Gleichen", I simply would have gone and tried to negotiate some kind of acceptable living arrangements. When he framed his proposal as a question, I naively took it to be just that. This regrettable interview was actually the last time we ever spoke. I continued my visits to Gleichen afterward, but within eight months I applied for the position of curate at All Saints' Cathedral in Edmonton, was interviewed, and subsequently appointed.

A Priest's Tale

✠

My position at All Saints' Cathedral, Edmonton, was really as a curate but the Dean decided that I should be given the pretentious, double-barrelled title: *'Vicar and Precentor'*. My engagement there came about after the previous assistant had been terminated. He had done some significant work with youth in Edmonton and some of their social activities took place in the Cathedral parish hall. Apparently, during one of these functions, one of the young men was found to have some marijuana in his possession. A great tempest in a teapot ensued resulting in the Dean firing him.

The Dean probably did not really want a curate, I suspect, as he was rather a one man band, but the vestry undoubtedly felt obliged to fill the position because there had been a curate on staff as long as anyone could remember. When I drove up to Edmonton for the interview, I was duly wined and dined and the decision to hire me seemed to come rather quickly. It was not until years later I realized I must have been of interest to the Dean because I was virtually without credentials; I had limited experience and came from a remote Indian Reserve. My new title—*Vicar and Precentor*—was undoubtedly chosen by the Dean to give the Cathedral a grandiose demeanour. One morning, I unintentionally overheard a telephone conversation in the office. Someone was apparently asking the Dean about my rather imposing title and he responded that a vicar was simply someone filling in for someone else, which certainly is the Latin derivation, but he added that I was just a *'go-fer'* —go for this, go for that. However, the Bishop of Edmonton on one occasion told me that when he was asked the same question, he answered, "Well, a Vicar is an assistant to the Dean, and as for Precentor...well, it just means that the Dean can't sing."

Almost from the beginning, my special niche was to be Evensong. I quite enjoyed those quiet evenings on my own with only the organist, Hugh Bancroft, the choir, and a small congregation of perhaps 30 or 40.

My formal introduction to the Cathedral came during the first Sunday service after my arrival in Edmonton. In the week that followed, I began the process of getting to know people by arranging a schedule of parish visits. Having a secretary and office staff was a completely new experience for me. I stood at her desk on that first Monday morning and asked if she could offer any suggestions as to where I might begin a round of visiting. She thumbed through her Rolodex and rattled off a few names which I dutifully jotted down. She hesitated for a

A Priest's Tale

moment or two as she glanced over one particular card and then looked up at me and remarked, "Oh, and you might want to visit Mr. Fryett. He's a bachelor, too." Hello, I thought; I wonder what that means?

I jotted down his name—*Barrie Fryett*—and his telephone number. That evening as I was telephoning around to set up visits, I called him. Mr. Fryett sounded extremely pleasant and happy to have received a call from the Cathedral. He told me we had actually met on the previous Sunday at coffee time after the service, but appreciated that I had been quite overwhelmed by hundreds of new faces. He described himself, but I was still unable to place him. However, we made an arrangement for me to visit him on an evening the following week. I had no idea this visit would prove to be a pivotal event in my life.

Barrie lived in a high-rise apartment in a fashionable part of Edmonton's west side. I arrived at his building promptly at the agreed upon time and was presently buzzed in. The moment he opened the apartment door, I remembered meeting him. He was a tall man with a bushy Afro-hairstyle that would have been difficult to forget. He welcomed me warmly into his home and we proceeded to the living room. I took him up on the offer of a drink, and as Barrie prepared two scotches, I surveyed the art and tasteful furnishings. He soon returned with a tray of drinks.

We toasted and began our introductory small talk. I liked him immediately. He obviously felt comfortable with the new Vicar, too, as our conversation flowed ever so smoothly.

After about an hour of pleasant chit-chat and several refreshments of the scotch, we had exchanged, in capsule form, our histories; mine recounting my life and some of the places I had served since ordination and his of growing up in Alberta and B.C. and his career as a department manager with the provincial telephone company. Barrie worked in an office tower just a few minutes walk from the Cathedral. He was also community conscious and began telling me about his latest volunteer project in which he would function as a mentor to people just released from prison—not in the capacity of a law officer or social worker, but rather as an ordinary citizen who could offer moral support, friendship and perhaps some direction. The programme was professionally monitored, and there had been a considerable amount of training and evaluation before he was assigned to anyone.

In the course of things Barrie also mentioned he had just completed several long sessions with a psychologist to, as he put it, "Find out what made me tick." I was feeling quite relaxed at this point in the evening and was so enjoying this open and pleasant man, I felt I simply could not let that statement go by without comment.

A Priest's Tale

I looked at him over my scotch glass, and asked, "And did they?"

Barrie's eyes widened in astonishment and he sputtered a bit before responding, "Oh, I need another drink on that."

Dissolving into hysterics, it was obvious that words and explanations were passé; we instinctively knew we had a bond with each other and a long and beautiful friendship began.

When I look back on my life, I see Barrie standing out ever so strongly for the pivotal role he played in my evolution as a gay person. Never before had I met a person so utterly comfortable and at ease with his own sexuality. Of course, I was then so very naive about my own nature; Barrie was like a bucket of ice water. His approach to life was refreshing, enlightening, and made an indelible impression on me. I feel fortunate to have learned the basic practicalities of gay life from such a delightful and dignified man.

In gay circles, such men are often called *'aunties'*—and Barrie was certainly mine. He taught me so much about gay life; the terminology, perspective, and humour. Much of what he had to teach me was crucial to my ability to cope with life as a gay man. Because we both were rooted in the Church, our friendship was that much closer. Barrie didn't seek to have the place of teacher and mentor in my life—it simply happened through what I see as natural affinity.

I was in my early thirties when we first met and was still in the process of addressing the issues of my sexuality. Barrie, on the other hand, was one of those people who had dealt with the question at a very early age. Actually, I had the impression he was one for whom the nature of sexuality had never caused any struggle for identity at all; a thing I envied.

I was regaled with laughter when he told me the story of his brief flirtation with the idea of a career in dance which began when he was sixteen or seventeen years of age. The Royal Winnipeg Ballet Company had come to his hometown for a performance. Barrie had been enthralled with dance from an early age. He was invited to an after concert cocktail party and was apparently courted to come to Winnipeg and take up the dance. I have seen photos of Barrie at that age and he was a rather appealing and lithe young man. It was easy to see why the members of the ballet were taken with him and could sense his potential. Barrie's father was a magistrate—described by Barrie as a rather strict, old school English gentleman. When he approached his father about going off with the ballet company his father went into a state of apoplexy and simply

A Priest's Tale

forbade it. Barrie often remarked to me that by now, he would be a long retired dame of the ballet—his *Red Shoes* long since hung up.

In the evolution of our friendship, one Saturday afternoon Barrie told me he would be going to a gay club that evening where there would be dancing and socializing. He said if I should like to go, he would be happy to introduce me to people. I declined immediately—my knee jerk reaction. I had never been to one of those places and was rather uneasy about going because of my position at the Cathedral. Barrie understood completely. However, he added, if ever I did want to go, I should just let him know.

On a Saturday some weeks later I was sitting in my basement suite after dinner, thumbing idly through the pages of a magazine and feeling a yearning to meet people—perhaps feeling a little lonely. I phoned Barrie around 8:00 o'clock and told him I just might take him up on his offer. He sounded quietly pleased and we arranged to meet in the parking lot of the club around 11:00 pm.

I was a little nervous going in. Would anyone from the church see me? Would I meet anyone? Would they recoil if they discovered what I 'did for a living'? Barrie seemed to know everyone in the place and it proved a rather interesting, if smoky, evening. As we left the coat check and walked toward the lounge, Barrie introduced me to several people in the entranceway. The atmosphere was rather exhilarating. This was my first experience in such an openly gay setting. It was also my first encounter with bitchy gay humour, which took me a few moments to compute.

Barrie saw someone he knew sitting alone at a table and we went over. He whispered to me over the din that this was 'Millie', and that he was a hair stylist. After introductions, Millie and Barrie chatted for a few moments during which I overheard Millie say, "Oh, Brenda! Your hair's the shits!" Barrie was always carefully groomed and proud of his bushy Afro. He laughed raucously at Millie's outrageous remark, obviously enjoying the good-natured ribbing. Camp names were another thing I had not encountered before and mercifully I was fortunate that no one ever tried to attach one to me.

During the course of the evening as we watched those on the dance floor, Barrie asked me if I danced at all. I said I did not, though I realized that was part of the reason for coming to the club—aside from the drinks. I was quite content to sit at our table and watch. There were some brief, shouted conversations with various people I met. But such was the volume of the music; I found a steady stream of conversation to be virtually impossible.

A Priest's Tale

At one point, I noticed an attractive young man on the dance floor about 20 feet from where we sat. I found him quite appealing, myself being, in the new language I was slowly acquiring, attracted to 'chicken'. This young man in white trousers and laced-up shirt apparently noticed my glances. Eyes, I was discovering, are particularly germane to gay communication. Later in the evening I was not a little startled to find the same young man appear suddenly beside my chair and, with his mouth very close to my ear so as to be heard, asked if I would like to dance.

Barrie knew full well what was happening, and remembering that I had already declined any notion of dancing, looked on approvingly—rather like a mother hen—as I stood up and was led off to the dance floor. I had no idea what to do except to begin gyrating. It didn't seem to matter much what one actually did amid the thunderous throbbing of the music and the rotating lights and pulsing strobes. To my surprise, after a few minutes of that, the music ended and a slow waltz began. Jackie—as I later learned was the young man's name—asked if I would like to stay on the dance floor for it. I said, sure, and was immediately enveloped in his arms. I readily reciprocated.

This dance was obviously intended to be an opportunity to just stand there making minimal motions and hold someone close—and, I must say, I found it preferable to the pin wheeling and gyrating. Jackie and I were about the same height and our cheeks were touching. He felt incredibly gentle, warm and vulnerable—the musky scent of his cologne still lingers in my memory. An open fire escape door brought a cool refreshing breeze to the hot summer evening. I felt light headed and extremely mellow. Leaving the dance floor finally, I waved across the hall to Barrie with a 'see you later' gesture and I joined Jackie and a few of his friends at their table.

At the end of the evening Jackie and I stood in the parking lot and talked for a long time both trying to tactfully discover more about each other and figure out what was to happen next. Eventually, we went back to my apartment. It was a wonderful experience to be with someone whom I genuinely liked and who liked me.

The next morning was Sunday. After the service at the Cathedral I encountered Barrie in the narthex looking as though he would explode if he didn't learn what had transpired the previous evening. Barrie had known Jackie from the club for some time and he quite approved of our meeting. When he asked me how things had gone the night before, I said that Jackie was at home in my bed. He let out a gasp throwing up his hands and rolling his eyes heavenward, "Oh my God, what have I done?"

A Priest's Tale

It was not very long before I was introducing Barrie to other friends. One of them was Nan, a parishioner at the Cathedral. Nan had heard all about Barrie and, of course, knew at least some of the details of my personal life. She invited me to bring Barrie to her house one evening for dinner. Nan was a very easy-going and gregarious person. Soon after arriving, we had drinks in hand and were launched into a relaxed conversation. It was still a tiny bit formal because it was the first meeting between them and they were getting acquainted. Although Nan knew we were both gay, Barrie had not yet revealed this to her himself, and one does not make assumptions. However, the moment of epiphany came quite soon after we sat down to dinner.

I was rambling on telling them about something rather foolish I had done. Nan graciously remarked, "Well, you're only human." As a comeback, I jokingly played on the theological concepts of humanity and divinity and retorted, "No, I'm Divine." Barrie's eyes lit up with anticipation and delight and, clutching his breast, he countered, "Oh, she's just divine!" The three of us shrieked with laughter and from that moment on, our mutual friendship was cemented.

I found Barrie to be a wonderful confidant. On a number of occasions, I discussed my career with him knowing he was a very organized and sensible person. He always knew just the right diplomatic solution to things. His experience was, of course, with the corporate world and he thought much in that vein. At one point, I wondered aloud if it might not be time for me to be interested in having a parish of my own. Being an assistant is the sort of position that usually lasts for a few years at most. Then, one needs to get on 'up the ladder', as they say. Barrie thought very much in that mode. On one occasion, when the subject of my career came up, I mentioned I had seen an ad in the church paper about a vacant parish in the country. It was the parish of Three Hills, Alberta.

"Why don't you apply for it?" Barrie asked.

I said, "Are you kidding? Who wants to be the Rector of Three Hills?"

Barrie responded instantly, "The Rector of Two Hills!"

We shared a laugh over this, but I am afraid I have never really been interested in that sort of personal advancement. At one stage in my career I left a position as Rector of a tiny country parish to be an assistant in a city parish. One person I spoke with could not quite figure out this situation (of course, she wasn't familiar with the parish to which I was going), and she asked, "Isn't that a step down the ladder?" I laughed, and replied, "I don't really think I am even on the ladder."

A Priest's Tale

Still, I always valued Barrie's advice and wisdom, his knack for seeing the wider picture was quite profound. This was, of course, always tempered by his delightful sense of humour. It was his way of viewing and framing the inconsistencies of the world. It was almost always expressed with gentleness and charity—and Barrie quite enjoyed his own idiosyncrasies.

On one occasion, I marvelled aloud at how he laughed so lustily at his own jokes and comments. To this he responded, "Well, I haven't heard them either."

Barrie quite embarrassed himself on one occasion, but retold the story with obvious zeal. It happened in the dead of the Edmonton winter. The temperature was around minus 40. At that time, I drove a little, red Datsun. Barrie was walking down Jasper Avenue, from his apartment to work, early one morning. Traffic was stalled and great billows of steam and exhaust wafted in the air.

A red Datsun had stopped in the stalled traffic just to Barrie's left and he, thinking it was me, walked over, opened the passenger door and climbed in with a cheery, "Good Morning, my Dear." Then he looked over at the driver, a rather horrified middle-aged man wearing a turban. Barrie babbled a profuse apology and made a hasty exit.

Always the devoted son, when Barrie's mother became bedridden he was a tremendous help to her understanding that in spite of her health she always wished to maintain her dignity and look presentable. The hospital staff would dress her each day and attend to her hair. He even took a sewing course so that he could alter her dresses—slitting them up the back—so that they could easily be put on in bed. He regaled me with stories of these sewing classes where he was the only man in a group of twelve or so women. He became so clever at it that he began making his own shirts.

On one occasion, Barrie was shopping in the Hudson's Bay store on Jasper Avenue for a new dress for his mother. He had browsed meticulously and in due course found one that he believed she would like and which was about the correct size. A sales lady approached him and he indicated which dress he wanted. The woman looked at the dress and then glanced at Barrie with a quizzical look and said, "But Sir, I think it will be a little small." He looked at her aghast and exclaimed, "It's not for me, it's for my mother."

Our friendship grew and ripened over the years we knew each other. We were neither each other's type and the friendship was entirely Platonic, which in a strange way made it even more precious and deep. I valued Barrie's sense of fairness and honesty just as his employees and fellow workers did. For that matter, everyone who knew

A Priest's Tale

Barrie felt that way. When he was in his sixties, he was diagnosed with cancer and he quickly became very ill. I flew out to Edmonton for a visit with him for a few days during those last months and although it was good to see him, I was quite shocked at his diminished state. He was now very frail and thin. One Sunday morning we went to the early service at the Cathedral and afterwards one of the men who had known Barrie quite well years before asked me who I had been with.

When Barrie died a few months later, I was not able to return to Edmonton to attend the funeral but I heard that the Cathedral was completely full. I missed him very much. This was the first time I had experienced the death of such a close friend.

✠

Hugh Bancroft was the Organist and Master of the Choir at All Saints' Cathedral during my time there. I had known his name since my teenage years, Hugh being a very distinguished organist and musician. Hugh had been organist in Cathedrals in Canada, Australia, and the Bahamas as well as parish churches in Britain. He was also a composer and some of his works are part of the standard church repertoire. While working on the committee of the

Canadian Book of Common Praise, 1938—Hugh made a significant contribution in a spontaneous moment.

They were dealing with a text that had no suitable tune to match it. The text was *"There's a voice in the Wilderness Crying"*. Hugh left the meeting for a half an hour, went to a battered, old, upright piano in the church basement, and soon emerged with the familiar tune we all know and have used for decades.

Hugh was a dour Lancashire man with seemingly no sense of humour at all. Many people thought him a grouch, but he did have a very sensitive side, which I was privileged to see on one or two occasions. We became friends through some strange process I shall never understand. Perhaps Hugh recognized and appreciated my interest in music. He gave me permission to practise on the cathedral organ when I had the opportunity.

During a Christmas Day visit one year we managed to get into quite a discussion about the relationship between clergy and organists. This seems to be a perpetual source of tension in many parishes. The Rector of a parish has the ultimate authority with regard to music and liturgy, but sometimes the organist has a much better knowledge of what is workable or even what is good and suitable. That was most certainly the case with reference to the situation at All Saints'. As Hugh and I talked about the difficulties that

A Priest's Tale

sometimes rear their ugly heads, he made the remark, "When you clergy get that collar 'round yer necks it cuts off the oxygen to the brain." I thought this spot on, and laughed heartily as I do appreciate the outrageous.

The Cathedral offices in those days were in the Parish Hall—an old ramshackle building adjoining the Cathedral. I was in the office one day when a long distance call came through for Hugh. I knew he was in the Cathedral practicing and went to call him to the telephone. The door from the Hall opened not far from where the organ console was. As I entered Hugh was just near the end of a magnificent composition by Cesar Franck. I was familiar with it and knew he was very near the end so I didn't attempt to disturb him. Hugh neither saw nor heard me approach the organ bench as he was into the thunderous climax of the *Pièce Heroïque*. I stood there just behind him waiting for the glorious final chords to fade. When there was silence I quietly said, "Hugh!" ...and he shot up about six inches above the organ bench and screamed "JESUS CHRIST." Mercifully, there was no one else in the cathedral at that moment. I'm sure he thought the Angel of Death had come to take him and I had difficulty containing my giggles as I told him of the long distance call.

One year it was decided the choir would stage a concert to raise money for the organ fund. It was to take place on a Friday and Saturday evening in the Parish Hall. The first part of the programme would consist of some secular choral music and the second half would be a production of Gilbert and Sullivan's "*Trial by Jury*". "Trial" was just the right length at forty-five minutes, for the second part of the programme. Hugh approached me and asked if I would sing the part of Edwin as I am a tenor. Edwin the Defendant, and a cad, is charged with breach of promise of marriage; hence the "Trial". I was intrigued by the thought. I pondered it and felt that it was not too long to pose a problem for memorization. I agreed to take the score home and look at it.

That evening I sat down after dinner to look at the score and I had a rather rude awakening. The story begins with a little preamble by the chorus, which is in this case the Jury, setting the scene for the trial, introducing the Judge and Bailiff, which then leads into Edwin's entrance. Edwin prances onto the stage from the wings strumming the obligatory ukulele. This was all fine. What made me sit up in shock were the first couple of lines I was supposed to sing. Edwin addresses the assembled jury:

"Is this the Court of the Exchequer?"
The Jury responds, *"It is."*
Then Edwin sings, *"Be firm, be firm my pecker."*

A Priest's Tale

Well, being unfamiliar with this operetta I can only say that my reaction was horror—and I am not easily horrified. I went to Hugh the next day and explained I could not possibly sing that. Hugh just looked at me with a deadpan face and said, in his grumpy Lancashire accent, "Don't b' daft." and took no further notice of me nor my complaint. I tried speaking to him over the next few days, but he simply wouldn't take me seriously. I then experimented with changing the phrase; attempting to retain the sense of the British idiom about keeping the head high, 'stiff upper lip and all that', and at the same time keeping the sound and metre of the word similar. I came up with, "Be firm, be firm my ticker", which would make more sense to a Canadian audience. However, at the next rehearsal I found that when one sings 'ticker' it sounds pretty much like 'pecker' anyway and because I was so distraught about it, I got the notes all wrong. The cast, being very familiar with the libretto, was regaled with fits of laughter. Hugh, who I had never known to laugh, collapsed over his card table podium, turned red in the face and howled. It may have been the only time in his life that he laughed so.

In preparation for our production of "Trial by Jury", someone got the bright idea we could get publicity through a local community events programme on CBC Edmonton. Hugh and the others involved in the production thought this a good idea and felt I would be the logical person to do the interview as I was in the production and also a priest on staff at the Cathedral. Jo Green, the wife of the principal flautist of the Edmonton Symphony, hosted the CBC's noon hour community events programme. I had seen her on TV many times. However, I had never had any exposure on this medium.

I was quite nervous as I drove up to the studios in south Edmonton. I had debated wearing my Edwin costume from the production. In the end, I went in my clerical blacks. Jo, wearing a black dress with a white lace choker, met me and took me to the make-up room. I expected there might be a review of just what would be happening during the broadcast. I was duly powdered and prepared for the bright lights as Jo and I chitchatted.

She asked some questions about me, and in the process discovered that I had built a harpsichord and was interested in Baroque music. She told me that she and her husband, Harlan, had built the very same Zuckermann spinet. We had a bond already. However, as fascinating as the small talk was, I was still nervous about what was to come. I asked her what the plan was once we were on air. She shrugged it off with a, "Well, we'll just relax and it will

A Priest's Tale

all fall into place, talking about the operetta and so on." She appeared to be quite oblivious to how distraught I was and her shrugging it off did not give me any assurance.

Finally, I was led to a small set, which was made to look like the corner of a comfy living room with a coffee table in the centre and some stuffed chairs. We took our seats ten minutes before airtime and tried to compose ourselves.

A studio person wearing a headset walked past and said "Three." I said to Jo, "Three what?" She said, "Three minutes." More idle fidgeting on my part and soon the man came back and said "One." My heart was pounding. Then he said, "Thirty."… and I knew my fate was sealed. There was a monitor almost at my feet on which I could see what was being transmitted. The camera initially zoomed in on Jo and she introduced the programme and talked a bit about some of the features coming up in the course of the hour—including our Cathedral production of "Trial by Jury".

After she finished, the terror really began. Sometimes when I am under stress, I cannot really be held responsible for what comes out of my mouth. I could see on my monitor that the camera had zeroed in with a close up of the coffee table and then slowly moved back. As the screen gradually showed more and more of the room and the two of us sitting there, an attendant brought in a tray complete with teapot, two cups, saucers, milk, and sugar.

Jo looked up at the camera and said ever so calmly, "Well, as you can see, today we have the Vicar to tea." She then proceeded to pour, asking me as she did, "Well, Vicar, do you take milk and sugar?" As I detest tea and never drink it, I said, "I'm really not sure. I'm a coffee drinker."

We managed to decide on just sugar for me. Then she posed a question to me—my poor heart pounding. "Well, I understand that we have something in common?" I knew she was referring to the building of the harpsichords, but for some unknown reason I opened my mouth and out came, "You mean that we're both wearing black and white?"

The camera operator and other crewmembers almost exploded but managed to make no sound. We finally got into the meat of the exercise and talked about the operetta. She tried to make connections between Edwin, the cad, who was being charged with 'breach of promise' and my role in the operetta. She asked me some rather personal questions about being a bachelor and asked whether I had young women of the parish pursuing me. It was all rather unfortunate. However, I answered her question by quoting the text of one of my arias in which Edwin explains why he should not be considered a very good catch. Gilbert's

A Priest's Tale

amusing libretto, in which Edwin appeals to the jury, explains it all:

> *"I smoke like a furnace – I'm always in liquor,*
> *A ruffian—a bully—a sot:*
> *I'm sure I should thrash her, perhaps I should kick her,*
> *I am such a very bad lot."*

Edwin also attempts to explain that variety in life is really the way of nature:

> *"Oh, gentlemen, listen, I pray,*
> *Though I own that my heart has been ranging,*
> *Of nature the laws I obey,*
> *For nature is constantly changing.*
>
> *The moon in her phases is found,*
> *The time, and the wind, and the weather.*
> *The months in succession come round,*
> *And you don't find two Mondays together.*
>
> *Consider the moral, I pray,*
> *Nor bring a young fellow to sorrow,*

> *Who loves this young lady to-day,*
> *And loves that young lady to-morrow."*

The broadcast was not live but aired one hour after it was taped. I managed to get home in time to view it. Others from the Cathedral who saw it thought the interview extremely funny, if not outrageous. It must have done its work of publicizing the operetta because for the two evenings it ran we had a full house each night.

There was one surprise I hadn't anticipated with this production. The background to this incident is that every July in Edmonton there is a celebration of "Klondike Days"—the local summer festival. Although Edmonton is rather removed from the Yukon, I am told in the gold rush days Edmonton was one of the major outfitting stops the prospectors used before proceeding to the gold fields. As a part of this festival, there is a Pantomime show, which runs each evening. It is the usual turn of the century pantomime in which a Villain tries to evict a poor and innocent Heroine. It is traditional for this show to be very interactive with the audience cheering on the Heroine and booing the Villain. Edmonton audiences were so used to this custom it spilled over into our production of "Trial". On opening night when I made my entrance I was already on edge knowing I had to sing that offending line, but I was even more unsettled when the audience started to 'boo' me the moment I appeared. It took me a moment to realize this was nothing personal. I realized this interaction would make the performance that much more alive. It was great fun and the booing actually egged me on to play up to the audience.

✠

After serving two years as Assistant at the Cathedral I began to contemplate the possibility of having a parish of my own and I spoke about it with my confessor, Archdeacon Ed Thain, and was able to talk candidly and confidentially about the situation. He was extremely pastoral and understanding—I suspect it was he who shared my concerns with the Primate, Edward Scott. They had been very close friends from college days and Ed, I presume, discussed with the Primate my previous history of work with Native People. This was what I believe led to my receiving a telephone call from Timothy Matthews, the Bishop of Québec, and the subsequent offer of parish work in Québec's north.

In a brief ten-minute telephone conversation, Bishop Matthews offered me the Incumbency of the Parish of

Schefferville. The parish was an assisted, northern mission which included the English speaking Parish of St. Peter in the town site as well as the care of the Naskapi congregation living on the adjacent Reserve. During our phone conversation the bishop was a little vague about Schefferville's precise location. When I put the question, he said it was "about 300 miles north of the river". I thought that sounded hopeful, imagining possible jaunts into one of the most beautiful of Canadian cities. As I was eager for such a position I accepted his offer without much hesitation.

I packed my belongings into the red Datsun and set out on the long drive across the country. Central Canada in February can be very bleak and indeed vast. I traversed Saskatchewan and Manitoba in almost one day along highways that ran straight as an arrow through flat, featureless, snow-covered fields. I entered Ontario near Dryden and was astounded at the width of that province. It seemed never-ending as I made my way along the northern shores of the Great Lakes. Eventually I arrived in Toronto and found my way to the home of friends from Alberta with whom I had arranged to stay for the night. I had occasion to visit with Father Bruce Stavert who was then the chaplain at Trinity College. He had been the missionary priest in Schefferville some years before and was able to give me some extremely useful information about the people and life in Ungava. Bruce later went on to become the Bishop and then the Archbishop of Québec.

After two very icy days in Toronto, I continued on my journey toward Québec. Passing from Ontario into Québec was somewhat un-nerving for me. The FLQ crisis and the War Measures Act episode had happened only a few years before. I was somewhat nervous about the reception I would receive as an Anglophone in Québec. Recent history had shown there were some very emotionally charged views about heritage. However, my worries quickly vanished as I negotiated with restaurant personnel and hotel clerks who were friendly and cordial to this *Anglais* with his hesitant, high school French.

It was not until I arrived in Québec City that I discovered where Schefferville actually was. Bishop Matthews had been quite right; Schefferville *was* 300 miles from the St. Lawrence River. However, that was the lower end of the St. Lawrence and the town was in fact about 700 miles north of Québec City in the Arctic part of the Ungava Peninsula. Bishop Matthew's remarks during our telephone conversation were very clever. I should make clear, however, that during my whole time in the parish the bishop was extremely supportive and well aware of the possible consequences of such isolation.

Eventually, I arrived in Québec City and found my way to the Bishop's Palace. The Matthews were very kind to me and we passed a pleasant evening in conversation. We talked about the work in Schefferville; the bishop giving me as much information as he could to supplement what Father Stavert had shared with me in Toronto. Mrs. Matthews was also supportive. Knowing I was a bachelor, she kindly gave me her copy of a small paperback cookbook which I still cherish. It is called the *"Appendix To The I Hate To Cook Book"* by Peg Bracken. Years later I would spend a lovely day with Peg and her husband on their launch on the Columbia River when I visited friends in Portland.

The next day, after breakfast with the Matthews, I continued on my journey, making the long drive north along the St. Lawrence River to Sept-Îles. This proved to be the most taxing leg of the journey because the weather was extremely blustery, approaching blizzard conditions. As there were no roads into Schefferville from Sept-Îles, I arranged transportation for my car on the Iron Ore Company Railway. I stayed overnight in the Rectory at Sept-Îles and flew to Schefferville the next day on the Iron Ore Company plane. The flight was very turbulent and tense as we passed through yet another winter storm. I arrived safely at the Schefferville airport and was met by Father Ross, the priest I was to replace, who took me to the

A Priest's Tale

Rectory to meet his wife and small children and settle into the guest room.

My first three days in Schefferville proved to be a dramatic introduction to the hostility of the Arctic climate. The winter storm through which we had flown continued and intensified. Within a couple of days, it became a fierce blizzard. For three days the entire town was compelled to remain indoors as the wind increased to around 90 miles per hour and the thermometer dipped to minus 40, which happens to be about the point where the Celsius and Fahrenheit scales match up. At one stage, we phoned the Department of Transport to enquire about the wind chill factor. They simply laughed and said it was off the chart. However, their guess was that it must be about minus 140 considering the wind and thermometer temperature. The rectory shook with the force of the wind and I seriously worried that the roof might not be torn off. I had visions of the wind entering the ventilation openings forcing the roof to explode with the pressure.

When the storm finally abated and we were able to venture outside, we discovered the landscape remade into mountains of snow. The rectory driveway was under a snowdrift about 12 feet deep. Other drifts in the town topped 25 feet, and some houses were almost completely buried. Once the snow clearing machinery began to work, a pickup truck was discovered under the drift in front of the Rectory where it had been abandoned. The driver was very lucky to have made it to a nearby house. During the storm, it was a complete whiteout with visibility reduced to a few inches. A crew at the mine had taken refuge in an unheated equipment shed on the site and the thirty or so men were trapped there without food for the three days. No casualties—although there were some who suffered emotional trauma because they were convinced they would freeze to death. Fortunately, no lives were lost.

My car had arrived and it sat in the rectory driveway during the storm. When we could finally go outside, I thought the car looked a little strange—the windows seemed to be frosted over in a peculiar way. I opened the door and discovered the car was completely filled with snow—every square inch. Apparently I had left one window open just an eighth of an inch and the wind had forced the powdery snow inside. We shovelled and swept the snow out and it seemed there was no harm at all done to the car.

The principal reason for having a resident priest in Schefferville was to care for the pastoral needs of the Naskapi People who were all Anglican. The reserve then lay about a mile from town. There was also the small frame church of St. Peter in the town itself, which had a tiny

A Priest's Tale

congregation of English speaking Anglicans, most of whom were from Newfoundland. Locally, St. Peter's seemed to be known as the 'white church', though at the time I arrived the Native people were also worshipping in St. Peter's while their own new church on the Reserve was under construction. It would be another year or so before that building would be completed to the point where we could begin using it.

The Naskapi had once been caribou hunters as the people to the south and west had been hunters of the buffalo. The Naskapi were nomadic, following the caribou herds in the Ungava Peninsula between the Labrador coast and Hudson Bay. The opening of a fur trading post in the Schefferville region in 1838 caused a major disruption to the Naskapi way of life. The fur traders settling in the Naskapi land encouraged them to abandon the caribou hunt to become pelt trappers.

Many Naskapi groups lost connection with each other and the lack of inter-tribal communication meant the hunters no longer knew what paths the caribou were travelling. As the market for pelts dwindled, and without the knowledge of the caribou herd migration, the Naskapi community faced starvation. In 1949, the federal government sent food rations and medical missionaries to Fort Chimo to help them.

It is not entirely clear why in 1956 practically all the Naskapi moved from Fort Chimo to the recently founded iron-ore mining community of Schefferville. Some say it was by order of officials of the Indian and Northern Affairs department. Others believe it was a decision of the Naskapi themselves, who made the move in hopes of finding employment, housing, medical assistance, and educational facilities for their children.

While the officials of Indian and Northern Affairs seemed to be aware of the Naskapi intent to move to Schefferville, and may even have been the force behind their move, they did practically nothing to prepare for the Naskapi arrival in Schefferville, not even informing the representatives of the Iron Ore Company of Canada or the municipality of Schefferville.

The Naskapi made the 400-mile journey from Fort Chimo to Wakuach Lake, 70 miles north of Schefferville, on foot, arriving in a desperate state; exhausted, ill, and near starvation. A rescue effort was mounted, which succeeded in providing food and medical attention. However, the only homes the Naskapi had were the rough shacks they built for themselves on the shores of Knob Lake out of salvaged and donated material.

In 1957, under the pretext that the water at Knob Lake was contaminated, the municipal authorities moved the Naskapi to a site adjacent to John Lake, four miles north, north-east of Schefferville. Here they lived without benefit of proper accommodation, and here, despite their hopes when making the journey to Schefferville, there was no school for their children, nor medical care. The Naskapi shared the site at John Lake with another group of Native People, the Montagnais, who had moved voluntarily from Sept-Îles to Schefferville with the completion of the railroad in the early 1950s.

Initially, the Naskapi lived in tiny shacks that they built for themselves, but by 1962 Indian and Northern Affairs had built 30 houses for them. In 1969, Indian and Northern Affairs acquired from the reluctant Municipality of Schefferville, a marshy, 39-acre site north of the town centre and adjacent to Pearce Lake. By 1972, 43 row-housing units had been built there for the Naskapi, and a further 63 for Montagnais, and most of the Naskapi and Montagnais moved to this new site, known as Village de Matimekosh.

Montagnais, meaning "mountaineers," was the name given this band of people by the French. They originated from the rugged St. Lawrence shoreline near the mouth of the Saguenay River where the French first encountered them. Montagnais and Naskapi today refer to themselves in Cree as the Innu, or "people" especially in north-eastern

Québec and Labrador. The Innu are not the same as the Inuit who most Montagnais regarded as enemies, although the origin of the two words is probably the same.

The Naskapi were Anglican and many of them spoke English although a large number of them spoke Naskapi only. The Montagnais were Roman Catholic and almost all of them spoke French as they had a much longer history of contact with French speakers. Oddly, because of the language situation, I was often better able to communicate with the Montagnais in French than with many of my own Naskapi parishioners in anything.

Father Ross and I spent ten days together, which was valuable as it provided a wonderful transition period. He introduced me to the two congregations at Sunday worship. This was most certainly not the usual Anglican situation where one could take a familiar Prayer Book service. The Catechist, Joseph Sandy, who spoke a little English but was well versed in church teaching, led most of the Naskapi service.

Anything said in English had to be translated into Naskapi. Sammy, the interpreter, was an old man who had been doing this job in the parish for many years and was paid a small honorarium for his service. At one time, decades before, he had been the most fluent English speaker in his community. However, as more and more of the

A Priest's Tale

community attended school it had become obvious that his knowledge of English was seriously limited. He would listen to the English with me pausing after every sentence, and then, supposedly, he would translate it for the congregation. It became apparent to me that he was just making up something religious sounding in Cree, and didn't really understand the English. I certainly couldn't understand enough Cree to know what Sammy was actually saying, but the giggles and expressions on the faces of the young people in the congregation indicated that he was not really able to do the job. Father Ross also knew it was no longer working but was reluctant to terminate the poor man. Inevitably, this unpleasant task fell to me as the "new broom".

    The situation reminded me of a story told by my Roman Catholic colleague, Père Cyr, who had been working with the Montagnais Cree in the area for 35 years, and who spoke the language fluently. In the early days, when the bishop would visit, Farther Cyr would act as translator when the bishop spoke. The bishop understood nothing of the language and knew almost nothing about the parish situation and the needs of the community. Father Cyr would use these visits to his advantage. The bishop might be saying, "My brothers and sisters, I urge you to be faithful to the Church and to attend Mass regularly".

Father Cyr would translate this as, "The bishop says he wants you to do something about the plumbing in the rectory and also to clean up the grave-yard."

Whether it was learning the nuances of Québec French or just working around the obstacle of various native tongues, the question of language seemed to dominate my existence in Schefferville. Shortly after my car arrived on the train, I drove to the gas station one extremely cold evening for a fill-up. I had once rented a car in France and remembered quite well the first time I went to a filling station for gas. When the attendant approached I panicked, and thought, Oh, my God, what do I say? I quickly rehearsed some verbs and remembered that '*remplir*' was the infinitive 'to fill'. So I said to the man, "*Remplir?*" with a large question mark. He smiled and politely said, "*Complet.*"

I was feeling rather confident when the young man at the filling station in Schefferville approached. However, little did I know!

The attendant was about 16 years old and was bundled up in a parka against the 40 below air. I opened the window a crack and said to him, "*Complet, s'il vous plaît,*" in the best French I could muster. The young man said not a word during the whole transaction, though he made considerable noise in banging the gas cap down on the trunk of the car and slamming the nozzle in to fill the tank. He collected payment, gave change, and hastened inside without speaking to me at all.

About two weeks later, I was back at the gas station and this time the owner was there. Although we had not yet met, he knew I was the new Anglican vicar. He greeted me warmly in English and introduced himself. Then he said, "You come here two week ago, eh?" I said I had. Then he said, "Jean-Pierre was not too please, eh?"

I answered, "No, he wasn't. I think he could tell from my accent that I am English."

He laughed heartily, slapped his thigh, and said, "Hell no—he tink you are French."

This was my first realization that there is often no love lost between the Continental French and the Québecois. However, I must admit I was rather delighted that Jean-Pierre thought I was French, but I was still a little perplexed about exactly what you do say when you want your tank filled in Québec, so I asked the station owner.

He responded, "You just say, *full.*" He pronounced it like 'fool'. I was to discover, although many people in Québec wish to keep their language free from the pollution of English, many English words and phrases have crept in unawares.

At the hospital in Schefferville, there was a resident doctor to handle the day-to-day needs of the sick and injured. The more complicated surgical procedures were done en masse by a team of surgeons which would descend upon the village a couple of times a year. People would be brought to Schefferville from all over the northern region of Québec and a marathon of surgeries would take place over the space of a week.

On one of these occasions as I visited the hospital before the round of surgeries, I met a number of Inuit people from the Fort Chimo area. I assumed they were Inuit and Anglican because many of them had Inuit prayer books on their bedside tables. In one room, there were three women; a Naskapi, a Montagnais, and an Inuit. The Montagnais woman spoke French and Cree, the Naskapi woman spoke Cree and Inuktitut, and the Inuit woman spoke Inuktitut only.

As I entered the room, it was rather like a little Pentecost. In order to communicate with the Anglican Inuit woman, who was scheduled for surgery, I had to speak in French to the Montagnais woman who then translated it into Cree for the Naskapi woman, who translated it into Inuktitut for the woman from Fort Chimo. We were basically chitchatting about where she was from and trying to arrange for me to bring her the Sacrament before her surgery. The questions and answers appeared to go up and down the chain with surprising accuracy. At one point, we all broke into fits of laughter at the convoluted situation. The amusing thing for me was that none of this was happening in English except in my head. The woman from Fort Chimo had a successful surgery and was soon sent back to her community on the isolated tip of the Ungava Peninsula.

Dealing with the Naskapi People and the Cree language was perhaps the most difficult linguistic challenge, but living in a French speaking community also added to the frustration. I desperately wanted to be able to function in French and it really was a necessity.

Soon after my arrival, I joined the community choir which was a rather good glee club. It was at that time a completely French group. It was helpful to have to function in French and I enjoyed it immensely. Music was the bridge in this case and my experience with choirs and orchestras proved to be valuable. My first rehearsal with the group was a turning point. I was welcomed and introduced by the director, Mme. Richard. As I sing tenor, I was seated in the appropriate section next to a young man named René. He was a teacher at the French High School. He spoke very good English and was very cordial. I explained to him that I wanted to begin using French, but that I was quite shy about it and it was difficult to begin. I didn't need to explain that we English have this prideful phobia about making mistakes in other languages. It often causes us simply to speak English more slowly and louder, believing that it will then be understood. René was sympathetic and assured me that when I was ready; I would begin to use French.

After I had been going to these rehearsals for about two months I came to the conclusion that I really must make some serious effort. At the next rehearsal, as I took my place in the tenor section, I approached René and said, "Bonsoir, René." He responded, "Bonsoir, ça va?" All seemed to be going quite well—so far so good.

When I met René at the post office one evening soon after this, I lapsed back into English after the obligatory "Bonsoirs" and "ça vas". René, however, responded to me in French and forced me to continue in French since I had made my initial attempt and he would simply not let me retreat. Actually, he never, ever spoke to me in English after that. I was quite impressed with the mature and wise attitude of this 25 year old. I tried to convince myself of that assessment in spite of the fact that he was also very cute and I thought could not possibly do any wrong. This was really the beginning of my use of French. I soon learned it did not matter if you got a gender or a tense wrong or mispronounced a word—it was still quite understandable. The problem was not so much in articulating something in French; it was in being able to comprehend the reply. Years later I thought about this while watching an episode of "The Muppets". The guest on this particular show was Jean-Pierre Rampal, the French flautist. Miss Piggy had always made a great to-do about her ability to speak French. "Moi?" When Monsieur Rampal made his entrance he greeted her with a long complimentary speech about how wonderful it was to meet her—in beautiful French of course. Miss Piggy looked completely perplexed. One of the other characters said, "But, Miss Piggy, we thought you spoke French?" To which she replied, "I do speak it. I just can't hear it."

My French was learned at high school in Vancouver in the 50's. In those days, the emphasis was not on speaking much at all, but more upon reading and writing good Parisian French. It is now taught with much more sensitivity to conversation and to the Canadian experience—not much about the Champs-Élysées, but more of beavers and snowshoeing.

One afternoon I was doing some mending on a set of vestments and discovered there were a few snap-fasteners missing. There was a Singer store in the town, but someone warned me that the owner refused to speak English, although she spoke it quite well. I was not concerned about that considering it to be another opportunity to use French.

I browsed around in my copy of Larousse to see if I could find what these fasteners are called in French. Despite thousands of helpful little pictures, I could find no reference at all to snap-fasteners. Finally, I decided to simply take one of the fasteners with me to show her. I approached the store with some confidence knowing I ought to be able to navigate around the situation without having to resort to English. As I entered, Madame was engaged in a conversation with another customer so I waited. Finally, the person left the store and we were alone. I approached her with my sample fastener on my fingertip and said, "*Madame, qu'appelez-vous ceci en français?*" in my rather formal French. She smiled pleasantly and said, "*Oh, mais oui Monsieur, c'est un* 'snap-on'."

I thought to myself, You just can't win.

·

Don ~ Ordination Picture, 1970

Dad, Mother and Don,
Easter 1940

Don at Crescent Beach, 1942

ATC College Picture, 1967
(Don 5th from right, back row)

Graduating Theological Class of 1968
Don (seated), Daniel Anonby, Ronald Sands

Bp. Goodman and Don
Priestly ordination at St. Augustine, Lethbridge

Ordination of Joseph Sandy
Don, Bp. Matthews and Joseph

Edwin, backstage with the
Judge for "Trial by Jury", 1972

St. Joseph's Seminary Chapel,
St. Albert, Alberta, 1976
(Photo: Kim O'Leary)

Leading a local protest - St. Albert (photo: Kim O'Leary)

Christ Church, Alert Bay

Cormorant Island "Killer Whale" Map

Don Censing the High Alter
St. James' Church, Vancouver
(photo: Kim O'Leary)

Clergy Team at St. James', 1990
Stephen Herbert, Donald Dodman, David Retter
(photo: Kim O'Leary)

Devan & Don wedding reception ~ 2003

Devan & Don ~ San Gimignano, Italy 2005

Devan & Don
wedding kiss, 2003

✠

Joseph Sandy, our Parish Catechist, was invaluable to my ministry in Schefferville. He led almost all of the Mass in Cree except for the Prayer of Consecration and Absolution, the things only a priest can do. It was Joseph who preached regularly as he knew the needs of the community far better than I. Gradually, as I developed an ear for the language, I was able to catch the drift of his sermons. He seemed to have about a dozen or so themes—standard sermons on Communion, the Bible, the Prayer Book and such basic teaching. Joseph was obviously well trained as a Catechist and every few years he would spend a month at the Henry Budd College in the Pas, Manitoba for further catechetical training.

Bishop Matthews and I discussed Joseph's ministry many times and came to the mutual conclusion that it would be appropriate to make him a deacon. The preparation for this was done mostly by audiotapes, which the priest at Great Whale River, Fr. Caleb Lawrence, would send. Fr. Lawrence was fluent in both Inuktitut and Cree. His tapes would contain a message to me, informing me about what Joseph was learning, and then a long session of training in Cree for Joseph. I found all of this quite remarkable.

A Priest's Tale

Joseph's ordination was rather a special event in the lives of the Naskapi people of the Village de Matimekosh. He was the first person from this community to be called to the clerical office. People came from all over to attend the service. Père Cyr preached the homily. He was able to adapt his Montagnais to the Naskapi ear and presented what sounded like a wonderful and encouraging sermon. During Father Cyr's sermon the power went out due to the coffee makers and ovens in the basement overloading the circuits. Father Cyr simply continued in the darkness without a pause as I rushed out to see if I could get the lights working again by unplugging the appliances and resetting the trippers. Luckily, it worked and we had light again.

After the service, a celebratory feast was held in the church basement. Men had been working for days smashing up caribou shinbones to make the traditional bone marrow 'dressing' that accompanied the meat and fish. This pulverized mixture had to be boiled for days. I had not tried the delicacy before and when I was given a great scoop of it, I found it to be so full of fat that it was difficult to choke down. However, as one of the other priests attending pointed out as he scooped his share onto my plate, "This is probably essential when you are out hunting in minus forty degree weather for hours on end." I often wondered if the bishop, who was the guest of honour at this feast, realized that it was Naskapi custom to serve the honoured guest the delicacy of the caribou—the caribou rectum. At least, that was the story I was told at a feast where I was the guest of honour. I made a point of looking closely at the bishop's plate, but the offering of meat didn't look any different from any other cut of meat to me. I wonder what I was expecting to see!

Once Joseph was in Deacon's orders, I was a little puzzled to know just how to utilize him in his new capacity because he had already been doing almost all of the things that deacons do. One thing that made sense, and which would enable people to see him assuming a new role, was to vest him in a cope when we had baptisms and for me to assist him, holding the book and attending the ewer and linens while Joseph baptized the candidates. This was always done in the context of the Mass and on one such occasion, a rather good photo was taken of Joseph at the font during a baptism. Some years later Joseph and his wife died in a tragic fire. I am told a sort of shrine was set up in the church in memory of Joseph, and that an enlargement of that picture was the centrepiece of the shrine. My informant reported I was there in the photo at Joseph's side.

I had been in Schefferville several years when the principal of the English Protestant School, Mary Reeves, asked me if I would act as a substitute teacher. I was one of the few people with a university degree who also had a flexible schedule. I agreed, thinking this would be a wonderful opportunity to interact with the Naskapi children as they all attended the school. Mary also asked if I would teach the Protestant Religion course to certain grades.

Initially, I thought this would be another wonderful opportunity, however, I soon learned otherwise. In the Province of Québec high school religion courses were mandatory at the time. Over the years, this class had been foisted on teachers with no inclination or interest in the subject. The curriculum, what there was of it, was pitifully flimsy and by the time I came along the students regarded MRI (Moral and Religious Instruction) as basically a free period. It was almost impossible to reverse the pattern and begin to inject any actual teaching or discussion. The students seemed of two sorts—those who just tuned it out or those who had an appallingly simplistic view of the Bible.

Eventually I changed my tack and tried to steer discussion toward topics that dealt with moral and ethical questions, but which were also contemporary—issues like war, drugs and dating. This captured the interest of a few of the students. There were still some who simply blocked out every attempt I made.

On one occasion, the discussion had turned to the subject of drugs. I was trying to impress upon them the dangers of impure drugs. I made the perhaps foolish comment that, if a person knew the chemical components of certain drugs, they could make them at home in the bathtub. A girl notorious for not paying attention to anything other than her nails or whispering with girlfriends managed to pluck this one remark from the whole of the discussion and went home and repeated what she thought she heard to her mother.

Apparently, it caused a stir at the bridge club when the girl's mother remarked to a fellow player who was a parishioner at St. Peter's, "What is this clergyman of yours teaching our kids anyway? Pamela tells me he told her class *'you can make it in the bathtub.'*"

Fortunately, my parishioner's son was also in the class and had been paying attention. At dinner that evening, the discussion from the bridge club came up. The young man burst out laughing and explained the whole situation—thank God he was paying attention. His father approached me in the post office one afternoon not long after and teased me about what I was teaching their kids, and quoted the fragment. I had no idea what he was talking about for a few moments and then it connected. It is frightening how easy it is for misunderstanding to spread.

A Priest's Tale

✠

St. Peter's Rectory had been built with the expectation that a family might sometimes inhabit it and consequently it was a fairly large house. As much as I revelled in the space it was a rather quiet life on my own—most evident at meal times—and eventually a situation arose whereby it came to my attention that a fellow I knew was in need of lodging. Daniel was the credit manager at *La Baie d'Hudson* and I was confident that he would be a responsible boarder. Apparently some months earlier a health problem had occurred and he was flown to Québec City for emergency surgery. Months later, when he came back I visited him in his tiny trailer some distance from the village. He was extremely weak and looked so thin although he was continuing to walk to and from work each day—quite a distance considering his condition. I was fond of Daniel and thought the company would be pleasant. I suggested he might come and stay at the Rectory at least until he had recovered more of his strength.

After discussing it for a while, Daniel agreed this arrangement would probably be best, especially as the rectory was near the Hudson's Bay store. There were no secrets or any hidden motives. Daniel and I had a mutual friend who also worked at The Bay and who was gay. So

Daniel knew all the details about me and that I understood he was straight. It was all above board. The move was a simple matter involving only a few clothes and a small trunk. A friend of Daniel's transported his belongings in his car and the move was accomplished in the space of half an hour. After carrying his things in I took him upstairs to introduce him to the guest room. After settling Daniel in we walked down the hallway toward the stairs and as we passed my room I opened the door to show Daniel. My room was the master bedroom and it was exceptionally large with a huge king sized bed. (Perhaps it was Queen sized; I somehow get those two confused!) I said, jokingly, "Now, Daniel, if you ever feel lonely..." We both giggled as we went downstairs. After dinner he went off somewhere to meet with his friends.

I retired that evening about 11:30 and read for a while as I listened to my usual dreamy, CBC radio programme of late night poetry and soothing music. I put the book down and turned off the radio and the light at about midnight. Not too long afterward, I heard the back door being locked and Daniel stamping the snow from his boots. It was comforting to know I was not alone in this large house and I was particularly pleased to have Daniel as a housemate as I found him quite charming.

A Priest's Tale

I heard the toilet flush and then the brushing of teeth. Comforting sounds. Daniel tiptoed up the stairs quietly, passed my door and went into his room. I felt deliciously content. I heard the muffled sounds as he undressed then the winding of his alarm clock and the click of the light switch. Then, to my utter astonishment, my bedroom door quietly opened and Daniel padded in on bare feet, placed his alarm clock on the headboard and climbed in beside me. He gave me a peck on the cheek and said good night. He certainly was a cuddly and affectionate young man. The warmth of his body was a delight and it was wonderful to feel someone I cared about so near. We slept together for most of the duration of Daniel's time at the Rectory; though only occasionally were we ever intimate.

Living with someone was something I had not experienced before, aside from my life at home when I was younger and when I was in residence at college. But, living closely with someone for whom I cared was a completely different thing. Although there were the odd times when we would be affectionate, I was delighted simply to have the company in all of the ordinary daily routines—preparing dinner; getting Daniel's bagged lunch together; entertaining guests together; doing grocery shopping; watching the evening news. These were things that I had not realized I missed so much. We were very compatible together and home life was pleasant. Such a change from the quiet and solitary life I lived before he joined me.

Daniel spoke English quite well and we developed the arrangement that he would help me with my French and I would help him with his English. We tried to set certain days when we would use each language. One Sunday evening as I was preparing a roast of pork, Daniel received a telephone call from one of his friends who was from Newfoundland. Daniel and I were in French mode that day. His friend did not speak French and so the telephone conversation was taking place in English. During the call, Daniel wondered if he might invite Mark over for dinner which was to be ready in about two hours.

He covered the mouthpiece with his hand as he spoke to me in French. *"Est-ce que je peut inviter Mark au souper ce soir?"*

I responded, *"D'accord."*

Then, speaking again into the receiver in English, Daniel offered Mark an invitation to dinner. There was a pause as Daniel listened. He covered the mouthpiece again and said to me, *"C'est quoi pour souper?"*

"Un rôti de porc." I answered.

Daniel returned to the phone and said enthusiastically, *"Yeah, come on over, we're having a pig."*

A Priest's Tale

✠

The building of a church on the reserve was a project that had begun before I arrived. While the foundation was in place and the concrete poured, the Pan Abode building had yet to be finished—piles of the logs were stacked up around the church—and the floors, detailing and furnishing were yet to be done. Then the cedar logs needed to be coated with linseed oil. A thousand other details had to be attended to and it took years before the building was actually complete.

In an effort to maintain a sense of continuity, we attempted to use some of the furniture from the original St. John's Church, which had been located in the first settlement of the Naskapi and which had fallen into disrepair when they were relocated to the present reserve. The altar was one of those items. I wanted to add a tabernacle for the Blessed Sacrament because of the frequent calls to take Holy Communion to the sick but also to be a focus in the church and on the Reserve of our Lord's Presence with the people. I mustered all the drafting skills I could remember from junior high school and designed a tabernacle that would complement the existing altar. I chose to have it done in light oak and it would have a secure door with a lock. My three dimensional design, complete with measurements, would be of assistance when I went to the local carpenter shop to commission the work. The man who ran the carpenter shop didn't speak any English, nor did the three young men working there.

I should interject here that cursing in Québec is, for the most part, not sexually oriented as it is in France but rather tends to be religiously oriented. I am not quite sure why, but swearing using church words seems to have become common after the '60s and "*la revolution tranquile*", when the authority of the Church was beginning to be seriously challenged. So, when one wants to talk really dirty in Québec today one uses epithets like, *calice, tabarnac, baptême,* and *estie*. To the English ear it sounds like nothing more than an inventory of church items—chalice, tabernacle, baptism, and host. Rather tame! But, to the Québecois ear such words are scandalous and carry the weight of the most vulgar words in English.

The head carpenter took my drawing, laid it out on a workbench, and together with his three young workers pored over it. Everything seemed to be going well. They seemed to understand my intent and knew what I wanted—that it was to be of fine, white oak and they understood my measurements and annotations. Finally, one of the younger men, out of curiosity pointed to the drawing and said, *"Père, quelle est cette chose ici"*? What is this thing?

A Priest's Tale

I had failed to label my design and answered without really thinking about it. *"C'est un tabernacle."* Their mouths dropped open in unison—astonishment in their eyes. Such language coming from a priest. I added indignantly, *"C'est un tabernacle d'église."*

The first service in the new building was on Christmas day of 1976. The church wasn't entirely finished but close enough that it was usable. The service Christmas Day was filled to capacity and everyone was in a celebratory mood. There was a general feeling of pride and success at having completed the new church. No longer did the people need to make the mile trek into town to go to St. Peter's, which the tiny white congregation barely wanted to begrudge them. Having their own building made a remarkable difference in many aspects of life on the Reserve.

Daniel and I had invited a group of people to a turkey dinner that Christmas evening. The group consisted of other people who were similarly a long way from home or otherwise alone, so we all shared a common bond. Wherever I have worked families have always been kind and generous in inviting me to share Christmas with them. However, I always seemed to find it somehow awkward—feeling rather like a fifth wheel. It seemed only to make it more pronounced that my family was far distant.

I eventually stopped going to family homes and began inviting others in similar situations to the rectory for Christmas dinner. Sharing an evening with other people far from their families, or without families, created a special atmosphere all of its own. On that particular Christmas, Daniel and I entertained guests who were from Newfoundland, Portugal, other parts of Québec and Ontario.

Dinner was pleasant, the conversation a delight, and the wine flowing. Near the end of dinner as we enjoyed dessert the telephone rang. It was one of the young Naskapi men of the reserve calling to invite me to come to the 'dance' in the basement of the new church. A week before, when the people of the reserve had asked me if they could have a 'dance' in the evening on Christmas Day, I had hesitated in my reply. But, what could I say? The new church was the only public building on the reserve that could be used for such events. I agreed to the dance though I stressed they must clean up any mess and lock up the building afterward. I thought the dance was going to be the usual sort of thing where a record player blasted rock and roll music and people imbibed in celebration.

I tried to explain to Johnny that I was in the midst of entertaining guests at a Christmas dinner. To my astonishment he suggested that we all come out to the church and join them. This surprised me a little because the people of the town and the native community generally kept their distance from one another and there were some animosities between them. Rumours routinely circulated amongst the town's people about their cars being stoned as they drove through the reserve. I personally never ever saw any such behaviour.

As the 'missionary' on the reserve, and yet living in the town of Schefferville, I had a sort of immunity and was able to move back and forth between the two communities with ease. I was somewhat hesitant to accept Johnny's invitation, but my guests, who were overhearing my side of the conversation, thought the idea was splendid and urged that we go. What could I say? We called a taxi to augment our vehicles and the 10 of us made our way to the reserve.

We were welcomed so warmly by the Naskapi when we entered the hall my guests were overwhelmed and I felt a little shamefaced for having had doubts about it. I had not seen the two communities coming together in such a way ever before. I was used to being there and knew the people well but I was worried that my guests might be rebuffed.

After Christmas greetings were exchanged in a mingling of Cree, French, and English, we settled quite naturally into the celebrations. The 'dancing' I had thought would be the usual sock hop turned out to be traditional

Naskapi drums and a long line of people chanting and dancing. We were physically pulled into the snaking conga line and everyone enjoyed themselves immensely. It was much like a potlatch on the West Coast. The difference of course was the food. Here it was caribou and Arctic char. We found ourselves having a second Christmas dinner, which, under the circumstances was slightly obligatory. However, it proved to be a breakthrough for the Naskapi People and for my dinner guests.

During the celebrations one of the teenage boys from the parish appeared in front of me with a huge smile and an open tin of beer for me. My first reaction was one of discomfort. I was certainly on the spot. The Naskapi onlookers were mildly aware of the tension this act caused and watched expectantly. Should I decline it in order to maintain a modicum of integrity for my position, especially as this related to one of the thorniest problems in the community? or, should I simply accept the beer in the spirit in which it was offered? Heaven only knows—it was Christmas, the Feast of the Birth of the Prince of Peace—I took the gift and drank.

A Priest's Tale

✠

Although I had never spoken to anyone in my family about my sexuality, the years of being asked, "When are you going to find a nice girl and settle down?" seemed to have come to a natural end. I was in my early forties by this time and for some unknown reason—perhaps it was sparked by a paperback book I had recently read about a gay boy's 'coming out' story—I thought I owed it to my family to let them know I was happy in my busy life. The book was called '*Consenting Adult*', and was written by a mother about her gay son. A very good television movie of the same name appeared a few years later.

As I read the book I was amazed to discover that so many of the incidents were almost identical to my own life and it gave me the eerie feeling I was reading about myself. When I finished the book I thought about the situation pondering whether it might be an appropriate way to inform my family and to assure them I was happy. The book might be just the opener I needed. I posted it off to my parents with a brief note telling them I was gay and happy and that we would talk later after they had read the novel and had time to digest it.

I received a phone call much sooner than I had anticipated. My mother assured me that they loved me and were comfortable with the news. Almost everyone in my family was accepting, compassionate, and understanding except for a couple who were not very comfortable with it and suggested I was 'just going through a phase' and that it could be 'cured with drugs'. As is often the case, some members of my family had already suspected that I might be gay so it was not a total surprise to everyone.

Mother, rather than my father, was the one who would talk about personal things with me. She confessed my father's initial reaction was one of concern. Had they done something wrong in my upbringing? When I spoke with him I assured him that was not the case at all. I fully believe I was born with this orientation. Over the years this opinion has become more and more certain in my mind. It was good to talk about it and to have my sexuality out in the open. There is always a fear that when one tells someone, regardless how long one has been out to other people, the revelation will provoke a negative reaction. When it comes to family, this fear is, of course, more worrisome. So many times one hears of a young person coming out to family and being disowned and even rejected. I was extremely fortunate that my parents and siblings were able to accept my revelation with such tolerance.

A Priest's Tale

✠

Isolated communities can tend to become claustrophobic especially where there is no road to the outside world. Bishop Matthews was well aware of this and was concerned about my situation. He phoned me from time to time; our conversations always seeming to end with, "Now, Donald, whenever you need to get out for a break just let me know and we will fly you to Québec City. You are always welcome to come and stay with us." I never actually took him up on that offer but just knowing an escape was possible was amazingly liberating.

When the bishop contacted me one spring, asking what plans I had for my annual vacation, he made an offer that I did accept. He proposed that, if I wished, I might consider coming to Québec for August and living in the Palace while he and his wife were off at their summer cottage in Gaspé. I took a day or two to ponder and then called him to confirm I would be delighted to spend August in Québec.

That first summer in Québec City was an extraordinary experience. I had not been in residence in the Palace for very long when I ran into Terry, a deacon, who was connected with the Cathedral. The Palace is in the Cathedral Close, so it was perhaps inevitable we would meet. He rang the doorbell one Sunday morning in his cassock and introduced himself. He had perhaps heard about me from a mutual friend, however in only a few minutes we knew we were 'birds of a feather' and shared the same bizarre sense of humour. When he was ordained to the priesthood I was present and assisted. That was an especially interesting event in its own right.

Following Terry's ordination there was a reception in the Parish Hall with the usual wine and cake and speeches. But then there was another gathering later in the evening. This one was hosted by Terry's Québecois friends. Terry worked at that time for the Québec government as a translator and was completely integrated into the French community. This party was hosted by a group of Roman clergy and it took place in a lovely apartment in Le Grand Séminaire. The seminary seemed to be almost empty at the time and the party was extremely jovial, relaxed and very gay. My French was certainly not up to the quick repartee but our hosts made me feel welcome indeed. A few of them stopped to chat with me in slow, measured, 'proper' French and I had a delightful time.

The Bishop's Residence was truly a palace—a delightful three story, 19th Century building in the Cathedral Close with eight bedrooms, various salons, a large dining room and the Bishop's Chapel. My month there was

A Priest's Tale

primarily to have someone present in the house as well as to tend to a few duties such as watering plants and feeding the cats. I certainly didn't mind playing housekeeper though. I would be able to host guests should I be able to convince anyone to come and visit. Québec City in my estimation is the most beautiful city in Canada. August there is pretty much like being in Europe. My parents came for a week and other friends visited at different times at one point filling most of the bedrooms.

One evening after my out of town visitors had gone, I arranged to have a dinner party at the Palace with six or seven local friends. In the late afternoon there was a horrendous thunderstorm followed by torrents of rain and the sky was black. I had put a roast of beef in the oven about six o'clock and my first guests were to arrive around half past six. They all appeared on schedule and I showed them into a salon opposite the dining room and served cocktails. We lounged before a lovely fire in the hearth, which was especially comfy with the wind and rain battering at the windows.

As we chatted the doorbell rang. I went to answer it presuming it might be someone wanting a food voucher. To my surprise it was the bishop, soaking wet, and with his overnight bag. He had returned to Québec to do some office work. As he entered he noticed the aroma of the roast which permeated the foyer. I explained I had some friends over for a dinner party and asked him if he would like to join us. He said he had eaten at the airport but would be happy to join us for a drink, just to be sociable, and would then retire.

As the bishop went upstairs to put away his coat and dry off I returned to the salon and informed my friends that the bishop had come home unexpectedly and would be joining us once he had settled in. One young man, Bobby, a friend from Schefferville, almost had a fit. He had never before even seen a bishop let alone had drinks with one. He had to be restrained from fleeing through the patio doors into the back garden. Of course, they were all feeling a little awkward as it was an unambiguously gay gathering. Several of my friends knew the Bishop but I quickly assured them the bishop knew me well and that he was completely understanding and supportive.

I knew the bishop's preference in drinks and when he came downstairs and introductions had been made I soon had a glass of gros gin in his hand. The conversation was relaxed and even young Bobby calmed down and quite took to this imposing man. After several rounds, I made off to the kitchen with Terry to get things into serving bowls and onto the table.

A Priest's Tale

Finally, we were ready and everyone moved from the salon to the dining room. The bishop said that he would join us after all but would just have a small snack. He seemed to be eating as usual to me; perhaps the roast beef and Yorkshire pudding proved too tempting. I seated him in his usual place at the head of the table, arranged the guests along the sides, and then sat at the other end opposite the bishop.

Before we sat, the bishop asked a blessing and we settled in. Someone made the rounds with wine as we began passing the serving platters. Although a few of my friends knew the bishop—two of them being clergy—the atmosphere was still a bit formal. However, the bishop soon put everyone at ease with a clever bit of theatrics to which he was prone. He said he would like to propose a toast. With that, we raised our glasses and the bishop, noticeably directing his glass toward me, said, "To the Queen…Or her nearest representative." Hearty laughter erupted and we were all able to settle down for a relaxed and pleasant dinner.

After dinner, we adjourned to yet another salon on the second floor for coffee and liqueurs. One of the guests, a visiting organist from Ottawa, played Beethoven piano sonatas until the bishop nodded off. Eventually, he excused himself and went off to bed. The party had been a great success and it was a pleasure to be able to lay it on in such elegant surroundings.

There was one duty that went along with my use of the house that summer, which was taking one service each Sunday. The bishop was again a little vague in his details on the phone. I thought the parish in question was close by but discovered it was 90 miles east, down the St. Lawrence River. It was the parish of La Malbaie, which seems also to go by the name Pointe au Pic. This village had long been the summer get-away spot for the wealthy of Montreal. The people there were most accommodating, providing me with a rented car each weekend for the long drive down the river and also paying me an honorarium of one hundred dollars for taking the service. I had never made that much money per hour in my life, nor have I since. Of course, this Sunday duty consumed the entire day.

After the service of Matins on the first Sunday, a petite, elderly woman remained afterward to chat with me. She asked if I might be able to come to her house on the following Sunday for a luncheon after the service. A few people from the parish and some friends would be gathering there for the occasion. I thanked her and happily accepted the invitation.

The next week she appeared at church and, after the service, explained that she lived a little distance down the

A Priest's Tale

river and that if I followed her car she would have the driver lead me to her home. We began a long drive through backcountry roads and the pretty St. Lawrence ranges. Finally, we came to a huge wrought iron gate, which a gatekeeper opened. I followed her car through and down the long driveway. I could see a large country mansion off in the distance as we drove along the stately, tree lined drive. The gardens reminded me of Versailles. I finally parked my car in a space that a man in tails indicated and approached the house.

I was met at the front entrance by a butler and led to the drawing room where for some strange reason on this hot August day there was a fire roaring on the hearth. The twelve luncheon guests were having cocktails and my gracious hostess introduced me to each of them. I felt a little out of my element—and class—as I surveyed the house and the number of black and white uniformed butlers and waiters. Some of the guests were Americans from Vermont and New York—one gentleman was a professor from Harvard. During the introductions I was caught particularly unprepared. Near the fireplace stood a middle-aged woman veiled in black who appeared to be alone. My hostess, in introducing us said, "Mr. Dodman, have you met the Duchess of Augensburg?"

I had not, and needless to say, I was not a little disarmed by this situation. I had not the slightest idea how one should address a Duchess. Some time later, I discovered it should have been *'Your Grace'*. She was a White Russian whose husband had died the previous winter after falling from the roof of the motel they were managing. They had apparently lost everything and had moved to the area to manage a friend's motel. The Duke had apparently been freeing ice from the gutters when he slipped and fell to his death on the pavement below.

Dinner conversation was extremely interesting and esoteric. I occupied myself mostly with listening and enjoying a very elaborate luncheon. I found it peculiar that in the midst of all our chatter in English, whenever anyone spoke to one of the servants it was always in French. I found myself following suit. It seemed a little patronizing, but then I thought, Perhaps they don't speak English. The whole affair seemed somewhat like a surreal dream sequence.

On some Sundays, I would take my dinner at a marvellous CP Railway chateau near Pointe Au Pic amidst the elegance of New France before beginning my drive back to Québec City. The 'Manoir Richelieu' was on the banks of the river and steamships would occasionally silently glide by. It seemed curious to find this place in such a remote

A Priest's Tale

part of the province. On one occasion while having dinner, I noticed two elderly ladies sitting a few tables away from me. They spoke quite loudly as is often the way with people who are gradually losing their hearing. They spoke in very clear and proper French. One of them noticed my clerical collar and mentioned to her friend that there was "*un Prêtre*" dining there—one they didn't recognize. Her friend responded, "Is he really a priest?" The answer, "I don't think so. He's too young." I was about 40 years old at that time. Little did she know how much she brightened my evening and cheered my 90-mile drive back home.

Deanery meetings, synods and other conferences were opportunities to get out of the north for a few days and meet with colleagues. These occasions were pleasant and it was good to share experiences with other priests who also worked in isolation. On one occasion our deanery chapter met in the Lower St. Lawrence port of Harrington Harbour. This place, which actually consists of a string of small islets, was fascinating. It is one of a number of tiny English speaking communities in the midst of French Canada. It is entirely isolated. So much so, the local people speak with a recognizable accent. The bishop was with us on this occasion and after a confirmation service we had a dinner reception in a parishioner's home.

We were having pre-dinner cocktails and chatting in small groups. I happened to be talking with two of my colleagues and was telling them a joke. I was speaking quietly and assumed that no one else would overhear. The joke was about a loud American businessman who was visiting a gentleman's club in London—one of those with high backed leather chairs, cognac, cigars and *The Financial Times*. Club members were sitting quietly reading their journals. The American tried in vain to strike up conversations with several men but to no avail. Finally, in frustration, he blurted out, "This place is the asshole of the earth." This caught the ear of one little chap sitting nearby. He lowered his paper, looked over his glasses and, in a very plummy English accent, said, "Just passing through?"

The next morning at our clergy meeting—all five of us with the bishop—I realized that his Lordship must have overheard my joke. In his little pastoral talk with us after Mass he said, in a patient, fatherly tone, "It so grieves me when I hear, on the lips of the clergy, words like 'shit' and 'fuck' and 'asshole'."

My colleague, Bruce Stavert, looked across the table at me with a twinkle in his eye, stifling a laugh. We all realized the remark was meant for me. I did, however, feel a little over-chastised as it had been a private conversation and I hadn't even used two of the those words.

A Priest's Tale

Another tale of 'inappropriate language' among the clergy was told to me while I visited my friend Terry in the Eastern Townships one summer after I had done two weeks as Chaplain at the summer camp in Gaspé. Terry invited a Roman Catholic colleague to dinner one evening while I was visiting. He was the superior of a religious community nearby and was a most engaging man. Fr. Claude was an American Francophone who had grown up in New York State. He was a master with the barbeque and attended to our steaks that evening. During this delightful evening of beer and steak on the rectory veranda, Fr. Claude recounted an incident that had happened in his community when he was a novice.

His story hinged on the monastic disciplines associated with the recitation of the Divine Office, which like most such traditions harks back to the Rule of St. Benedict. For instance, during the recitation or singing of the psalms, if a brother makes a mistake in singing or of pronunciation, he must make a profound bow. If he arrives late for any office, he must make a full prostration before the Father Abbot before taking his place in choir.

Fr. Claude's story involved the Father Abbot himself, who for some reason arrived late for Vespers one evening. While he need not have done the prostration before his own empty chair, out of humility, he did. The

Abbot kept a beautiful, gold pocket watch, which had been his father's, in the inside breast pocket of his habit. Before the assembled community, the Abbot made his prostration and out tumbled the watch, clattering on the stone floor, causing him to utter a rather audible, "Son of a bitch." I should think that incident likely served to endear the Abbot and his humanity to the members of his community.

During the summer of 1977, I spent part of my holiday time visiting friends in Edmonton. While there, I spoke with Bishop John Langstone about the possibility of parish work in the Diocese of Edmonton. There was one possibility it seemed, in St. Matthew's parish. Bishop Langstone arranged for me to meet with the vestry of St. Matthew's in the town of St. Albert, which is about 10 miles north-west of the City of Edmonton. The thought of returning to Alberta was only an idea at the time as I had longed to get back to my home province, British Columbia. But, this was certainly a step in the right direction. My meeting with the people at St. Albert was very relaxed and informal. Sometimes when one is intent on landing a position such meetings can be rather angst filled. This meeting was certainly not like that.

After the interview, I continued with the final week of my holiday and then returned to Québec. The parish decided in favour of my appointment to St. Albert and

A Priest's Tale

Bishop Langstone ratified the decision. I resigned my position in the Diocese of Québec in the fall of 1977, and prepared to move back to Alberta.

As I have recounted, my time in Schefferville seemed to be dominated by the question of language and the difficulties of dealing with a multi-lingual community. It should have been no surprise that before I left Schefferville to take the position in St. Albert I would find myself once more tangled in the minutiae of language.

There would sometimes be social events in the community to which the clergy, school principals, doctors and other professionals were invited. Not long before my time in Schefferville was to end, I was invited to such an evening. I was not quite sure of the significance of the occasion at the time, but dinner at the Director's Lodge sounded rather pleasant. The Lodge was a grand house on the shores of Knob Lake.

Monsieur Achille Houde the mine manager hosted the evening. The table in the dining salon was magnificently set. My eyes widened at the array of Waterford crystal at each place setting. I knew most of the guests, a few of whom were close friends from my parish and from the English High School. However, the majority of those present were French and the talk around the fireplace and then in the dining room was mostly in French.

After a wonderful dinner, just before coffee and liqueurs were to be served, M. Houde rose and addressed us. After his affable introduction, I had a horrifying epiphany. The dinner was, among other things, an occasion for bidding me farewell. My horror was multiplied as I thought about it because Monsieur Houde was making a speech in my honour and that meant I would have to respond to it in kind—and in French. Huge surges of adrenaline! I have rarely known a moment of such anxiety.

When Monsieur Houde came to the end of his speech, there was nothing to do but rise and begin. All went fairly well for the first few minutes. Then I made a remark that drew a rather sharp comment from one of the mining company officials, known for his separatist views. I had said that it was '*funny*' I was leaving Schefferville to take up work in a Francophone town in Alberta. I unfortunately used the word *drôle*—perhaps a poor choice—and could probably have avoided this situation if only I had just said '*curieux*' instead. The perils of speaking off the cuff. I had not intended the remark to be controversial in any sense. My critic immediately shouted out "So why is that so funny?" It was like an arrow through my heart because I had worked so hard during the past four years trying to be a part of Québec society and to cultivating an appreciation for the issues of language and culture. I credit another adrenaline surge for what happened next.

There are times when I say things that seem to come out of the blue, and this was certainly one of those times. I responded with words to this effect:

"Well, it is funny because in Alberta, if one does not speak English, one usually speaks Ukrainian."

I was making a guess at the French word for 'Ukrainian' but apparently I hit on the right one—mind you, it is only one letter removed from the English. The guests laughed heartily and the problem was dismissed. They all seemed to appreciate that my critic had been overly harsh in his reaction. Monsieur Houde presented me with a lovely, framed aerial photograph of Schefferville and the evening ended most pleasantly with liqueurs, coffee and more conversation. I returned home elated that the community had acknowledged me so warmly and appreciated my efforts with French and my involvement in the community.

✠

The City of St. Albert has a rich history dating back almost 150 years and has often been called Alberta's Finest City. Founded in 1861 by Father Albert Lacombe, St. Albert is the oldest, non-fortified community in Alberta and was the largest agricultural settlement west of Winnipeg. Not many years before my arrival, St. Albert was a predominantly Francophone town with a population of only about 5,000. With the explosion of the Alberta oil industry in the sixties and seventies, the population of St. Albert began to soar. The influx of English speaking residents encouraged the Anglican Diocese of Edmonton to appoint a temporary non-resident mission priest to the parish which became known as St. Matthew's.

I was the first resident incumbent priest for the parish, and the people of St. Albert responded enthusiastically to having a priest of their own. I was warmly welcomed and found everyone extremely supportive. As there was no church and no rectory I stayed with a family for a few days while the apartment they had found for me was cleaned and painted. Another parishioner was kind enough to locate a suitable used car for me to purchase.

At the time I arrived, services were being conducted in the United Church at the rather inconvenient hour of 12:30 pm, which was understandable as the United Church congregation met at the customary church time, 11:00 am—'holy hour' as one of my friends used to call it. The building was certainly large enough for our growing congregation but from a liturgical point of view it was quite awkward. The people of St. Matthew's were a relaxed group and quite responsive to my style of leadership and worship which tends to be formal and intentional but with ample room for the informal.

On a Sunday shortly after I arrived, a rather spontaneous 'breaking of the ice' occurred between the congregation and me. As in most Anglican parishes at the time, notices about upcoming events were read out just before the sermon. One Sunday, someone handed me a sheet of paper just before the service containing quite a bit of information about a Cub and Scout event. I had no opportunity to read it over carefully beforehand and so approached it cold.

It was information about a fund raising event the young people were putting on involving the sale of bagged fertilizer. The juxtaposition of this notice, coming as it did just before the sermon, had something to do with the congregation's reaction. As I read the preamble to the notice my mind drifted to thoughts of bags of manure and at one point, I giggled a bit. This was not lost on the congregation. They responded with hearty laughter. Then, as I tried to continue reading, every additional statement sounded like it could be taken in the context of what was coming next—the sermon.

"This fertilizer is very good for your garden, especially at Springtime…It can be bought in 5 or 10 pound bags…We can deliver right to your door." I barely managed to get to the end of the notice; I was in such a state of hilarity as was the congregation. It is possible this completely serendipitous accident was more beneficial and bonding for us than the fertilizer ever was.

Encountering difficulties when reading a prepared text is one thing. The risk of speaking off the cuff presents even more possibilities for disaster. On one occasion, I was trying to encourage the people to be more forthcoming about letting me know when they were sick or going into the hospital so that they could be remembered in our prayers and also that I might visit them. We had experienced an unfortunate situation, which probably occurs in parishes all the time. Someone apparently had taken ill and been in the hospital and I was unaware of it. There were the usual hurt feelings and a bit of nattering about it in coffee klatches. I addressed the issue the following Sunday in a sermon. I stressed that the intention of the clergy was to be available to them in whatever ways were appropriate including visiting them and ministering to them when there was any special need. I underscored that it was vitally important that we be informed about illnesses and hospitalization. I unfortunately concluded my remarks with the comment, "You know the clergy don't have crystal balls." The double-

A Priest's Tale

entendre didn't even occur to me until I heard loud giggles from the congregation.

Recounting this incident reminds me of another situation that relates to the stereotypical ideas about clergy that some people continue to harbour. It was told to me by the Rector of Holy Trinity Church in Edmonton and concerned an incident that happened to him in the early years of his ministry. Dr. Thomas Leadbeater was, in the very best sense, an erudite, low churchman; a scholar who knew his theology and precisely where he stood on issues. It was a great privilege to know and work with him. His style of oratory was extremely articulate—and his sermons were fascinating. We were from very different quarters within the Anglican spectrum but I was in awe of his intellectual acumen. In spite of his august stature and grey hair, he possessed a wonderful sense of humour and humility. The incident happened to him when he was a young priest working in rural Saskatchewan.

Following the service one Sunday, he was invited to breakfast at a farmhouse some miles from the church. It was one of those log houses that had no room dividers but was homey and filled with hand-woven rugs and home crafted furniture. Thomas sat in the living room area while the farmer's wife busied herself with the preparation of brunch. The sun was streaming in through the large living room window and as Thomas sat there engaged in pleasantries with the farmer's wife, a cat wandered into the room and lay down in a patch of sunshine on the rug. It stretched out languorously enjoying the warmth. Thomas made the off-hand remark, "Isn't it too bad we can't do that?" He meant, of course, being able to relax so completely. The woman turned around to see what he meant. But by that time the cat had shot its hind leg into the air, as cats are wont to do, and had begun to lick itself. Thomas was at a complete loss for words—probably one of the very few occasions in his life.

St. Albert was in a rapid growth period due in large part to the oil industry. The suburbs were expanding in leaps and bounds. The community was bustling with young families who were, for the most part progressive professionals launching out on their careers. The town had become a 'city' and the population easily doubled in a few years. The United Church congregation was growing just as St. Matthew's was and eventually the day came when they had to ask us to find other accommodation. They were extremely courteous and we knew what the logistical problems were. However, what to do? In a sense, one part of me was glad. In the United Church building I had begun to feel very restrained, in the liturgical sense, simply not having enough room to do Anglican worship with a proper sense of decorum. For a few weeks I was at a loss as to what we were going to do.

Then, out of the blue, an idea occurred to me. There was a Catholic seminary just south of town, which trained priests and offered theological education in that part of the prairies. It had a very large and rather gorgeous chapel. I thought it might be worth making an enquiry. I made an appointment with the Rector and met with him to put forth my idea. It seemed the timing could not have been better. The college had been hosting an Orthodox congregation for some years, which had only one month earlier acquired a church building in Edmonton. As it happened, it would be quite possible for them to accommodate St. Matthew's.

After a few vestry meetings, we came to the happy decision to move services to the seminary chapel. The chapel was spacious, seating around 250 people, with very high ceilings and lovely, tall stained glass windows and a sanctuary to kill for, so to speak. That was just the beginning. We would also have access to the cafeteria beneath the chapel for the occasional large meeting and also to the classrooms for our Sunday school. Our church school was large and reflected the growth of St. Albert. We had 80 to 100 children involved in a vigorous programme.

On three Sundays of each month the children attended the first part of the Sung Eucharist and would leave for classes before the sermon. The fourth Sunday was a Family Eucharist and the young people would stay for the whole Mass which on those occasions was one of the contemporary liturgies in use at the time. My sermon on those occasions was directed toward the children and in this wonderful, carpeted worship space I took to having the children move to the centre—the chapel was rather in the round or at least in a "U" configuration—and sit cross legged on the floor. On the very first attempt at this, I realized how high I stood above them, and instinctively sat down on the sanctuary step to address them. I should not really say address because the physical setting immediately lent itself to having an informal conversation with the kids. This allowed for dialogue and interaction. We noticed attendance at those Family services was noticeably higher, not only because the children were there, but also because the adults seemed to be fascinated with the spontaneous nature of the event. When you ask questions of children you enter into a totally unpredictable space. Of course, it was obvious that I was in reality speaking to the adults as well as the children.

On one particular Sunday, I recall the Old Testament reading was about Noah and the Flood. I talked about the usual things including the rainbow and the concept of signs from God in the course of which I asked the question, "Do you know of any other types of 'bows'?" Hands went up with enthusiasm. "A bow in your shoelace." "A bow and arrow." Then a precocious little boy at the back waving his arm offered, "Bo Derek." I believe the increased numbers on those Sundays was in some measure brought about because people were curious to see how I was going to talk myself out of the blind alleys which were of my own creation.

On another Sunday I was spared a sticky theological debate by a bright little boy who was kind enough to wait until after Mass to throw a rather thoughtful and brilliant question at me. The theme that day was God as Creator—the Creator of everything. Outside the chapel, as people were departing, seven-year-old Jason shook my hand and asked, "Father, if God created everything, then who created God?"

I looked at him and considered my response carefully and then said, "Well, Jason…that is a very good question. Let me see; I don't quite know where to begin…" Such a philosophical question from a seven year old! Before I could even begin to attempt to answer this impossible question Jason let me off the hook by saying with a very compassionate but condescending tone, "Its okay, Father, you don't have to answer." He knew full well that there was no logical answer and his parents and those within earshot seemed to relish my dilemma. Little swine, who is the Rector here? A budding Thomas Aquinas or René Descartes.

Music remained one of my passions. When I went to St. Matthew's I retained the oversight of the choir and music. It is always a struggle in parishes to try to guide musical affairs. When we began worshipping in the Seminary Chapel the opportunities for musical growth were opened incredibly with its high ceiling and wonderful acoustics. The choir work proved to be a very therapeutic outlet for me. The group was small but able to handle a modest, standard repertoire of liturgical music. On one occasion, the Archdeacon was with us and he remarked that we had probably the most accomplished parish choir in the Diocese after the Cathedral. We attempted some fairly challenging things and had good fun in the process. On the occasion of my birthday one year, the choir gave me a lovely Pinwheel crystal decanter and two matching cocktail glasses, along with three symbolic conducting batons. One was very long and professional, and labelled, "For those grand moments"; another was medium length and marked "For regular use"; for the third, someone had made another very short baton from a toothpick with a little stub end marked,

"For when you're very picky". Choir practices were pleasant evenings which I personally found to be restorative and the choir accomplished some laudable work.

I had never tried my hand at composing before, but one year for our patronal festival, I wrote a "Missa Brevis" for the occasion. It was sung at the Mass that day and was used only that one time. Although I had done an introductory course in composition and had a rudimentary understanding of the principles, I was really simply writing what I thought sounded good. I was rather pleased with it. I even gave a copy of it to Hugh Bancroft for his thoughts. I should have known better. Several months went by before I finally asked him outright if he had looked at it. He was probably hoping I would just forget about it. However, responding to such a direct question, he answered in his inimitable, blunt way. "I wouldn't write any more music." He said I had broken all the rules of composition. When I remarked that Poulenc and Hindemith had also violated the classical rules of composition, Hugh retorted, "Yes, but you have to know the rules before you can break them."

Parish affairs were naturally my first priority while I was Rector of St. Matthew's but I was also involved in things on a Diocesan level. In the course of events I was nominated by the clergy in my deanery to be Regional Dean of Pembina. Regional Deans—in this case it could quite properly have been the old term 'Rural Dean' because the area was farmland—have a rather high-sounding title, but it is an office which has no actual jurisdictional implication. It is more a position in which one is able to gather clergy together for support and personal fellowship.

I had become friendly with Archdeacon Ed Thain during these years and, unknown to me then, I would later serve in Alert Bay where he had also once been Rector.

Ed was so excited one day about a book that had just been published which had been written by a friend from Toronto. He had a copy and was excited to show it to me. During his time in Toronto he had become acquainted with Rabbi Gunther Plaut of Holy Blossom Temple. Plaut was a Torah scholar who had recently completed this major commentary on it entitled simply "*The Torah*". Hearing Ed's enthusiasm about it, I was encouraged to find a copy. I went to the Canadian Bible Society store in Edmonton to see if they had it or possibly might order a copy for me. Instead of wasting time hunting around the store I went directly to the front desk to speak to a clerk. A young, clean cut, very 'Christian' looking fellow full of enthusiasm and fervour attempted to assist me. I explained I wanted to order a copy of the book '*The Torah*', by Rabbi Gunther Plaut. He looked me in the eye and said haughtily, "This is a Christian bookstore." I was rendered speechless for a moment but simply let the issue drop and filled in an order form.

Living in St. Albert was a good change for me after having worked in the north, particularly because of the social dimension. Isolation can grow a little wearisome. Here I was thrown into a completely different style of work. Because of the good economy the community was growing rapidly and I found it to be a refreshing approach to ministry. Many members of St. Matthew's parish tended to be younger, newly married people just launching out on their careers and families. There were scores of young professionals and a high degree of interest in the parish and the social interaction it provided. Although I was only in my early 40s, I was feeling old, which was a new experience for me. This new sense of the generation gap was brought home to me one evening rather bluntly.

I was visiting a young family in their spacious suburban home. They had a little girl about five years old and an infant son. They were part of that progressive generation who embraced the avant-garde, liberal discussion of all manner of things with even the smallest children. The coffee was served and we were having a pleasant conversation in the living room. Soon their little five-year-old girl appeared in the living room in her night attire. She was very precocious and approached me without the slightest shyness. We were introduced and before long, she looked me in the eye and said quite casually, "Do you want to see my vagina?" For one who is not often lost for words, all I could muster was, "Not now, dear." The parents didn't seem to flinch at all. I just hope the full implications of this sort of familiarity occurred to them.

The seven years I was at St. Matthew's were dominated by the search for a property on which to build a church. Countless hours were spent in meetings and brainstorming, sifting through every possibility. At one point we considered purchasing a large house and using it for worship and a parish centre although we realized that it would before long become far too small for our needs. Then there was the possibility of using a warehouse in the industrial area where there would be some advantages. We had meetings with the city council to have bylaws changed so a church could be located in other than residential areas. Then we realized a parish in a non-residential area would not really work well. The quest seemed never ending.

Along with the search for a building location were endless fund raising projects. The Church groups were eager and extremely determined about raising money. The list of fund raising projects would be far too long and tedious to enumerate here. Bingo was one notable project which seemed to work well but which caused much debate

A Priest's Tale

and soul-searching. A local bingo hall had an arrangement where groups could host and manage certain evenings in the month and claim a portion of the revenue.

The bingo idea didn't sit well with everyone, however, and the issue was continually challenged at vestry meetings and especially at the annual meeting. One notable antagonist was a woman who seemed determined to oppose every idea we entertained. At one annual meeting, it came to quite a climax. I have always dreaded annual meetings or chairing any meeting in general. I have never been good at it. I could never seem to get my mind around Roberts' Rules of Order and use them effectively. I believe it is the same blockage that prevents me from being able to be interested in card games. However, on this one occasion Roberts did come to my aid. Again, this woman raised the question of the bingos as we suspected she would. She gave quite a speech about the evils of gambling and how there is no 'free lunch' and how it was ethically wrong for the church to participate in or support gambling. She did not, however, mention anything about the frequent raffles the Anglican Church Women—of which she was the president—was so keen on running. Much discussion followed her speech. For the most part, everyone else appeared to have no problem with the bingo idea. However, she would simply not let it go. Eventually, she made a very uncompromising motion to the effect that we disband any involvement with the bingo immediately. Her husband seconded the motion and no one attempted to amend it.

After a suitable pause for comments, I called for a vote and the entire assembly, except for the woman and her husband, defeated the motion. I was rather thankful for Mr. Roberts just then. Following that, there was not much to say, but that didn't stop her from rising to her feet again and continuing the argument. She reiterated that as Christians we should be aware that getting something for nothing is quite out of keeping with the Gospel. It was the typical protestant work ethic rearing its self-righteous head. I can be pushed only so far and that remark did it for me. I reminded the meeting that at the very heart of the Gospel is the belief that God's love is unconditional; that our Lord's sacrifice on Calvary was offered without any strings attached…it was, indeed, something for nothing.

Eventually, we purchased land in a residential neighbourhood in the northern part of St. Albert; engaged architects and a contractor and the actual building project began. It was a long, wearying process. When the new church was in the process of being finished and the interior work was well underway, exhausted after seven long years of constant effort on this project, I felt the need of a change.

A Priest's Tale

Coincidentally, just at that time, I received a telephone call from a friend in the Diocese of British Columbia about a parish appointment in his Archdeaconry. I was without a doubt intrigued. For some time I had longed to go home to B.C. We set a date for me to visit the parish, Alert Bay, and I flew out for a meeting with the people and Archdeacon Lancaster. Things went well and I flew back to St. Albert feeling optimistic about the possibility of working on the West Coast.

I had scarcely returned from the trip, however, when all hell broke loose. A number of problems had arisen with regard to the building project that needed attention and I didn't feel it would be responsible to leave if things were becoming complicated so, with some reluctance, I called my friend, Archdeacon Lancaster and explained the predicament and begged off the appointment in Alert Bay. Disappointing, to be sure, however, little did I know that another disaster was lurking just around the corner.

One morning I received a call from the Synod Office and was asked to come in to talk with the bishop. He sat me down and called in his executive assistant to witness the discussion. With no idea what was going on I was a little disoriented. The Bishop then proceeded to drop a bombshell in my lap. The information he imparted to me was somewhat vague but concerned somebody's report to him that there was an issue involving a young man, Sean, whom I had known since I first arrived in the parish. He didn't say anything concrete about what he thought had happened nor did he make any accusations except that someone thought there was some kind of personal connection between Sean and me.

As no one was willing to provide any factual information, all I was able to do was to piece together the sequence of events from what I presumed had happened. It was a shocking and painful situation for me as a gay man. The most frustrating aspect of it was that I never had any idea what people were really thinking, what they had been told, or what assumptions were being made. It sounded to me like some people thought a serious and criminal incident had taken place although nothing specific was ever implied.

As far as I can tell, the gossip began at a dinner party. Because the parish was in a period of rapid growth and development, we worked extremely hard to provide all the social means necessary for a church community. It would have been impossible for me as Rector to be in close contact with so many people, although I always maintained a programme of pastoral visitation. One of the ways we tried to encourage fellowship in the parish was through a series of social evenings—dinner parties involving three or four couples at a time. They would visit each other's homes every few weeks for dinner and an evening together.

The concept came from the people and they formed a committee to plan and facilitate the dinners. I fully endorsed it and thought it was extremely creative. People who were interested in the concept would sign up and they were then randomly linked with other couples. It was a pleasant way for them to get to know each other and to interact. The programme had already been functioning for several years by the time this unfortunate incident occurred. I was not expected to go to these affairs—indeed, it would have been impossible as there were so many individual occasions and they were happening simultaneously. We all believed it was a marvellous venture in lay ministry and I was particularly delighted to see such initiative in the parish. Unfortunately, in the course of one of these parties, a rather insidious discussion developed.

From piecing together the limited information I had, a man who was not actually Anglican but married to an Anglican woman, was present at one of these dinners. I knew this man was not really comfortable with my leadership and especially with my having encouraged and stressed the importance of Eucharistic worship, which he in his tradition was not accustomed to. We had moved from alternating Matins and Mass each week to having a

Eucharistic celebration each Sunday but with the introductory part of Matins, which included the well-loved and familiar canticles and psalm singing. It seemed to incorporate the best of both worlds and made for a good preparation for receiving the sacrament. I should underscore that all of this had been decided in consultation with the Parish Council. Everyone seemed comfortable with this; our attendance was constantly growing and interest in the parish was high. But, apparently not quite everyone. Little did I realize church people will often utilize the same malicious techniques that manifest themselves in political life. When you are incapable of rationally dealing with an issue, then simply go for the jugular and attack the person. We see this technique in operation on the evening news almost every day.

At the dinner gathering in question the conversation apparently drifted around for some time touching on many subjects but eventually gravitating toward issues of relationships and marriage. And then—the zinger! As I understand it, the man who had questions about my style of leadership, and who knew as everyone else did, that I was a bachelor, *innocently* slipped in a question. "Do you think the Rector might be gay?" From reports of the event, I gather a thoughtful discussion ensued with everyone present mulling over that possibility.

A Priest's Tale

Now, I must backtrack slightly to set the scene for what came next. This, of course, involved Sean. I had known him since my first week in the parish and watched him grow up. I was friendly with his family and lived near them. Over the years Sean and I found we had mutual interests—photography and 8mm movie filming in particular. In later years, we would sometimes go on filming outings in the countryside. When Sean graduated from high school we went out for a nice dinner in celebration and had a wonderful time. It is true; I was quite fond of him and cherished our friendship. I had a sense Sean liked me as well and quite naturally the thought that he might also be gay had crossed my mind. However, for one in my position, caution and discretion are the rule.

Sean would sometimes drop by my apartment to have a coffee and chat. On one particular occasion as he was putting on his coat in preparation to walk the few blocks home, we stood at the door and continued to talk. I felt ever so close to Sean as we chatted and said our goodbyes. In an unthinking moment, I gave him a hug. I realized right away that I had made him uncomfortable as he became oddly silent for just a few moments. He didn't say anything, however, and we said our goodbyes and he was off into the night. After Sean left, I thought to myself, You must be more careful and not allow your feelings to run away with you.

About a week later, Sean phoned me sounding his usual relaxed self and asked if he could drop over for a coffee to show me the new jacket his parents had bought for him. I was delighted and relieved that he had not been offended and our friendship was still intact.

Sean arrived, showed me the new leather jacket and we had coffee and talked for a couple of hours. I was extremely happy that all was fine between us. Eventually, after a pleasant evening, Sean prepared to head home. After donning his boots and jacket, he was ready to go. Remembering our last leave-taking, I was very careful to offer only a simple 'goodbye'. I was reaching to open the door for him when all of a sudden he flung his arms around me and gave me a big hug. He pressed himself against me and I could not help but notice he had an erection.

"What is *that*?" I whispered in his ear, sounding a little like Mae West saying, *"Is that a gun in your pocket?"*

He giggled and said sheepishly, "I don't know."

He continued to hold me; pressing himself against me. It was an extraordinary beautiful moment. I felt I shouldn't move or speak for fear of breaking the spell. But he wasn't letting me go. I didn't want him to. Eventually, our passions prevailed and nature took its course. I knew at the time that I cared for Sean deeply and had felt that way for some time. I also realized that he was just beginning the process of exploring and reckoning with his own sexuality. Heaven only knows, I identify with that and know how traumatic it can be.

Sean and I got together occasionally to go for dinner or out taking pictures, but there was a distance between us I wasn't sure how to cross. I wanted to give Sean time and space to work through his feelings. In the end we were never able to bridge that distance between us. Needless to say, there was no repeat of that one evening's sweet passion.

Now, I backtrack momentarily to pick up the thread of the dinner party. Sean's parents had been at that dinner. My understanding of it is that the next link in the chain took place in the kitchen of Sean's home several days after the dinner party when his mother was chatting with his sister as they tidied up the supper dishes. The subject of the party arose and they were discussing the gay phenomenon with, from what I gather, a good degree of acceptance and understanding. Sean was in the dining room at the table engrossed in writing something. Sean's mother remarked that there were lots of gay people around and you never really know who may or may not be gay. Unfortunately, she added the phrase, "You never know; Don Dodman might be gay."

Sean's sister, perhaps amazed at the possibility this idea presented, burst into the dining room and declared, "Sean, did you know Don Dodman is gay." Sean, unaware of what preceded this exuberant outburst and already tied in knots by his own feelings misinterpreted the whole thing—had a panic attack—and broke down sobbing.

From that point on I am not at all certain of where it went from there. Somehow, the situation became more and more convoluted as the gossip mill began. The end result was my meeting in the Bishop's office and my being confronted about it.

There was no accusation of any wrong-doing or any specific event—the problem seemed to be simply the fact that I was gay. The bishop declared I would have to resign the parish. It was all so disturbing and chaotic I didn't even think to ask about legal advice or any such thing. However, it then dawned on me why the bishop had asked his assistant to witness the conversation. I was offered no opportunity to safeguard my own position.

After an unpleasant drive through the afternoon traffic I arrived home and began thinking about calling the Archdeacon on Vancouver Island. That evening I telephoned him and simply asked if it was too late to be considered for the parish in Alert Bay after all. He assured me that no action had been taken with regard to the

A Priest's Tale

position and that we could surely pick up from where we left off and continue to pursue the possibility.

After deliberations with the wardens the bishop insisted I give two months notice before departing. I discovered later that the bishop had also demanded that the people concerned refrain from speaking of the issue so as not to fuel gossip. When the time came for me to leave, the parish hosted a going away reception—if that is the correct term considering the situation—with all the usual speeches. That was undoubtedly one of the most uncomfortable experiences I have ever known.

I had absolutely no idea who knew what, or what they thought they knew. I was completely in the dark and didn't know how to respond, except to speak of my desire to return to my home province. Sean, quite naturally, was not present although his parents were there and everyone was extremely kind. We had spent seven very good and productive years together and it was saddening and demoralizing that it had to end like this.

I ran into Sean many years later during a visit to Edmonton and he was very kind and gave me a big hug. Sean and I caught up on things. Neither of us made any allusion to those fateful few hours we spent together. And in the course of our conversation I realized, for Sean, that evening had been merely his first fumbling attempt at establishing his sexual identity with which he now seemed quite at ease. Sean managed a gay nightclub and had assumed the mantle of *'Mr. Gay Edmonton'* by becoming quite a prominent figure in championing gay rights.

✠

It is now over 200 years since Captain George Vancouver anchored his vessel, *H.M.S. Discovery,* at the mouth of the Nimpkish River at the north end of the island that bears his name. While Captain Vancouver visited with the inhabitants of Cheslakee's village, the island that would be known as Cormorant Island lay uninhabited just a few miles away. In 1846, the island received its name from a coastal cruiser, *H.M.S. Cormorant,* and later, about 1858, the Bay was named for *H.M.S. Alert,* which was then stationed on the Northwest coast.

The late 1860's saw the first settlement on Cormorant Island. In 1870, a small fish saltery was established to mild-cure local salmon before being sent to Victoria. As the industry began to grow, a community sprang up. The Reverend James Hall, an Anglican missionary with the Church Missionary Society, who had just established a mission at Fort Rupert, recognized the prospects and decided to establish a mission at Alert Bay as

A Priest's Tale

well. In 1878, he relocated to Cormorant Island and built a mission house where a school was opened. In 1881, the construction of a store and a cannery were begun while Mr. Hall supervised the construction of Christ Church.

Hall also established a sawmill there in 1887. Lumber was produced which would be used in the construction of homes and a new school for boys. Government recognition of the growing community came in 1890 with the relocation of the Indian Agency from Fort Rupert to Alert Bay. That same year saw the arrival of the first provincial police constable.

Transportation on the coast was always a vital element for Alert Bay. In 1896 the Union Steamship "Comox" made its first regular call at Alert Bay while steaming toward Rivers Inlet further north. When the community was at its peak, as the centre of the region, regular ferry access was provided from Kelsey Bay via Beaver Cove. Ferry service is now provided from Port McNeill, with the direct runs to Alert Bay interspersed with trips to Sointula on neighbouring Malcolm Island.

Christ Church, at the time I was there in the late 1980's, was about one hundred years old and a very beautiful wooden building with gingerbread fretwork adorning the ridges of the roof. Pictures of this historic church have appeared in numerous coffee table books depicting British

Columbia places of worship. Considering the age of the church, it was in remarkable condition.

During my incumbency, Alert Bay was home to about 1,300 people. The population was almost evenly divided between Caucasian and Kwaguilth people with the latter, for the most part, living at the west end of the island and the former at the east end. The name Kwaguilth, or sometimes Kwakiutl, seems to be the preferred spelling for most people of this Nation although changes seem to crop up from time to time. The Church played a significant role in the early days of the community, judging by the size of Christ Church and St. Michael's School, which in my time had become a 'back to basics' school operated by the Nimpkish Band. In addition, St. George's Hospital, still bearing its church related name but under the aegis of the Provincial Government, ministered to the medical needs of the region.

Christ Church and the rectory are on Reserve land on the bay almost at the midpoint of the island. The parish was integrated and mercifully, no one had attempted to have separate services for the two segments of the community, even though many of the elderly people were fluent only in Kwak'wala. With the able assistance of Sam Hunt, a Lay Reader, parts of the service were in Kwak'wala as were some of the hymns. The congregation was small, but it was proportionate to the general population compared to other Anglican communities on Vancouver Island. I went there with great ideas of doing things that would involve more people. However, in the scheme of things I regard myself as having been a sort of caretaker rector principally doing maintenance. Unfortunately, not a great deal of anything I initiated actually took root.

In the first few months after arriving in the parish, I made a concerted effort to walk around the island and visit people door-to-door; especially the Nimpkish people who I sensed felt they had been neglected. There were some curious looks from people from time to time, wondering what I was up to. Sometimes I encountered downright anger simply by appearing at the door. I believe now I was rather naive about why there was such a deep-seated problem. I came to realize over time it was a combination of the white insensitivity to native culture and the lingering stain of the Residential School scandal mixed with the resentment of the Native people about the government's suppression of the potlatch in the early decades of the last century. The parish situation had taken on parallel attitudes and had become similarly polarized.

In his zeal to enliven and wake up the community, my predecessor had taken an extremely rigid position on church membership and on baptism in particular. He must have had a problem with infant baptism and the way it is often regarded as just a social event—a rite of passage. I, of course, also have concerns about that issue but feel there must be ways of dealing with it other than simply closing doors and severing the lines of communication. He refused to baptize anyone unless they or their families were seriously involved in the life of the church, which probably also meant, unless they thought as he did. This approach resulted in almost no baptisms taking place during his incumbency and a congregation that dwindled to a very tiny group, which consisted of his devoted supporters.

During the first autumn of my incumbency I set up a series of teaching sessions and baptismal preparation classes with interested parents and families. On the occasion of the first batch of baptisms we had a remarkable 21 candidates. It was a logistical nightmare for me as it meant 21 sets of parents and godparents, 21 candles, 21 certificates and entries in the Register. However, the occasion was a joyous one for the community and Christ Church was packed to overflowing. Even the second crop of candidates six months later was a respectable gathering of some nineteen candidates.

A short while after the first round of baptisms, I received a pleasant surprise in the form of a letter from the well-known Fort Rupert artist, Tony Hunt accompanied by a beautiful print. Tony had family scattered all over the communities of the North Island. In his letter he related how his nephew had been amongst those baptized and that he had been present. He was so happy about this change in attitude at Christ Church he wanted the parish to have one of his prints—"*The Baptism of Jesus by John in the Jordan*". It was a magnanimous offer and I immediately thought the print might be framed and placed near the font at the back of the church. There had never been any representation of Native culture or art in the Church and I realized this idea was likely to raise some eyebrows. I approached the Parish Council as is customary when dealing with church furnishings. I took the print and displayed it as I told the story about Tony Hunt. I half expected the request to be rejected but, to my astonishment they were unanimous in support. The print would be framed and placed in the church near the baptismal font.

When we celebrated the next baptisms, I contacted Tony and asked if he could possibly come down from Fort Rupert and be present when we officially unveiled and blessed the print. He was happy to come and it was a rather significant occasion, especially for the Kwak'wala speaking members of the parish who were astonished that such a thing would ever happen.

Shortly after this event, a lady who had been one of the former incumbent's devotees was heard to say that she was going to pray to God to send a fireball to burn up the print. I encouraged the person who had passed on this remark to convey back to her my response which was: Yes, she might well take that thought to the Lord *but*, if no fireball appears, then she should accept that as God's answer. (I uttered a silent prayer that no one would be tempted to play around with matches.)

The community had retained the use of its language, Kwak'wala, with the aid of a wonderful language programme in the local school. Numbers of the senior members of Christ Church congregation were Kwak'wala speakers. I attempted to learn some Kwak'wala as I had done with Cree and Blackfoot, but it always seemed a little daunting and frustrating. Aboriginal languages are not 'primitive', as some seem to think, consisting of ughs and grunts. They are phenomenally complex; much more so than English grammar or that of any other European language. However, the ability merely to exchange greetings and to communicate in even a minimal way was amazingly worthwhile. One June I attended a Band School graduation exercise which was held in the Big House. The Big House was where the Nimpkish community held all special gatherings. There was much dancing and singing around a crackling fire in the centre. There was much good-natured laughter when the teacher of Kwak'wala gave out the prize for the best achievement for grade four. The boy who received it was Chinese, the son and grandson of long time merchants in the Bay. The teacher took the opportunity to humiliate the Namgis students for their efforts, or lack thereof, in their own native tongue.

Stressful situations are not unusual in parish work as with any encounter with people. Here on this tiny island I found myself directly in the crossfire between two cultures. The tension between the two parts of the community, although not articulated in words, was very palpable. In retrospect it was like a harbinger of the religious divisions that are now playing themselves out in the Anglican Communion. One evening I attended a potlatch at the Big House which was in celebration of a wedding anniversary—60 years together for a couple who were parishioners. News of my attendance spread quickly around the island with the result that the evangelical guard of the parish felt thoroughly offended. I imagine they perceived it as the Rector siding with the opposition.

The potlatch is a focal point in the communal life of the people of the Pacific Northwest. Many threads are woven together in this celebration. It has implications of social status, the hierarchical relationship between clans and tends somehow to be connected mostly with the winter season involving feasts, music and dance. Potlatch traditionally took place when a family hosted a festivity in honour of a specific occasion like a marriage or birth to which everyone in the community would be invited. However, there is one critical and remarkable difference between this and the typical European or western celebration of such events. Instead of the guests bringing gifts, the family hosting the potlatch would *give* gifts to all attending. The social status of the family was determined by how much they gave away. It always sounded to me rather like something Jesus would have liked. In ancient times, when a person gave a potlatch, blankets, furs, coppers and other goods were distributed to the guests. Coppers were ceremonial shields, which came to be recognized as the gold standard of wealth in this society.

Giving rather than receiving is without a doubt laudable but the practice was prone to get out of hand when taken to the extreme. Those who received gifts were then obliged to host more potlatches to match or exceed the display of giving in order to maintain or increase their own status. This tended to reduce many to a state of poverty so that they became reliant on the government.

In 1884 the potlatch was banned by the Canadian government. This issue is interpreted in various ways

A Priest's Tale

depending on one's point of view. Many native people feel the government banned the potlatch in order to crush their culture. Elements of the potlatch represent the exact opposite of western society's concept of status where the more goods or money you accumulate the more status you have. Is it possible that the North Coast way was an embarrassment to materialistic European thinking? Whatever the case, potlatches survive today and continue to celebrate the ethos of the various clans and their wonderful legends. The gifts, however, are but tokens. Whenever I have attended a potlatch, each person would be given a small sum of money according to his or her dignity. At one potlatch I attended with some friends who were visiting from Vancouver, they each received a one-dollar bill and I, presumably because I was the Vicar, received two dollars. Benefit of the clergy!

Although the evangelicals were riled by my attendance at the potlatch, a worse affront to their sensibilities was yet to come. A woman's body—a skeleton actually—was discovered on a beach and identified by clothing and dental work. She had apparently fallen overboard from a fishing boat five years earlier and had never been found. She was one of our people from Turnour Island. One of her brothers telephoned me and asked if I would take the burial on Turnour Island. The Alert Bay

RCMP had recovered the body and it was arranged that we would travel with it aboard a seine boat, the *Izumi II*, the following Saturday morning together with friends and relatives from Alert Bay.

The weather was ideal. It was a bright, summer morning when Gregg, my Lay Reader, and I carried the processional cross, vestments and other ecclesiastical paraphernalia down to the wharf. Seine boats are quite large. The coffin was respectfully placed on the main hatch cover and there was ample room for the fifty or so of us who set out on the two-hour voyage. As we sailed through the scenic passes between lush spruce and cedar carpeted islands it brought back to my mind the book "*I Heard the Owl Call My Name*" by Margaret Craven. I had read her book some years before and many times since. It was not until I lived in Alert Bay that I came to grasp how very accurate and sensitive is her portrayal of the Kwakwaka'wakw People. (Kwakwaka'wakw, literally translated means Kwak'wala speaking people belonging to several distinctive groups; the Alert Bay People being called Namgis and those in Fort Rupert, Kwagulth). Margaret Craven candidly reveals the hardships North Coast People have faced in the collision of cultures and she compassionately reveals the depth of their stoic wisdom and serenity. Her delightful story captures the life of the North Coast in an extraordinarily moving way.

A Priest's Tale

Actually, I had known the priest after whom the character of Father Mark was based. He was Eric Powell who went himself as a young priest to the parish of Kingcome Inlet many years before and the bishop who sent him there was Godfrey Gower who had confirmed me. The mysterious terminal disease that threatened Father Mark was a clever use of poetic licence for the purposes of the story line, because Fr. Powell actually lived well into his senior years.

At one point during this leisurely passage to Turnour Island, I was on the flying bridge chatting with the skipper and soaking in the sun and scenery. Glancing down at those sitting on the foredeck, I noticed that some of the young men had tins of beer in spite of the fact it was only around ten in the morning. Recalling my predecessor and his harsh approach to morality, I could not resist doing what I did next.

I climbed down to the foredeck, sat beside one of the young men, and introduced myself. The poor lad was furtively trying to conceal his beer from the prying eyes of this vicar. After a bit of chitchat, I said, with all the casualness I could muster, "I see you have a beer." He nodded sheepishly. I then said, "How would one go about getting one?" His eyes went slightly blank for just a few seconds as he tried to compute this. Then they widened and he smiled broadly. He leapt to his feet and said, "Just wait a minute." He disappeared below decks and in a flash he was back proudly offering me a tin of Molson's. Everyone on the forward deck seemed to breathe a sigh of relief.

As we approached the dock at Turnour Island, I could see there was a throng of people on the jetty waiting for us. Gregg and I made our way to the galley and vested in albs, preparing to lead the coffin with the processional cross up to the community hall where the service was to take place. As we neared the dock, I could see that the Pentecostal mission boat and the Pastor from Alert Bay were also there. As we stepped onto the dock in all our regalia we were suddenly face to face with the Pastor and I furtively tried to distance myself from him on the narrow float for fear he might smell my beer breath.

The Pastor immediately asserted that he had been telephoned and asked to take the funeral. The woman's brother, who had called me, was also standing nearby. I thought, Now, we don't want an altercation here. Motioning toward the man who had called me, I said, "Her brother here telephoned me and asked if I would officiate at the service. Who called you?" The pastor pointed to another man who was standing nearby—possibly another family member. "Well, I think *they* have a problem," I

A Priest's Tale

remarked, and waited for one of them to enter into the discussion.

After a somewhat awkward pause, it was obvious no one was going to take any initiative, so I turned to the Pastor and said, "Well, what were you planning to do?" He recited a litany of things: his wife was going to play *Amazing Grace* on her accordion; he was going to preach; someone else was going to read the 23rd Psalm; another relative from the Turnour Island community was going to give a eulogy. "Alright", I said, "I'll tell you what. We'll do everything you suggested, but within the framework of the Anglican Burial Office which I am obliged to use, and I will also say some words of comfort to the family". Without waiting for further discussion, I looked at Gregg and motioned with my eyes for him to lead the way with the processional cross—the pallbearers with the coffin and everyone else simply followed us up the hill to the community hall. I felt justified in taking charge of the situation as we *did* have the body. Isn't that what *'habeas corpus'* is all about, I thought?

The service was horrendous—a ghastly mixture of the worst of all the funeral traditions—and the accordion rendition of *Amazing Grace* proved to be the climax of my apprehension. I had the feeling, however, that the people of Turnour Island were enjoying every moment of it immensely; after all, such entertainment was not a frequent occurrence on the Island. During the service, one of the family members announced there would be a *'reception'* in the community hall following the burial. I took that to be code for a potlatch and I presume the Pastor picked up on that as well because he and his good wife retired to their launch immediately after the burial obviously not intending to be present.

The committal took place in the lush forest perhaps a few hundred metres from the Community Hall. There did not seem to be any recognizable pathway through the bush, however someone who knew precisely where the grave had been dug led us on. The forest floor was wet, lush and rather muddy. The grave appeared to be on its own amidst the tranquillity of the cedars rather than in a designated graveyard. Perhaps other burials had taken place in that location but had since become absorbed into the forest. Immediately following the committal, in the earthy way that things are done on the coast, shovels appeared and six men filled in the grave as everyone watched. The true reality of the situation is acknowledged and closure is embraced. I had always found city burials slightly obnoxious with their plastic grass disguising any bare earth and attempts to pretend that death was not a reality. Clergy frequently try to circumvent that kind of avoidance, but alas, funeral

A Priest's Tale

directors seem to believe they are somehow more acquainted with what they imagine to be good psychology.

There was to be an hour to spare between the burial and the *reception*. In that interval I celebrated a Mass in a schoolroom for a small group of the Anglican faithful of the Island. In preparation for the Mass, I passed an empty water cruet to one of the men who offered to go and fill it for me. He soon returned with it full of what looked to me like urine. My consternation must have been obvious because he chuckled and said, "It's our cedar water." During the course of the Mass, my thoughts were distracted by the question of whether or not cedar water might have the same properties as hemlock.

When Mass was finished we wandered back to the community hall where the reception was getting underway. As we approached, we could hear the drums—deep, rich, throbbing drums. Gregg and I took seats in the sports bleachers near the back of the hall and watched the dancing which was interspersed with breaks for Kwak'wala speeches and sandwiches and tea. At one point, I noticed Gregg having a conversation with one of the women from Kingcome Inlet and then a little later she approached me and asked if I might like to join in the dancing. Gregg knew I was interested in and open to the culture and traditions of these people. I responded that I would be deeply honoured to dance, but was afraid I wouldn't know what I was doing and might look a bit ridiculous. She said, "Soon they are going to do the Peace Dance and it is very simple—you would just follow the gestures of the other men." That sounded reasonable enough. I agreed and was led off to a back room and vested in a button blanket along with five other men. The movements and steps were truly no problem, but having the vicar a willing participant was such a novelty that the amused drummers seemed as though they would never stop.

We arrived back in Alert Bay late on that summer evening at twilight. To my astonishment, news of the day's events had preceded us by radiophone. I puzzled over who might have broadcast this news. Unfortunately, I was again in the bad books of the evangelical group; this time for the more heinous sin of having actually participated in a potlatch.

✠

For all the polarization in the community regarding heritage and religion, a few people stand out in my mind as maintaining a position quite apart from the fracture. Next door to the Rectory, on the opposite side to the church, was a large, imposing grey house. Once the Mission House, it

A Priest's Tale

had been the home of the Kenmuir family for many decades. The current Kenmuir in residence was a delightful lady in her 90s who I came to know as 'Auntie Emma'.

Auntie Emma was one of the matriarchs of the community. Her father had been an English settler and her mother a Nootka princess. Auntie Emma had lived in Alert Bay for most, if not all, her life. For a large portion of that time, she had lived in the Mission House. For many years, she had worked as a radio dispatcher for floatplanes working in the North Island region including Port Hardy, Port McNeill, the Nimpkish Valley and the many scattered islands. She was known to the pilots as 'Mrs. K' and operated from a home radio as a sort of flight control centre.

Auntie Emma had a boarder who, although a little younger than she, was her protector and faithful companion. In the beginning, I thought Bob was Auntie Emma's husband. Bob had come to Alert Bay when he was 18 years old to work on the British American marine oil float. Bob had boarded with the Kenmuirs for almost 60 years; except for a 10-year period when he was the manager of the BA bulk plant in Nanaimo. Bob was ardently attentive to Auntie Emma.

After I had been in Alert Bay for several months, I was invited to drop by Auntie Emma's some afternoons for tea. Tea is not my favourite beverage, I must confess.

Perhaps Bob sensed this because on one occasion he hesitantly asked if I would like a scotch instead. I told him I thought he would never ask. From that time onward it became a daily ritual; I would ring the church bell and say Evensong at 5:00 PM, and afterward make my way across the Rectory lawn to Auntie Emma's house. The worn path across the lawn became quite defined as the months and years passed. Bob and I would have a scotch—or two—and Auntie Emma, a Bailey's Irish Cream, which she seemed to believe to be a non-alcoholic drink. I assume this tradition had been established long before my arrival, and probably continued after I left the Bay. It was a wonderful and relaxing diversion for me. We would talk about Island and parish gossip and Bob and I alternated in supplying the scotch.

On one occasion, when I was not very flush with cash I bought a cheap bottle of scotch called "Two Feathers" or perhaps it was "Two Crowns". I apologized when I presented it to Bob. He laughed and made the delightful comment, "There is no such thing as a bad scotch".

Auntie Emma was a very discreet and noble woman who didn't talk much about her native ancestry. However, at a church function one evening, I overheard her speaking with one of the very old women of the island and they were conversing in Kwak'wala. I had not realized she spoke the

A Priest's Tale

language so fluently. I imagined she might have perhaps spoken Nootka in her early years. I was impressed by the way her dual heritage, English and North Coast, was so happily joined and how completely she was accepted and revered by both cultures.

In small settlements like this there are times when something is common knowledge but never addressed openly. It was well known there was a drug problem in the Bay. The police were aware of it and, as the ferry was about the only way to gain access to the island, the authorities kept a close watch on it. However, with so many fishing boats and planes coming into the Bay it was impossible to keep the trafficking problem under control. At one point, after a long period of investigation, there was a huge series of arrests and the problem was kept in check temporarily.

I might never have felt the need to speak out about this obvious problem had it not affected one of my parishioners—a woman who was a youth counsellor with the Native Band. Her son had committed suicide. The young man was using drugs and it seemed to be common knowledge. When I spoke with the parents a few days before the funeral they urged me to speak out about the perils and consequences of drug use.

On the morning of the funeral, the church began to fill to capacity. There were people standing everywhere, even outside in the churchyard. The whole community came out to funerals because, ultimately, almost everyone was related in some way or other and despite the underlying cultural tensions, there was a strong sense of community on the island. I noticed that one particular young, Caucasian man, not originally from Alert Bay was a pallbearer. He was a very clean-cut, handsome young man who was widely known to be dealing on the island. I was rather surprised to see that he was involved in the funeral. The pallbearers were seated in the choir stalls in the chancel but the dealer was a little bit behind my line of vision from the pulpit. I asked my friend Paula, who would be sitting in the congregation, to watch this fellow's reaction as I spoke because I intended to bring the issue out into the open. One doesn't get many chances to speak to a whole community on such a level.

During my homily, I waded right into the tragedy of drug use. The congregation fell into absolute silence. I spoke firmly but in a measured and deliberate way and used pauses to heighten the dramatic effect. It was a tense moment for everyone—certainly, it was for me. Throughout the entire oration I saw nothing but a sea of stony, blank faces. I had no idea what anyone was thinking. Paula told me later that the nice looking young man who was a dealer looked straight ahead and didn't evince the slightest emotion.

In the days following the funeral, I noticed a definite change in people's attitude toward me and it varied greatly. I would be walking into town; passing people on the road, some of whom would glare and give me decidedly disgusted, dagger-like looks, while others would smile and sort of nod, which I assumed was a kind of silent approval. However, no one dared talk about it—certainly not to me. It was such a tight and inbred community; people simply could not afford to speak openly about such a volatile issue, which probably touched the lives of almost every family. That idea in itself was frightening. With some people's reaction to my candid approach, I worried for a time the rectory or church might be damaged or even torched. It was in situations like this that I was always thankful I was not married with a family. I was a free agent, able to take risks, convinced that such problems needed to be articulated. Fortunately, there was no retaliation, probably because I posed no real threat, and was simply ignored.

Another suicide that occurred during my time in Alert Bay was even more disturbing to me, perhaps because it struck a more personal note. The young man in question had returned to the community after several years' absence. I was at a church bake sale and bazaar in the community hall one evening just before Christmas when I first saw him. One does tend to notice strangers on a small island, especially the way this young man was dressed. He wore a punky outfit with a black leather jacket and spiked hair. I was quite curious.

    Later in the evening, I was at the concession counter where he was getting some coffee and we chatted. I introduced myself and he did the same. His name was Luke. He was exceptionally friendly and polite. Luke explained he was originally from Alert Bay but had been living in London for several years. This struck me as quite remarkable because in this insular place people tended to stay very near home—quite a number of people never ever leaving the island. It was, I thought, rather unusual to encounter a native of Alert Bay who was a world traveller. I was quite intrigued. As we parted, I remarked that there would always be coffee on at the Rectory if he wanted to drop by to chat. For some reason, I didn't really expect that we would.

    Some weeks later the doorbell rang and there was Luke. I invited him in. We had coffee and talked for an hour or two. Our conversation was pleasant and easy—this black clad vicar and equally black clad punker. We were very much on a wavelength, I thought, both seeming to discern, without articulating anything, that we were birds of

A Priest's Tale

a feather. He told me about his travels, life in London, and about how he had a passion to work with young people. I can remember thinking to myself; This is going to be a pleasant friendship. When Luke left, I told him I hoped he would visit again.

A week or so later I was appalled to hear of Luke's death by suicide. Why? I thought. Was it because he was struggling with questions of sexuality? Was it perhaps cultural identity? Why had he not come back to talk to me since we seemed to be making a connection? I felt a horrible sense of missed opportunity—even personal failure. Why hadn't I sensed the turmoil Luke had been struggling with? As well, I felt a sickening sense of déjà vu, recalling my own bleak and anguished struggle in coming to terms with my sexuality and personal identity.

I officiated at his funeral and buried him in the Christ Church cemetery on a dreary cold and windy morning. As usual, the entire community came out in force. Wind moaned through the lofty, ancient cedars as we stood in silence after the committal—in the distance ravens cawed. Luke had been a member of the Wolf clan and after a few moments, four young men stepped forward and began a mournful, ceremonial wolf howl. It was unearthly and I became overwhelmed with emotion. The gothic setting seemed particularly appropriate to mark the passing of this young man.

For me, in this funeral rite, there was as well a glimpse of how the two cultures, so often seen in tension, could entwine and compliment one another. During my walk down the dirt road toward the church I could not eradicate the scene from my mind. I brooded on it for days. How truly sad it is that such insignificant issues as race, culture and sexuality have been allowed to drive wedges between us—we who are all children of the same Creator.

✠

Life in a small, insular community like Alert Bay can be extremely lonely for a gay person and especially for a gay priest. One must be circumspect and sensitive to the other members of the community which means, in essence, that one must live a completely secret and guarded life. The need for companionship and affirmation was overwhelming at times, but my work occupied me and life was pleasant enough for the most part. I am sure there were many times parishioners speculated about my bachelorhood. Speculation, however, is one thing but when it becomes gossip with the intent to hurt, that is another factor all together.

A Priest's Tale

My years of work in the church have taught me that, all too often, when a person or group begins circulating malicious gossip, it is often because they have taken issue with your style of leadership. If people are unable to articulate their concerns and preferences, then they sometimes resort to gossip and personal attack as the only way to respond. It is like the defamation of character that happens so often in politics when one party finds they are unable to present a reasonable or logical challenge and so, instead, attack their opponent's character.

The brief storm of gossip about me while I was in St. Albert could be said to be mostly my own fault, if only in that I gave into temptation when Sean held me in his arms. There is a story—quite possibly apocryphal—that circulates among some clergy about a young curate who, on his first day on the job in an Anglo-Catholic parish in a large American city, was being welcomed and advised by his new Rector—a seasoned, elderly priest. After explaining the basic outline of duties and life in the parish, the Rector said, "Oh, and Father, just one word of advice…Don't fuck the customers."

Whilst in Alert Bay another situation arose which again involved gossip but this time there was absolutely no substance to it whatever. It would seem that there are occasions when you're damned if you do, and damned if you don't. But, let me flesh out the details of this situation which for no earthly reason seemed to turn into a little crisis. But first, just a brief sketch of background information. In the course of my work on the board of St. George's Hospital, I had come to be friendly with the administrator. He was not a church member or an overtly religious person, but we thought quite alike and were in agreement about many things and I quite liked him. I valued his professionalism and attitude as well as his charming personality and our engaging conversations. He, of course, was not the problem I allude to; simply one of the participants in a crazy and unfortunate unfolding of events.

One beautiful, sunny, Saturday morning I was cycling along Front Street near the hospital when I saw my friend Butch, the hospital administrator, out on the water testing his brand new wooden kayak which had recently been built for him by an artisan on neighbouring Malcolm Island. It was a gorgeous piece of workmanship and he was rightly proud of it. He paddled around for a while as a few of his friends and I watched and cheered from the pebbly beach. Eventually, he came ashore, pulled the kayak up on the beach and approached us. In the course of things, Butch introduced me to the one person I had not met—a distinguished, grey haired woman about my age. She had recently arrived and was to be the resident doctor for the

A Priest's Tale

native health clinic on the reserve which worked in concert with St. George's Hospital. She was quite pleasant and we had an engaging chat. I discovered later she was on the rebound from a messy divorce and was working in the north to get away from Vancouver—a scenario I had seen enacted so many times in the north. Nevertheless, she was warm and friendly and I thought to myself how nice she was and how well she would fit into our community. Little did I realize the consequences that would follow from this innocent encounter.

Sometime during the next week, I heard from a friend that there was a rumour circulating around that I was gay. In a small community, it is not very difficult to trace the source of such a thing. I was not at all surprised to discover that the source was a couple who had been sympathizers of my predecessor's evangelical approach. I telephoned them and more or less summoned them to the rectory to talk.

At first, they would not mention the gay issue at all, but instead went on about how I had been seen in Port McNeill 'drinking'. I used to go to Port McNeill on most Friday's for grocery shopping at the super market and would then go for a fish and chip lunch with a glass of beer. They had apparently seen me at my table from the street level as they passed by. During our discussion they persisted in referred to it as "*your drinking*", which I took to imply "drinking problem". I had really never given a second thought about having a drink and thoughts flashed through my head of a comment my friend Paula made on one occasion; "Fancy Christians being concerned with that when the central act of worship in the church revolves around an alcoholic beverage". Finally, I dragged out of them all the details of the gossip including the gay comment which they were apparently too reticent to mention.

It seems their daughter, who I also knew, worked as a receptionist in the native clinic with the new doctor. One morning, in the course of idle chattering, they began to speculate whether or not I might be gay because apparently, when the doctor and I had met on the beach that Saturday morning, I had not *'come onto her'*, as they put it. That was the extent of it! To put it mildly I was absolutely livid although I believe I did not outwardly show it.

I pointed out to them that if I had in fact actually *'come onto her'*, they would undoubtedly now be here accusing me of improper sexual behaviour in my capacity as Rector of Christ Church. Then I became downright aggressive, wishing to put this to rest once and for all and I asked them if they understood what libel meant. After a few more stern words, I ushered them out of the rectory

A Priest's Tale

with not a little fear that such baseless gossip could easily destroy my work in that place.

To my knowledge, there seemed to be no further gossip, but for many months after I felt extremely uneasy and often fretted about it. As to the couple in question and their daughter, I realized the gossip had been primarily a means of discrediting me because they didn't really like the "Anglican" direction I was pursuing and also because I was not very sympathetic toward the born again, pentecostal style of religion that they preferred. I also knew, incidentally, that there had been a history of alcoholism in their family and, to top it all off, the husband's brother had apparently been homosexual. Projection can be such an insidious and damning thing! It brought back memories of St. Albert, where in the final analysis; I had been forced to resign my position, not because I had done anything in particular, but simply because I was gay. It was extremely frustrating to think that my ability to perform my duties faithfully to God and the community were being discounted on such preposterous grounds.

✠

My friend Barrie came on one occasion for a week's holiday in Alert Bay and to check up on his protégé. We had a wonderful reunion and a time to catch up on Edmonton gossip. He seemed to thoroughly enjoy the tranquilly of life on this remote coastal island and it was a delight to have him share with me the daily morning and evening offices at Christ Church. We did the brief tourist circuit of the island and it's attractions. As we approached St. George's Hospital I showed him the sign, which had a graphic map of Cormorant Island. I explained that the local people claimed the island had the shape of a killer whale. Barrie looked at the map, then looked at me and said, "That doesn't look like a killer whale to me!"

We dissolved into a fit of giggles. It was nice to know I wasn't the only person to have entertained that thought.

✠

As recounted earlier in these pages, I discovered St. James' Parish in my youth and had been deeply impacted by its teaching and spiritual discipline. In 1987, near the end

A Priest's Tale

of my third year in Alert Bay, I heard news that Father Lloyd Wright, a college friend and assistant priest at St. James, was going to retire. I was well aware of the opening for an assistant at St. James' as I had kept up with what was happening in the parish since my student days and of course I knew that Lloyd was nearing his 65th birthday. I talked to him about the possibility on several occasions during those years and he encouraged me to apply. The advertisement then appeared in the *Anglican Journal*. By this time the church had moved to the business model of job competition including advertising positions and interviews. It seemed a rather slow process with letters going back and forth, finally culminating in a meeting with the canonical committee at St. James'. I flew to Vancouver for the evening meeting and was a guest at the Clergy House overnight. For weeks I had prepared myself to speak to them about my thoughts and philosophy regarding ministry, the church, and the social dimensions of parish work in the downtown. People began to arrive; wine and cheese were served in the refectory; conversation was very relaxed and laid back. I was a little distracted, however, expecting to hear the Rector announce at any moment that the meeting would begin in the sitting room. The evening wore on and on and before I knew it the grandfather clock was striking eleven and people began to collect their coats and take their leave.

After they had all departed, Father Gardiner poured a couple of scotches and sat down with me, assuring me that all was going well and the canonical committee was very happy with our meeting. I hadn't noticed at the time, but every member of the committee had managed to engage me in conversation during the evening. It was a rather clever and civil interview technique.

The following day I returned home to Alert Bay and within a week or so received a letter from the Archbishop offering me the position at St. James', which I naturally accepted immediately. It felt like the fulfilment of some sort of destiny and I was walking on air for the three remaining months in Alert Bay. However, my appointment was not all that surprising as it seems I had actually been the only applicant. I gave the customary notice of my resignation to the Bishop of British Columbia and it was agreed with the Rector of St. James' I would make the announcement of my resignation on Sunday at about the same time my appointment was announced at the High Mass at St. James', thus avoiding any misinformation or rumour.

I had a great fondness for the small congregation at Christ Church and for Alert Bay, which caused me to feel somewhat awkward about announcing my departure. Customarily, announcements during services were made just

A Priest's Tale

before the sermon. However, on this occasion, I waited until the very end of Mass, just before the last hymn as I did not want the surprise of my leaving to disrupt the flow and mood of worship.

After the service, we went to the rectory where I had coffee and pastries ready for the small group who gathered each Sunday. I was a little on edge about what sort of conversation might evolve, but to my surprise, no one said a word about the announcement for a full half hour. Then finally, one of the dear souls, an elderly lady, anxiously said, "Why are you leaving us?"

I took the opportunity to explain to them a bit about the nature of St. James' and the opportunity of working there as well as my desire to return to my hometown. Rather diplomatically, I described the parish, its worship and its location in the depressed East End of Vancouver. For some of these people, insulated in this little corner of the north coast, I'm afraid my explanation must have sounded a little flimsy.

✠

A Brief History of St. James'...

People have lived on the shores of Burrard Inlet for aeons. European contact began in 1791 when the Spanish visited and then with Captain George Vancouver's exploration and charting of the British Columbia coast in 1792. By the 1860's, and especially during the last two decades of the 19th century, the area became a town and a significant centre of activity for the region. The discovery of gold in the Fraser and the Yukon caught the attention of the world. The history of St. James' begins around 1876 when a small frame church was built on the waterfront near what is now Main and Alexander Streets. The town was called successively Hastings Mill, Granville, Gastown, and finally Vancouver.

The first church—a small, wooden frame building right on the shore of Burrard Inlet—was burned along with almost everything else in the Great Fire of 1886. After the fire, the Canadian Pacific Railway, which employed many of the people living in Vancouver, donated land for a church. The new location was a few blocks from the original site at what is now the corner of Gore Avenue and Cordova Street. The new wooden-frame St. James' seated 250, far more than the tiny church on the waterfront.

Captain James Raymur, owner of the mill, was very much involved in the town, its development, and in church affairs. When it came time to choose a name for the church, Raymur's wife suggested that it be called St. James' after her husband. So much for any sentimental musings about that question. In fact, when it was pointed out to Mrs. Raymur that there were actually two James's, the Great and the Less, she was asked which one it should be. She responded unhesitatingly, "The Great, of course".

If new Anglican churches were to be built, the founders of what was to become Christ Church were adamant about the type of Anglicanism they wanted preached and practised—'low-church'. The rector of St. James', Father Henry Feinnes-Clinton, was of the opposite persuasion. However, he encouraged the founding of another parish with a low-church style, realizing that not everyone was comfortable with Anglo-Catholic practice. He probably realized as well that if another parish was to be established along more moderate lines, St. James' would be able to maintain her catholic tradition more easily.

Fr. Clinton, a graduate of Keble College, Oxford, was of the second generation of the Oxford Movement. That movement fifty years earlier had established Anglo-Catholicism in England. As much as was possible in a frontier community, St. James' reflected that tradition. Father Clinton put stress on ceremony and catholic discipline. Fine linens and colourful frontals imported from England adorned the altar, but most importantly, the Mass was held to be the focus of worship.

☩

For me, returning to Vancouver and being on staff at St. James' was truly a homecoming. Living in the Clergy House in the midst of Vancouver's depressed East End was certainly a different experience after so many years of rural and northern isolation. But city living was not the only change. As had been the custom at St. James' since the earliest days, the parish wanted a single priest who would reside in the Clergy House with the Rector and another priest, forming a staff of three. The idea of living with other clergy in community was extremely appealing to me. No more saying the daily office and eating alone. We each had our own suite of rooms, but meals, chapel and parish activities were shared in a pleasant 'family' style of living. Another delightful aspect of this arrangement was having colleagues with whom to share problems and vent frustrations.

Being the new kid on the block was a little awkward at first. Rather than being told exactly what duties I should take up, I was left to find my own niche. All of this seemed to unfold naturally as I took on particular jobs in the management of the house and parish. Of course, from the very beginning the schedule of Masses and preaching formed the hub around which everything else turned. In the

A Priest's Tale

same vein, I believe the life of the Clergy House and the cycle of worship was the heart of the parish around which everything else revolved.

When I joined Fathers Gardiner and Retter in the Clergy House, there was a housekeeper who came in each day to prepare meals and do laundry, though she had plans to retire within the year. Meals were quite formal and wonderful but there was a sense in which our meetings and appointments had to be scheduled to conform to them. Before the actual date of the housekeeper's retirement, I suggested to the other two that we might consider taking on the duties ourselves. Fr. David and I felt we could handle the situation provided we had slightly more casual and individual lunches while still maintaining the formal evening meal. The Rector initially had doubts about the arrangement since he did not cook, but we assured him that we believed it would work and he agreed to give it a try. It was indeed a workable plan and it freed up our noon hour schedules considerably even though there were some added duties like grocery shopping and laundry. Despite our communal living, there were times when the house and meals were very quiet. I recall one Friday evening in particular. From the entry in my journal:

"I prepared a dinner this evening of sole almandine with broccoli. The rector and I are on our own this evening as it is David's day off and he is away. Fr. Gardiner is not given to chattiness, so the quiet seemed even more pronounced as we sat at the refectory table, the rector in his traditional place at the head. Fr. Gardiner has a habit of feeding scraps to the cat during meals, which never fails to surprise me because in every other aspect of his life he is a man of rigid discipline. This evening I was unaware the cat had arrived and sat down between our chairs, having come in on her 'little cat feet'. The Rector noticed her. He turned—I thought towards me—and said in a saccharine tone, "What do you want, Sweetie-pie?" Startled, I looked at him wide-eyed and said, "I beg your pardon!"

I had known Father Gardiner for decades and had been at his induction at St. James' in the days when I was a student. When I accepted the appointment to St. James' as an assistant I realized Fr. Gardiner would be retiring quite soon as he was almost 65. As it happened, he announced his retirement about eight months after I joined the staff.

Father's retirement caused quite a disruption in our lives. He had been rector at St. James' for twenty-two years. The daily round of worship, meals, meetings and social events bound the three of us together in a unique way. Once Fr. Gardiner had officially retired and moved out of

A Priest's Tale

the Clergy House, Father David was appointed by the Archbishop to be priest-in-charge while the search for a new rector began. David and I dealt with the operation of the parish for almost a year as this process continued with the ever-dependable help of Fr. Wright who lived next door at St. Luke's Court. As staff members, neither David nor I had anything to do with the process of searching for a new rector nor were we certain at all what lay ahead for us. We felt uncertain about the future knowing that, when a new rector was selected, he would have the option of retaining or letting go any staff. The Diocesan process hinged upon the principle of advertising the position, priests making application and then the usual interviews and finally a decision which is agreeable to the parish canonical committee and the bishop.

Applications are the *modus operandi* of this process. By nature, David was very reserved and offered little of what he was thinking so I had not the slightest idea where he stood with respect to the situation. One day I finally put the question to him outright, asking him if he was going to apply for the position or not. He seemed reluctant to talk about it. However, I really did need to know. I explained that if he was going to apply then I definitely would not. But, if for some reason he was not going to, then I would. It would have been awkward if we both applied, and conversely, unfortunate if neither of us did. When I put it that way he finally confessed that, yes, he was going to submit an application. I was very pleased and relieved.

Eventually, the process ran its course. One evening as David and I were in the kitchen putting together our evening meal the phone rang. I answered. It was the Archbishop asking for David. Our hearts skipped a beat knowing what it must be about. David took the receiver and after a few tense moments the call ended and David told me he had been appointed. I gave him a big hug and we opened a couple of celebratory beers; the uncertainty of the past year was lifted. David was inducted as Rector on a weekday Festival evening. The church overflowed with parishioners, friends and about twenty of the city clergy.

Once David had assumed his new role, the next step was to begin searching for a third priest. A carefully designed advertisement was submitted to church publications in Canada, the US and Britain. The English newspaper, the *Church Times*, has a worldwide circulation. Finding a priest who was single, catholic, and willing to live in a communal situation in a depressed neighbourhood proved a slow process. We received twelve applications, which David and the wardens shared with me. Three of them were interesting and good possibilities. The others were either completely bizarre or simply did not meet the requirements outlined in our advertisement. One was local, one from Britain and one from the US. As it happened, the British applicant was visiting friends in Seattle and was able to stop over in Vancouver for an interview, which saved us a considerable sum on the airfare. The local priest was easily interviewed and the parish arranged to fly the American priest out from Pennsylvania for several days.

It did not take very long to realize that the priest from Pennsylvania was the obvious person to join our staff. Naturally, we also needed to discern whether he was interested in the parish after having spent a few days in our house and being involved in things. It happened that there was a parish funeral during his visit, which was an opportunity for him to see us at work on a day-to-day basis. Stephen had been the last of the three interviewed and it was obvious to everyone involved in the process that he was the one to complement our staff. And so it was that Fr. Stephen Herbert came to join our team in 1989 bringing his cat, Friedeswide—or Frieda for short—with him. He was then about 35 years old and had a background in teaching. He was scholarly, with interests in social outreach, music, and preaching. We were delighted and fortunate to have him join us.

With Stephen's arrival our meals took a notable upturn. He was an excellent cook and was especially talented in preparing meals for larger numbers. We began the practice of having dinner parties once each month and inviting six or seven parishioners at a time in an endeavour to strengthen the bond between us and the parish. The long refectory table seated 8 or 10 comfortably, and this was an excellent way to get to know people and to express our gratitude for their hospitality and kindness to us. One of my tasks was to keep track of dinner guests on my word processor and to send out the invitations. Over the course of those years, I estimate that we had more than 200 people to dinner parties. These were extremely pleasant occasions, beginning with cocktails in the drawing room and eventually moving to the dining room. Dinner conversations were spirited and witty; an extremely pleasant way for us to relate to people, and they to us. There surely is no better way to socialize than to do it as food is shared. I have always felt it no accident that Our Lord chose to enshrine the most profound experience of His life in a meal.

Each of us had our special chores on these dinner occasions; Stephen usually supervised the main meat or fish dish; I laundered and ironed the linen table napkins and prepared vegetables; David made salads, did the polishing of silver and setting the table.

On one of these occasions, the first two guests arrived at the appointed time and we took their coats and

A Priest's Tale

led the two ladies into the sitting room. Soon drinks were poured at the sideboard and sherry served. As Stephen and I sat chatting with the ladies, Frieda, the Clergy House cat, strolled into the room and went immediately toward one of the two women. She was also a cat fancier and thought she knew why Frieda had gone to her so decisively. She said to Frieda, "Oh, hello. Do you smell my pussy?"

I nearly choked on my Scotch and quickly excused myself to go to the kitchen to check on the roast. Stephen soon followed me and we had a dreadful time trying to regain our composure and calm down. It was several minutes before we dared return to the drawing room.

Fr. Wright, who I had replaced, moved to St. Luke's Court next door and continued to have a very active involvement in the parish. I had known Lloyd since I was about 19 years old at college. He was then in his early 40's. Our time at the Anglican Theological College of BC overlapped a little. Lloyd was an 'older vocation'—a phenomenon that later became more the rule than the exception. I have always been impressed with Lloyd's holiness, sincerity and his devotion to the parish and to the priesthood.

After Lloyd's retirement, we began the custom of having him over to the Clergy House for dinner on Sundays before Evensong. Lloyd in turn would have us over for dinner on Saturday evenings. Lloyd was always a very methodical person and he took up cooking when he moved into his own quarters. He was very good at assiduously following recipes and he created some delicious meals.

My own approach to cooking is much more experimental; a pinch of this and a dash of that, making it a little risky. Lloyd was particularly skilled with stews and I always envied his talent with them. Over the many years we exchanged dinners, we often commented on his culinary expertise. At some point during our discussions over dinner we began to refer to Lloyd as the *'Stew King'*. The banter about his being the 'Stew King' was gradually woven into our frequent dinner conversations, especially on those occasions when his delicious stews were featured.

One Sunday evening when Lloyd was at dinner at the Clergy House, I had prepared dinner—a chicken cacciatore dish. Lloyd liked it and during the meal with David, Stephen and me, he remarked, "Don, you are the Chicken King."

I exploded with uncontrollable laughter, as did Stephen and David. I simply couldn't stop. The more I tried, the worse it got. Poor Lloyd looked at us incredulously asking, "What's so funny?" Of course, we couldn't explain it and I don't think he ever knew quite what evoked all the frivolity.

A Priest's Tale

✠

During the second summer I was back in Vancouver a gay friend invited me to a barbeque. I didn't know anyone except my host. But the dozen or so people who attended were a rather eclectic group spanning the spectrum in age as well as lifestyle and occupation. I became involved in a delightful conversation with a woman who was about my age and who taught at the university. We discovered we knew some people in common and we had various similar interests. As we chatted, I couldn't help but notice a young man who had just arrived and was talking to the host near the back gate. He looked to be about 18 years old and was one of the most handsome young men I had ever seen. He was dressed in stylish slacks and a casual shirt and looked like he had just stepped out of a GQ advertisement. I was a little distracted and hoped my interest was not too noticeable to the woman I was talking with.

As people circulated to greet one another my attention kept wandering back to this vision of beauty. Eventually, our host gripped my elbow and led me over to where the phantom of delight was refilling his glass at the drinks table.

"Don, I would like you to meet Jason!"

Jason smiled and we shook hands. Our host drifted off. As we made small talk, Jason and I discovered we each had an interest in the sea; he was a Cadet at the same naval base where I had done my Naval Reserve service. He was not long out of school and was working at a summer job. When Jason asked me about myself, what I did, he seemed unusually interested and intrigued that I was a priest. When food was ready Jason and I became separated in the normal course of mixing and mingling and finding a place to sit for dinner.

Later, when the host and I found ourselves alone for a moment, he dropped me a wink and said, "Jason is a straight boy you know. At least, he says he is!"

We giggled over that. He knew full well how Jason was just my cup of tea. After a pleasant evening and delicious food the night came to an end and people began to disperse. Jason and I stood talking at the front gate. I didn't want it to end and chattered on as long as I could about this and that. Eventually, he asked how I was getting home.

I told him that my car was parked a few blocks away and he kindly offered to drop me off there, which I happily accepted. We drove over and parked behind my car and continued talking. Finally, as I got out Jason suggested we keep in touch. This, of course, pleased me immensely. I gave him my card and said, "Why don't you give me a call and we can get together for a coffee." I left his car feeling rather elated—such a delightful, handsome young man seemed to be showing an interest in *me*.

Within the week I received a phone call from Jason. After a brief chat we arranged to meet and have dinner the following weekend. I was in especially good spirits since it was Jason who initiated this rendezvous. It was certainly different from my usual situation of being smitten by some young man who wasn't at all interested in me.

On the weekend we went for a wonderful dinner at his favourite Greek restaurant. Afterward, we drove around and stopped to enjoy the starry evening and have a walk along the beach at Spanish Banks. We both seemed to feel comfortable with each other. Inevitably, the question of my sexuality came up and I was quite at ease, and answered him honestly. And although my friend had told me he thought Jason was straight, I played dumb and asked him about himself.

He smiled and said, "Well, I really don't know yet. I'm young." We laughed and continued talking. Over time, I came to realize that Jason was quite relaxed about the question of sexuality. In fact, it was a little disturbing to me when he would recount incidents involving girls he dated in all their lurid detail. He seemed to have a lot of sex and it was certainly no mystery to me why these young women would throw themselves at him. During the ten years of our friendship there were times when Jason was extremely tactile and affectionate. He had no problem with touching and being affectionate, even kissing on the lips. And yet, Jason would often assert he was not really gay, which made me think to myself, *You could have fooled me!* Perhaps he was just very sexually inclined.

One evening after we had spent a very affectionate and sensuous time together I made the comment that I enjoyed making love with him. Jason picked up on that and made a correction to satisfy his own sensibilities. "We weren't making love. We were just having sex!" Interesting how we can split hairs to maintain our self-perception. The times Jason and I spent together were wonderful and I didn't want to make an issue of it.

We made the rounds of most of the classy restaurants over the years and enjoyed those evenings out. When Jason got his new, red convertible he would come by to pick me up. I think my colleagues were duly impressed. One particularly memorable occasion was when I took him to dinner on his 21st birthday. I think it meant a lot to Jason because his parents were divorced and it didn't seem like there was much of a connection between him and his father.

A Priest's Tale

One evening we decided to go to a movie and planned to have a quick supper beforehand. Jason wanted to go to a particular Boston Pizza outlet because he had worked there and wanted to see if any of the people he knew were still around. En route Jason suggested we should try their garlic bread, which he claimed was fantastic.

We arrived and the place was almost empty so we took a booth and settled in. Soon a very young girl came to take our order. She approached from behind my line of vision so I didn't see her until she was beside our table. Jason saw her coming and by the look of interest on his face I could tell that she must be quite attractive. She asked what she could bring for us and Jason suddenly became transformed and I sensed that he was attempting to be suave.

He spoke very slowly and deliberately trying to be Mr. Cool. "Yes, well, let's see. I think we'll begin with an order of the garlic breasts." He immediately corrected himself and went a noticeable shade of red. We have both since made ample use of that story and his delicious Freudian slip.

Jason went on to study navigation and acquired his 'papers' and is now a ship's officer. I don't believe he ever felt inclined to settle down with one person of whatever sexuality and I have not heard from him for years.

✠

St. James' Parish, from its founding, had always been a bastion of Anglo-Catholic faith and it functioned like a well-oiled machine—the day to day operation cemented by a century of sound and disciplined principles. Around the parish, one often heard the phrase, "But...we've always done it this way." Although that attitude sometimes restricted innovation, the principle served the clergy and the parish remarkably well.

During my curacy, a modest attempt was made to involve lay people more in the decision-making and also the general operation of the parish. It was a time when lay people were encouraged to organize and run things like the parish newsletter, many of the social outreach programmes and providing meals for the homeless. Things never went completely out of control as was the case in so many churches at that time, where sometimes outlandish and I dare say, silly activities were allowed to play themselves out. It was a time of many fads in the church which I fear were latched onto out of a sense of desperation in the face of dwindling congregations and an honest desire to appear to be contemporary.

A rather amusing incident resulted from one such project. The Trustees decided to do a parish survey to

A Priest's Tale

determine the congregation's *'level of satisfaction'*. In the 1980s and 90s the national Church seemed to be preoccupied with imitating the corporate world. A parishioner, a competent consultant from the business sector, was chosen to prepare a questionnaire that would reveal where our strengths and weaknesses lay. The poll was quite voluminous and much of it was in the form of "yes" or "no" questions, or answers that could easily be categorized and thus represented as numbers. However, there was also a provision for people to express their thoughts about the parish in essay form. These were more difficult to assess and tabulate for the final results, which were then made available to the members of the parish.

    One morning the clergy and wardens met in the Clergy House to attack the mound of questionnaires on the dining room table in an attempt to codify and evaluate the information. We spent hours sipping coffee and sifting through all of the written responses. The reports were anonymous but on occasion we had a reasonably good idea who might have written certain comments. When anyone found something of interest, it would be shared with the others around the table. All of a sudden Stephen burst out in a fit of laughter. The rest of us waited for him to regain his composure and when he had, he read us the response that had set him off. It was from a section about worship—suggestions about sermons in particular—and simply said, "MORE SERMONS ON MASTURBATION".

We all exploded. We wondered at first if it was a joke. Then someone wondered aloud if the writer was requesting a 'How-to' type of sermon. We thought we knew where that one might have come from but were never really certain.

The end result of this laborious survey proved quite encouraging. It revealed that there was about a 90% level of satisfaction throughout the parish. I thought to myself that after going through all those hoops and such a great amount of work and organization, it didn't actually result in the need for very much change in the operation of the parish, although it did lead to some adjustment.

☨

The daily round of worship was the glue that held everything together at St. James'. Six-thirty in the morning in the Blessed Sacrament Chapel, sitting or kneeling in silence, waiting for Matins to begin, was a beautiful and calming experience. Traffic noise from Cordova Street was the only intrusion aside from the occasional sound of the outer door opening and closing as people gathered for Mass.

A Priest's Tale

After Matins, Angelus was rung on the largest bell in the tower, a reminder to those living and working in the surrounding area that God's Incarnate Presence is here amongst the bustle and turmoil of the neighbourhood. My friend, Brother Savio, of the Friars of the Atonement, who resided at the other end of our block, once told me how they regulate their offices and routine in accordance with the bells of St. James'—morning, noon, and night. We shared a common purpose and always considered our efforts as complimentary.

The Sunday routine of offices and Masses were always an immense pleasure and blessing. Kneeling in the preacher's stall during High Mass, my thoughts would flash back to the days when I was in my teens and had just discovered St. James'. Past and present overlapped as St. James' seemed to remain the same over the decades. Fading chords of the Sanctus and Benedictus reverberate through the church as shafts of sunlight, glowing in the smoke of pungent incense stream into the sanctuary from the high clerestory windows. We are momentarily transported into the Presence of the Eternal—a foretaste of heaven. The Host is elevated; sanctus bells jangle; curls of incense drift in the still air; the tower bell tolls thrice announcing to the neighbourhood that Christ is present. Only the occasional siren nudges us back to reality. Little did I know in those early years I would one day serve here.

Early morning mid-week Masses were wonderful times of devotion and quiet contemplation. My spirit was prepared and refreshed for the busy day. The idyllic atmosphere was frequently interrupted. Visitors from the street would wander in, mystified about what was happening, sometimes disrupting things. On occasion when I was the celebrant of the Mass, I would be praying the words of the Liturgy, but at the same time wondering what was happening behind me and to the other worshippers, sometimes plotting out how I would eventually have to deal with the visitor. It is truly amazing how the mind can be doing two completely different things at the same time.

There were times during worship when my mind would wander to things erotic and intimate, which caused some consternation. It was particularly troubling when I would be in the middle of the Prayer of Consecration, saying the most holy words of the Mass—and some image would come into my mind. I would fight against it and chastise myself but came to comprehend that God can cope with our human frailties and lapses. It is another instance of living in a world which encompasses both the sublime and the profane.

A Priest's Tale

In reminiscing about things sacred and profane, I am reminded of an incident that happened one year at the time of Vancouver's July "Sea Festival". For some time there has been a week-long celebration of the sea which on occasion includes visits of tall ships and naval vessels from all parts of the world. When such visits occur churches in the city, especially those near the harbour, attempt to make the seafarers feel welcome. St. James', in particular, has had a century-long involvement with the Missions to Seamen, the facilities of which are a short walk from the church.

One year during the Sea Festival, parishioners were encouraged to take a personal interest in the visitors and perhaps invite someone to dinner. The Rector, in promoting this programme, put a notice in the Sunday leaflet about visitors to the Sea Festival with the dubious heading, 'DIAL-A-SAILOR'. Needless to say, many in the parish found this more than a little amusing, especially the members of the Server's Guild. Perhaps not so strangely, the programme was redefined the next year.

Holy Week was an intense spiritual exercise and it has always given me such joy to see the large numbers of people who come to participate throughout the week. After Stations of the Cross on Wednesday evenings during Lent, there were rehearsals for the clergy and sanctuary party for the services of Holy Week, which are rather liturgically complex. Because of the length of the Palm Sunday liturgy with its blessing of palms, procession and the singing of the Passion, it was necessary to try to make the sermon as brief as possible. On one of the occasions when I was to preach, I prepared a normal sermon, trying to keep it succinct, but alas, the result was not really very much shorter than usual. I then tried to prune it by removing superfluous words and phrases. The more I persisted with this reduction, the more salient the piece seemed to be as it evolved from prose into poetry. Truly, it was a moment of revelation to me and I began to have a glimpse into what actually sets apart poetry from prose. The result surprised and intrigued me although I never seemed to have the time to take up the pen to repeat the experience.

THE GIBBET

Wooden beams await
on the incline
of Calvary; rough
hewn lumber, not yet assembled;
intended for a house or barn;
destiny uncertain; shape obscure.

Their origin the same as all

A Priest's Tale

created things; brought into being
in love—the purpose, noble—to
glorify the Creator; made to reflect
the Majesty of the Architect.

By chance or fate, perhaps by design,
it becomes the gibbet upon which
that very Architect will draw
a final breath and expire.

What has begun must be finished.
Beams assembled, the instrument of
death takes shape, its form rudimentary,
infinitely simple, a sign of shame
and infamy which will come to be the
sign of powerful love—of
reconciliation.

Cursing and lamenting intermingled,
the defiant mob drags its Victim toward
the place of final humiliation.
He complies, there is no struggle, the
die is cast.

Creator and creature, joined in strange

      array so as to bind together once more
         that which had been pitifully
        estranged in mist of eons past.

              It is finished—
            it is accomplished.

Because of the nature of our communal life at St. James', and in particular of the Clergy House, we were occasionally called upon to be a haven for clergy who were in need of support. Priests from isolated northern villages or those who were experiencing some sort of emotional difficulty were able to stay with us and to share in the life of devotion and community.

One year we had a student from the theological college stay with us for a four-month period. Michael was doing a parish intern placement for a pastoral theology component of his studies. Before details were firmed up he came to have lunch with us one day giving us all an opportunity to assess whether or not this arrangement might be workable. We prepared a soup and salad lunch and opened a bottle of white wine and quickly discovered that Michael was indeed the sort of person we could happily share our lives with for the duration of his placement. We

A Priest's Tale

discovered he was more than just 'compatible'—he was a splendid addition to our 'family'. He proved also to be a very able chef in addition to his ebullient and outrageous sense of humour.

Michael seemed to delight in being a part of the clergy team. He participated in the cycle of preaching and in officiating at the Daily Offices and generally brought a bright presence to our lives. While he was staying with us, the Rector was experiencing some unsolicited attention from a number of women of the parish, one of whom was sending him torrid love letters. David was far too kind to do anything to put an end this attention which of course only served to encourage it. There was a good deal of dinnertime teasing and banter about it. The saga unfortunately seemed to dominate daily life for a time. On one occasion Michael disappeared to his room after dinner and returned in about twenty minutes with a rather clever limerick he had written on the topic. As a connoisseur of limericks, I thought it was one of the better ones I had read.

> *"An eminent priest of St. James'*
> *Was pursued by importunate dames,*
> *For, though almost a monk,*
> *The Reverend hunk*
> *Had ignited their hormonal flames."*

Michael's sense of humour was a delight. He once told me about being up very late one evening at seminary working on an essay for his Christology course. It dealt with our Lord's nature—human and Divine—and Michael had simply named the file "Jesus". He began to tire shortly after midnight and decided to continue his writing the next day. In closing down his computer up popped the usual window, "DO YOU WANT TO SAVE 'JESUS'?" Michael went to bed having a good chuckle.

Not long after Father Stephen had arrived we made a few minor changes to the liturgy. We knew this sort of thing was a touchy issue and consequently we planned an all day workshop to prepare the way for what came to be derisively called "*The Changes*". One thing that was changed was the whispered preparation before Low Masses said at the pavement before the altar steps. This entailed the celebrant and server bobbing and weaving back and forth as they said the confiteor and Psalm 43. No one else could hear it in any case but a few diehards missed it because it did have a certain mystical appeal. From that time forward we continued to use the preparation, but audibly in the vestry. Some of the other changes were the Gospel Procession to the nave, the exchange of the Peace amongst the congregation, and the involvement of Lay People in the readings and intercessions.

Although there was nattering for a while, these changes were generally accepted. Some feared that the Passing of the Peace would get out of control as it did in so many places and would come to resemble coffee hour with people greeting each other and catching up on news. This was never what the Pax was intended to be. It is a simple acknowledgement of our unity in the sharing of Christ's Peace. At St. James' it did not get out of control thanks to Gordon Atkinson's skill in beginning the offertory hymn after just a brief pause.

Because St. James' Church was of such a unique design, there were frequently requests from movie companies to use the building for location shooting. The parish decided years ago not to allow any interior filming so as not to intrude on the spiritual life of the parish and to avoid any desecration of a holy place where the Sacrament is reserved. On occasion, the exterior was used and the film crews would block off Cordova Street. On one occasion it was used to represent a synagogue and the properties people made a few quite significant changes to the front of the church for the occasion. This happened not long after *'The Changes'* had taken place when some were still a little touchy about the innovations.

David and I walked to the corner of Gore and Cordova, stepping over thick cables and equipment, to see what was going on. Over the front doors the properties crew had placed what looked like huge bronze letters spelling, "TEMPLE BETH IACOV", which I thought was a very clever twist. It meant, 'Temple of the house of James'. Obviously, somebody in the art department knew Hebrew. I turned to David and said that I hoped none of those who had been so upset about the recent 'changes' happened to drive past right at that moment. I never did discover the name of the movie in which these shots were used.

One of the joys of a busy parish is the sheer variety of things that happen in the course of a day's work. Someone will come to the door with a long story of hardship, eventually working up to the root of the thing—a request for 'just enough money to get out to White Rock'—a favourite destination it seemed—where a job was waiting, or perhaps for enough money to buy a gallon of gas to get the car home. One becomes a little immune to this scamming. We were fortunate that we were almost always able to refer people to our Social Service offices on Powell Street or to food sources. More often than not, the scammers came to us in the evening when they knew full well that our social service offices were closed because they

A Priest's Tale

really wanted money rather than food or assistance. There were also unexpected encounters to brighten the day.

One day, dressed in my cassock, I answered the Clergy House door and the young man standing on the step, obviously a little taken aback by my attire, blurted out enthusiastically, "Oh, love your outfit!" He happened to be from a local theatre company and had come by to ask if we would put up a few posters around the parish.

An encounter of a stranger sort was with a young man who persisted in visiting the church for several weeks. He was a very attractive and affable young man, always dressed neatly, and rather intriguing which made it difficult not to want to spend time listening to him. But first impressions can be misleading.

He carried with him scribblers and papers with many of his notes which he wanted to discuss. He believed they were messages from God, and at other times from aliens with important messages and warnings for us. After reading several of these notes I realized that they were truly nonsense and that he had deep problems. In due course, I discovered he was a resident in one of our facilities and that he had been diagnosed as bipolar amongst other things.

One Sunday he insisted on talking with me just after the High Mass. He seemed particularly addled and wanted to talk privately. We went back through the corridor behind the High Altar into the Blessed Sacrament Chapel. I noticed Robert, from our social services office, keeping an eye on us. Robert knew this young man was an unpredictable and troubled person, possibly even dangerous. Discussions with the youth rather fascinated me because he was so bizarre. He even once described in detail the alien beings that had revealed themselves to him, and had somewhat plausible reasons for the whole scenario. I assumed these images had come to him by way of television or books.

That particular Sunday things took a rather comical turn. He must have sensed I was skeptical about his tales and he became a little defensive. At one point in our discussion, he looked me in the eye and asked, "Are you gay?" Somewhat startled, I responded, "Whatever makes you ask that?" He said, "Well, I can tell anyway because of the powers I have been given." Then, he asked me to stand up with my arms outstretched as if in a security check and dramatically ran his hands around my outline—my aura perhaps—slowly from the top of my head to my feet. I was intrigued to know what was coming next. Finally, he sat down and said, "OK, you're not." What a relief! We sat down and continued our weird conversation, which really had no beginning, middle or end.

A Priest's Tale

Most of the work of any parish is not quite as exotic as that, but rather, consists in visiting people in hospital or at home; doing administrative things in the office; writing letters; and organizing meetings or events and then attending them. There was a lot of driving involved as St. James' is a gathered parish with members living all over the city and outlying communities. During my time at St. James' I drove a cute, white Honda Civic. I had to buy a new car when I arrived at St. James', as I had no need of a vehicle while living on Cormorant Island and had sold my former car. Actually, Fr. David and I both had Honda Civics; his black and mine white. Over time, we discovered a rather strange phenomenon—perhaps one of those inscrutable mysteries of the universe. When birds defecated on our cars, on his car it was always white, while on mine it was always black.

When I bought my new Civic I had a radio installed because finally, living in the city, I could get good reception. It made my frequent drives between parish visits rather pleasant. One sunny day as I made my way to a visit, I had the radio tuned to CBC to listen to my favourite early afternoon classical music programme. It happened to be the host's 75th birthday and there was a special celebration for him. This programme had run for decades and he offered a volume of detailed information about the music. Some people used to complain about that and thought him pretentious. I enjoyed him because the chatter was educational and extremely well informed. I felt I knew this man because of the familiar voice I had heard over so many years. I had never actually met this man but my friend Barrie had apparently known him in Calgary in the 50s.

On the programme that particular afternoon he was talking about his latest discovery; a disc featuring a Spanish conductor who was only 21 years old, which certainly is unusual. From his glowing description of the young man, I pictured him sitting with the CD case in his hand as he talked and the cover bearing a photo of the young conductor. After a very long and complimentary introduction he finally said, "Well, now, let's get to the music. We will be listening to the Concertgebouw Orchestra under the baton of this *very* interesting 21 inch conductor." The air went dead for a moment—then the symphony began. I all but drove off the road in hysterics and had visions of the hilarity that must have erupted in the control booth. After the symphony he made absolutely no mention of this slip of the tongue, and the programme continued with the customary CBC decorum.

My interest in orchestral music was again picked up while I was at St. James'. Stephen was a gifted pianist and we often practised works for violin and piano together. For

A Priest's Tale

a few of those years I also played in the Vancouver Philharmonic Orchestra. I played second violin. As a youth of seventeen I had played in the Vancouver Junior Symphony—also second fiddle. At one of the Philharmonic concerts—a benefit for Eyesight International—we were honoured to have as a guest artist Jane Coop playing Beethoven's Fourth Piano Concerto. As an amateur orchestra we were feeling some angst playing with Ms. Coop. Our adrenalin was running high that evening and we managed to do quite a presentable job. On the same programme, we played Beethoven's First Symphony. For me, this was a nostalgic moment. I had played it on the very same stage in Point Grey High School when I was a teenager and a member of the Vancouver Junior Symphony. Music was a very therapeutic outlet for me in a situation where work was often intense and the days long. I felt I needed to have a social life separate from the Parish and friends who were not associated with the church.

Anglican Church structures tend to be quite complex from the figurehead position of the Archbishop of Canterbury down through national Primates, Archbishops of Provinces, Bishops of Dioceses and then down to the various Deaneries and Parishes. In addition, there are boards and committees to deal with education, social outreach, liturgy and worship and a plethora of other endeavours. Parishes are grouped together in Deaneries for the purpose of keeping the clergy informed and providing fellowship and support for them. It seems to have been the rule that Regional Deans were usually appointed from the ranks of associate priests or curates. And so, in the course of time, during my work as an associate priest at St. James', I was appointed as Regional Dean of Burrard.

It is a grand sounding title but in truth it is a position having no teeth or authority. The purpose is more to gather the clergy of the Deanery together and provide encouragement, professional development and fellowship. There was a small honorarium attached to the job, both for me and for the parish, to compensate for the time spent on Deanery matters as well as to enable us to host going away receptions for clergy and other such events. The honorarium also allowed me to take new clergy out for lunch or dinner to welcome them. This is how I met Fr. Peter Elliott when he came to be Dean and Rector of Christ Church Cathedral in Vancouver.

I arranged to meet Peter at the Cathedral just before noon one sunny day, and we walked over to the Georgia Hotel for lunch. We had only just settled in and begun to chat when Peter made a remark that got my attention, not so much for its content but for the assumption behind it. I don't now recall what we were actually talking about, but

A Priest's Tale

Peter said something like, "...*and we gay clergy need to keep this in mind!*"

I suspected Peter might have done a background check on me and may have even talked with Fr. Neil Gray, who was a magnet for Diocesan *news*. However, I was a little surprised, nonetheless, and couldn't resist having a bit of fun.

I looked at Peter and said in the most serious tone I could muster, "Excuse me, I'm not gay."

Peter's face went ashen for several seconds before he realized I was having him on, and then he burst out laughing.

✠

In the first week or so after joining the staff at St. James', I was introduced to Maude Palmer, one of the most remarkable people I have ever known. At the time we first met, Maude was about 90 years old and had only minimal vision and hearing. She still worshipped at St. James' at that time, being driven to church each Sunday by a neighbour who sang in the choir. I found Maude to be full of the joy of living and she communicated that to everyone around her. In spite of her diminished senses, Maude was completely cognizant of the world and of current issues.

She lived alone in her home on Yew Street which concerned me a good deal. Once when I went to visit her I found a note, probably intended for me, pinned to the front door written in her large, slightly shaky hand, "BLIND AND DEAF—DO COME IN." When I asked her about it she assured me she had only just unlocked the door knowing I was coming. On one occasion, some burglars did enter her house during a bright summer afternoon through a basement window. They were in her bedroom going through things on her dresser when she moved in her bed and frightened them off. She was very tiny and they probably hadn't realized there was anyone home.

When she was no longer able to come to attend church I would visit Maude on Fridays and take Holy Communion to her. Those Fridays were a marvellous opportunity for me to get back to reality. I was enormously impressed with Maude's deep spirituality; her life was one steeped in prayer and contemplation. Because of her blindness Maude had memorized huge portions of the liturgy and other prayers as well as poetry. I resolved at that time to make a point of trying to expand and utilize my own memory. Her interests were very diverse. Aside from memorizing Christian prayers and devotions she was committing to her memory portions of the Rubayat of Omar Khayyam and other writings.

A Priest's Tale

Our Friday visits were cherished and I looked forward to them each week. The visits began with the administration of Holy Communion and then expanded into delightful conversation accompanied by sherry or cognac. I don't know how we conversed as we did because her level of sight and hearing was so reduced. She was very astute at asking intelligent questions and then detecting the nods—yeas or nays.

During one of my visits a rather odd and disturbing thing happened. The telephone rang but, of course, she could not hear it. Maude had a telephone primarily to make outgoing calls in case of emergency. I mimed to her and gestured toward the phone. She thought I wanted to make a call and was asking permission.

"Yes, Dear, Go ahead."

I shook my head and mimed with my hand to my ear that the phone was ringing. She said, "Oh, will you answer it, please?" So I did. I should add here that her telephone number had remained unchanged in the directory since her husband's death—for her own protection—and the directory listing was still for "*George Palmer*".

I picked up the receiver and the conversation with a male caller went like this:

"Hello."

"Oh, hello, may I speak to George please?"

"I'm sorry. He's not here."

"Oh. Well, I was talking to him the other day, and I promised I would get back to him."

"Oh, I see. Then you haven't heard the news?"

"What news?"

"Well...George died."

"Oh. I am so sorry. When did he die?"

"In 1964."

[Click.]

After I hung up and somehow managed to explain the conversation to Maude, she shrieked with laughter. She knew full well, as did I, it was someone trying to work a scam through the telephone directory.

✠

There is much to be said about the church's need to offer good, spiritual leadership and decent worship. However, no matter how magnificent the liturgy might be, the church's life needs always to be grounded in the world of the everyday experience of her people. Many decades ago, a St. James' parishioner, May Gutteridge, believed the church could assist some of the men who lived in the neighbourhood with the management of their tiny welfare

A Priest's Tale

cheques. The Rector offered a small room in the basement of the church hall where May and a companion could receive guests for coffee and play checkers.

May was remarkably insightful and dedicated and before too long the operation expanded to provide other services and programmes for the needy. Over a thirty-year period it simply grew and grew, as May herself used to say, "Like Topsy". In the end it became one of the major social service ventures in East Vancouver. In fact, it became a model of this type of agency. Groups from as far away as New Zealand came to study our operation. From the humble beginnings of two women in a dingy basement room it blossomed into a corporation employing over 200 full time workers providing dozens of residential facilities and multi-faceted services to those marginalized by society, especially those who fell through the cracks of the provincial system.

Being part of the team at St. James' had so many facets. The liturgical and musical aspects of the parish were extraordinarily nourishing for the spirit. Balancing that and allowing it all to work was our involvement in social outreach through parish programmes and those of the St. James' Community Service. Sometimes ideas and interests were born from the activities of small groups.

Stephen had been a teacher and had some very fine gifts in that sphere. He conducted a Bible study group, which at one stage focussed on the Old Testament. Out of this group came an amazing development. One year, at the end of the classes, someone asked about the possibility of doing an introduction to Biblical Hebrew. Stephen had studied Hebrew and told them that, of course, anything was possible, but was well aware of the necessary level of commitment. He asked, "And, how many of you would actually participate?" Most of the dozen or so indicated they would like to. He decided to give it a try and the Hebrew study group was advertised in the newsletter and bulletin.

When fall arrived, dates were set and the first class convened. I had never done any Hebrew myself and was also interested. Stephen decided the course would work best if it was of ten weeks duration—meeting each week for two hours. On the first evening a group of 22 people gathered which was a pleasant surprise to all of us. The classes were replete with instruction, handouts, exercises and note taking. By the end of the sessions, we were actually able to attempt some translation of texts from Exodus and Isaiah. The original group of 22 became 12 by the end but that in itself was rather spectacular considering the normal pattern of drop-offs in similar classes.

A Priest's Tale

During the following year, some in the Bible Study group were keen to venture into a little introductory New Testament Greek. I took that on with not a little trepidation. I fashioned the Greek studies after Stephen's Hebrew, as a ten-week, intensive study. By the end of our sessions, we were able to translate bits of the Greek text of St. John's Gospel. One of the interesting things about this exercise was that a couple of local street people came and were involved for a time.

The normal Bible study groups continued during the time of these language seminars. During one term I led a small group of about 8 women who were examining Paul's Epistle to the Romans. I treasured those small intimate groups and there were moments when one had to think very quickly.

We were in the midst of discussing Paul's thoughts and teaching on married life when, out of the blue, one of the women asked, "Father, what do you think about what St. Paul says about homosexuality?"

I was usually quite comfortable when confronted with direct questions. But I have to admit, for a few moments I was not quite sure what to say. Perhaps the pause was not so long as to be noticeable. Many thoughts flashed through my head. How honest can I be about the question? Should I simply say the question is off the topic with regard to this particular text? Did I really wish to sidestep a perfectly good and honest question? I really have no idea where the inspiration came from, but I responded with words similar to these:

"Well, by way of answering your question, let me tell you a story about two different situations I encountered during my parish visiting in a previous parish". (I added that spurious bit about it having happened in another parish simply to prevent them from trying to guess who I might be referring to).

"In my visiting around the parish I happened to encounter two very different couples both within the same week. The first couple lived in a nice home in the suburbs. They had two teenage children, a lake cottage, a boat, two cars, and both had careers and good jobs. I happened to know that their marriage was going sour and that they were extremely unhappy. However, they remained together because of the children, although life was hellish for them. A very sad situation to be sure. The second couple was two elderly men; one in his 70s and the other in his 80s. They lived in a lovely vintage house in a quiet middle class neighbourhood. They welcomed me warmly. We sat on their sundeck and they served coffee and home made apple pie with ice cream. We chatted about their crop of broad beans and raspberries and discussed recent parish news.

One of them had a patio suite on the lower floor and was a 'boarder' as far as the neighbours were concerned. There was an enormous sense of love and respect between them. They had been together for 30 years."

"So, to answer your question, I would simply put to you another question: Which of those two couples would you think was in a viable and healthy relationship?"

No answers or comments were forthcoming; nor were they necessary. We simply got back to the text and continued with our study.

☩

During my last few years at St. James' I began to be deeply concerned about emerging trends in the Church; I don't mean at St. James' itself but in the Anglican Church globally. I had the inexplicable feeling that it was headed for serious problems as I noticed a definite deterioration with respect to its catholicity and order. It was not that any one particular thing had suddenly become a catastrophe but I perceived the gradual letting go of one tradition or discipline after another. For decades I had experienced the little bouts of *Roman Fever*, but it was now for some reason becoming a more serious issue for me. My faith in the Anglican Church had always been rooted in the fact that I believed the church was truly a part of 'catholic' Christendom—grounded in scripture, tradition, and reason—the classical Anglican foundation stones. Now it seemed tradition and reason were being largely abandoned leaving scripture as the sole basis of faith like most other protestant, confessional churches. With things moving in this direction, I felt it was only a matter of time before bishops and jurisdictional authority would be contested. At the time I had not the slightest notion the question of homosexuality would emerge as an issue. Actually, I do not believe it *is* the real issue but rather an excuse for the machinations behind this present turmoil—which, of course, returns me to my original suspicions about authority and power brokering.

I must emphasize that I loved being at St. James'. In my estimation, St. James' was the way the church ought to be everywhere. As much as I loved the parish and all it stood for, I had to concede it was just a tiny island of catholic presence in a Church that was becoming increasingly diluted. My desire from the very beginning of my faith journey was to be in communion and fellowship with the Church universal, not just a small portion of it.

Because of the uncertainty I was experiencing, and because I was financially secure, in 1997 I decided to take early retirement. My departure from the Parish of St.

A Priest's Tale

James' was a bittersweet event for me. The Feast of Corpus Christi was my last day. The evening began with a High Mass at which I was celebrant. I had begun my time at St. James' doing the same thing on Pentecost Sunday almost exactly ten years earlier. The parish came out in large numbers, as did the choir and servers. Mass was followed by a lovely dinner and heart-warming reception. It was a wonderful way to end my ministry. Naturally, I did not burden the good people of the parish with my anxiety about the direction of the Church.

Three

During the years leading up to retirement I had read numerous articles about how one should approach this new phase in life. Some even suggested one might need counselling in order to cope with the radical change. While I have known a few people who did have a rough time coping with the transition, for me it seemed relatively straightforward.

For the space of about a year I did have the feeling I should be doing something productive each day. Initially I felt guilty about all the leisure time and each month when my pension was electronically transferred to my bank account I was inclined to feel it was somehow unearned, even though I was perfectly aware of how pension plans operate. Frequently, when I speak about my retirement, people ask, "But what do you do with all the time?" I often jokingly reply, "Nothing. That's what retirement is all about." Of course, I do go on to explain just what it is I do—and the list of activities continues to grow. Nevertheless, the wonderful thing about retirement is, you don't *have* to do anything if you don't want to.

All the dreams I had about retirement have for the most part fallen into place; puttering with and practising the harpsichord; reading; learning Latin; night school courses in things like Italian, modern Greek and screen writing. As well I have kept busy with photography and cooking. Retirement has been much more stimulating and rich than I had ever expected it to be, and then to my delight, I discovered there were more surprises to come—but more of that in due course.

My mindset during those first months of retirement remained quite naturally church oriented. For a time I was mentally aware of what was happening at St. James' hour-by-hour, throughout each day. It took a while to get the daily routine of St. James's out of my system. I would often find myself thinking; now the Angelus is being rung after Matins; now a small group is having breakfast in the Bishop's Room following Mass. I kept abreast of church news on the internet, but as is customary after retiring from a position, I stayed away from St. James' and had little if any contact with parishioners.

Being retired and considering the numerous doubts I entertained as to the future of the Anglican Church, I felt, insofar as worship was concerned, I was free to roam around and attend services in a number of churches. For a short time, I was tempted and intrigued with the Greek Orthodox Church. However, I soon realized, in spite of the rich and ineffable faith of Eastern Orthodoxy, it is scrupulously ethnic. For one steeped in western culture and music it would have been far too radical a change. My spots could not be altered to such a degree. Over time, and not without deep deliberation and agonizing, I came to realize the Church of Rome was by far closer to the faith and order I had always loved and practised. That is not in any way to say there are not difficulties to be found there as well. However, one must weigh all the factors and decide what is comfortable.

For me, the basic elements I expected in my faith life were; a strong belief in the sacramental life; Christ recognized as truly present in the Eucharist; the fellowship of the Communion of Saints; the catholic creeds and a life rooted in devotion and prayer. This had been the basis of my religious experience since my teenage years. I was in effect not changing my thinking or values, but rather, continuing to live out the faith I had embraced in my youth.

Over the course of a year, I gradually prepared myself for what had to be done. I worshipped in my local Catholic parish church and became a part of that community. I was prepared in the usual way for reception into the church and was treated most kindly by the priest and people there, even sharing in some teaching in the preparation classes by presenting meditations and some commentary on Biblical and historical subjects. I became

A Priest's Tale

involved in the liturgy as a lector and administer of the Sacrament. And it felt wonderful to have that connection again.

My departure from the Anglican Church was without bad feeling or malice, and I recognize that a part of my heart still dwells in Anglicanism. I miss, in particular, the freedom to discuss and debate issues openly without the fear of reprimand or censure.

After my reception into the Church of Rome, I had endless conversations with people who were perplexed and even angry about my decision. I certainly understood their reaction. When you have been a part of a community there is a natural sense of alienation that comes when one takes a different course. For some people there is even perhaps a sense of betrayal. One friend, upon hearing what I had done blurted out, "You traitor."

I had never in my life felt the Anglican and Catholic Churches were enemies, but rather fellow workers in the Lord's Vineyard. I had always considered my church life as living and preaching the catholic, orthodox faith of the historic church. I continue to hold to that faith and am delighted to worship with others who are steeped in the spirituality of sacramental living. The faith of the church embraces inclusiveness even though it is often seen to be blatantly exclusive. Obviously, any church made up of human beings is going to have its problems and issues and one must choose where to find nurturing and community. As one friend put it, in the context of an unrelated discussion, *"...there is a charm and majesty about Venice which one can appreciate in spite of some smelly canals."* Likewise, there is no perfect church—at least on this side of the veil. One needs to discover a place where needs are realized to the greatest degree, but where the associated doctrinal baggage is the least objectionable. For me, as a gay person, the catholic understanding of grace perfecting nature is appropriate over against the protestant inclination toward the depravity of human nature. Church life is much the same as family life. You can love your relatives without necessarily agreeing with them.

✠

Despite my move to the Catholic Church, I remained in touch with Anglican news and was ever fascinated by the many groups that have splintered from the main body of the church and from each other—each one believing that it is the 'True Anglican Church'.

For a while it seemed each week there was a new 'reformed', 'authentic', 'evangelical', 'orthodox', or 'traditional' Anglican Church coming into existence.

A Priest's Tale

Names became more and more complex for these splinter factions as more of them came into being—many of their titles containing most (sometimes all) of those aforementioned adjectives. They are all listed on the 'Anglicans Online' website in the "*Not In The Communion*" category.

This splitting away phenomenon has always appeared to me suspiciously like a way of fast tracking the due process of the Church in order to achieve the purple. Many of these bogus churches have extensive web sites with pictures of their bishops and archbishops, wearing extravagant vestments and frequently enthroned in their cathedrals, which appear to be in rumpus rooms or garages. I have a curious feeling that many of these *churches* only actually exist on the Internet. They frequently list the same three people as the archbishop, dean, principal of the theological seminary, director of vocations, abbots of religious communities, treasurers, and so on. The last time I counted, there were some 78 of these bodies. The number seems to be dropping. Three years ago, I counted 147 groups on that web site. I assume they come into existence in a rush and then expire as quickly.

At one point I caught wind that a priest of the diocese was going to be consecrated a bishop in one of the stranger, local independent churches and I decided to send a spoof e-mail to a few of my friends as a way of expressing my disdain for this splintering tendency. I intentionally made the message as outrageous as possible so that it would be clear I was writing it with tongue in cheek. However, perhaps I underestimated the climate of susceptibility. The joke nearly backfired on me in a couple of instances. This was the e-mail message I sent out:

"Hello Friends.

I want to take this opportunity to let you know that I have been approached by the offices of Pope Shenouda III of the Coptic Church of Egypt and asked if I would consider being consecrated as the Titular Bishop of Mitylene. I am delighted to have been chosen and have happily agreed. My consecration will take place in Cairo's Coptic Orthodox Cathedral of the Holy Prepuce on April 25, 1998. Please remember me in your prayers.

Sincerely, Don"

I sent a copy to the editor of "*Topic*", the Anglican Diocesan newspaper, as I thought she might get a kick out of it. I received an e-mail response almost immediately from another friend in Alberta. It was a little embarrassing because she didn't get the joke. After some congratulatory remarks, she wrote, "And will you be living in Cairo?" Of course, I then had to explain that it was all just a prank.

A Priest's Tale

The other misunderstanding could have been even more embarrassing had a friend who worked in the Synod Office not spotted it. Fr. Matthew Johnson saw a draft copy of *"Topic"*, which was ready to go to print. It contained a congratulatory notice on the occasion of my imminent consecration. He gasped and said, "Oh My God, you have to take that out. It's not true, it's a joke."

By way of chance, when composing the e-mail, I referred to the Acts of the Apostles to find an exotic name from one of Paul's missionary journeys. I chose Mitylene, which sounded rather glamorous to me. It was a city on one of the islands in the Greek Archipelago. It was the name of the "Titular See" to which I would supposedly be consecrated. However, what I had failed to notice was that the now non-existent city had been in ancient times the capital of the Island of Lesbos. I giggled to myself as I mused on the fact that if all this fabrication had actually been true I might now be a Lesbian.

✠

During my lifetime, I have had the good fortune to have many friends and even a few short-term, intimate companions. Most were fairly brief and more often than not I found myself falling into one-sided infatuations where the person in question was not inclined or able to reciprocate. Despite this, I certainly didn't give up on finding "that special person". I must admit, however, once I retired and passed the 60-year mark, the idea of finding my "one true love" did seem much less likely and I was content to enjoy the quiet lifestyle of an elderly gentleman. Little did I know!

Towards the end of my working days, I was introduced to the computer and took the sharp learning curve to make use of it. As so many have, I discovered a whole world opened before me on the internet. A wealth of information was instantly available making my den a virtual library beyond imaginable scope. Articles, news, recipes, books, preaching resources...just about anything one wanted to know about was at one's finger tips. Inevitably, I stumbled upon the personal ad sites, which I found intriguing if only for the sheer number of postings. I never found meeting people that easy in the gay community—especially not being interested in the meat market atmosphere of the clubs and bars. I figured I might as well try a few of the gay personal sites. Although I did correspond with a few nice men, nothing really ever came of those contacts. Quite often my age was an immediate disqualifier. But, generally, there were more 'mind games' being played than actual interest in meeting in person.

Then one evening while browsing I discovered a website called "*The Apollo Network*"—a site dedicated to matching up younger and older men. I was delighted and somewhat surprised to discover how many younger men were interested in mature gentlemen. Not many were necessarily to my taste. But I was greatly reassured just by the fact that they were out there. It became my habit to scan through the section of younger-looking-for-older, occasionally even sending off a 'hello' to those that sounded interesting, all of which amounted to very little until one auspicious evening.

Scanning through the postings on *Apollo* in May of 2001, I came across one that caught my eye. It was a very brief paragraph posted by a young man in Virginia. He stated he was interested in e-mail pen pals. He didn't have a photo posted, but his concluding remark arrested my attention, *"A picture of thee gets a picture of me."* Perhaps it was the use of that one word, 'thee', that tweaked my imagination.

The next day, being unable to get the thought of it out of my head, I returned to the site and found the posting again. It contained his e-mail address. So, I thought, What the heck. He sounds very nice and there's surely no harm in sending a friendly 'hello' from far away. I sent a short message and attached a discrete photograph of myself.

I received a reply the following day, which had the promised *picture of me* attached. His name was Devan Burnett and he sounded extremely nice in his email. I opened the attached photograph thinking, '*As nice as he sounds he is probably not going to be my cup of tea*'—only to discover I was very mistaken. He was *precisely* my cup of tea.

We began to exchange e-mails and started the process of getting to know more about each other. We exchanged more photographs, and they got better as we went. Now, I didn't mean *that*! The additional pictures simply gave a more all-round, comprehensive view—after all, one photo captures only a split second. I was delighted that this twenty-four year old man and I had so much in common and shared such similar world views.

It wasn't too long before I felt I should tell Devan more about myself, particularly that I was a priest. I decided, instead of trying to explain it, I would simply send him a picture of myself in my *work clothes*. I have discovered that this revelation can have the effect of either being an enticement or being completely off-putting. Fortunately, Devan was intrigued. He wrote back and explained while he himself was not religious, the idea of seducing a supposedly unattainable, older priest—the quintessential 'forbidden fruit'—had always intrigued him.

Telephone conversations began soon thereafter, along with the daily e-mails shooting back and forth. Even though we had been communicating for only a short time, I was feeling I may have found what I had always dreamed about. Devan was a little more cautious. He had already made a move across the U.S. to pursue a relationship which had not worked out as he expected and was rightly wary about our situation.

However, after a few months of e-mails and telephone conversations, we both knew we were feeling quite in-tune and began thinking of making arrangements to meet and see where things would go. It was more convenient for Devan to make the trip to Vancouver, so in August of 2001 he flew up for a visit.

Meeting him at the airport was both nerve wracking and extremely exciting. I knew what he looked like, of course. But when he came through the international gate I discovered Devan's real-life smile and bright eyes much more than the pictures could do justice. We spent a delightful nine days together, getting to know each other. We rented a car so I could show Devan a bit of Vancouver, and the surrounding area, revisiting some of the places I had not been to for years. By the end of the holiday we both knew our feelings for each other were serious.

Despite my intense pleasure at having found such a wonderful young man—one who seemed to feel just as I did and was as interested in me as I was in him—I continued to have one lingering doubt. Not about our relationship but what would come of it. When I actually stopped and thought about it, I realized I was an old man, or getting there. I wondered about the ethics of entangling this young man in my life when the odds were that my life span would be so much shorter than his. More than just that, though that in and of itself was troubling enough to think about, I also had to contend with the idea of being a burden on Devan in my old age. What if I went doddery, as my own mother showed signs of doing? Would I want Devan to feel obligated to look after me?

When I voiced these concerns to Devan, he laughed a bit and said something to the effect that, "But who's to say you'll outlive me? I could step in front of a bus tomorrow, and that would be that. Besides, if you weren't the age you are, I don't know that we would even be together since I wouldn't have been attracted to you in the first place."

I must admit the idea of someone finding me attractive at my age is still something of a novelty. Even considering Devan and I met on a website devoted to

A Priest's Tale

linking up younger and older men, I still feel it a bit surreal to have this lovely young man telling me he thinks I am attractive.

In the end, my conscience was assuaged. I had been mostly concerned that Devan might not realize what he could be getting into. His response told me that he did.

Not all was as idyllic as it may sound, however. Life has a way of balancing out great joy with setbacks. Just when the age question seemed to have been settled, I received news that sent me back into a dither. In late 2001, during an examination, my doctor suggested that the gradual enlargement of my prostate, so common in older men, might be indicative of cancer. He suggested I have a biopsy done to verify whether there was a problem or not. I had dreaded the thought of this procedure when he had mentioned it in the past as I had heard horror stories about it.

An appointment was made with a specialist at the General Hospital and I went in for the biopsy. I undressed and was directed to lie on an examination table in the foetal position. The doctor and nurse performing the procedure were trying to be chatty and casual, which I appreciated. I was, however, in a state of high anxiety although I probably didn't show it. The probe they inserted produced an ultrasound image that allowed the doctor to see the prostate on a screen. It also incorporated a needle to freeze the gland and to take samples. The doctor gave me a running commentary about what he was doing and what he could see on the monitor. It was a nice pastoral touch. Once he had mapped the prostate and decided just where he would gather samples he told me that he would be 'freezing' the prostate. My anxiety level was rising higher and higher. Then he announced, "Now, Donald, you're going to feel a little prick." Under other circumstances I would not have been able to let such a remark go by without offering a wry retort, but I was so distraught I just let it go. I did feel it. And then, five or ten minutes later, when it had numbed, the doctor began taking samples. The device sounded a bit like a staple gun each time he 'fired' it—but there was no pain. Mercifully, it was soon over.

Once the diagnosis had been returned to my surgeon, I met with him to discuss the results. I truly believed he was going to say it was benign and everything was fine. Not so. The surgeon was very much to the point. He told me that it was malignant, but in the very early stages and had not likely metastasized. He then explained to me the three possible treatments; there was a lengthy programme of daily radiation sessions; the insertion of small radio-active 'seeds' into the prostate which gradually emit cancer killing rays; and surgery to remove the prostate gland.

A Priest's Tale

I asked him which treatment he would recommend. He said he could offer no recommendations, as it was my decision to make, which I understood. However, he did respond to my question by saying, "Well, I *am* a surgeon."

As I made my way home on the bus, I was in a daze. I have always had the good fortune to have excellent health so this unexpected diagnosis rather stunned me. I now fully understand why the "C" word strikes such dread in the heart.

I met with my personal physician to seek his advice and discovered his inclination was definitely for the surgery option. Naturally, I also discussed my situation with Devan in some depth. As our relationship was in its infancy, I told him he might want to rethink our getting involved. I would completely understand if he wanted to back out of this before it went any further. Devan told me later he did consider my suggestion. The conclusion he came to, however, was what he told me at the time. He felt our love was a reality; it was not something from which he could simply walk away. He wanted to be with me, come what may. We would get through it together.

In the end I decided on the surgery to remove the prostate. I wanted the cancer out of my body and could not see going through any of the other, more exhaustive treatments, only to run the risk of the cancer recurring. A surgery date was set for March of 2002.

Some time after the surgery, when everything had been resolved, I was having lunch with a friend, who I had not seen for several years. In order to catch him up on current news, I found myself explaining all the details that led up to the surgery. He commented that it must have been very difficult to decide which treatment to go with. I responded, "Actually, it was relatively easy because in the end it all seemed to boil down to one fundamental question…Do you want to live or have an erection?"

On New Year's Eve, 2001, during Devan's second visit, we privately pledged ourselves to each other with simple, spontaneous vows and the exchange of silver bands. We both felt absolutely sure of our feelings for each other and our intention that this was an absolute commitment. That feeling has grown and developed with time.

As my surgery date drew near, I knew that Devan might think of flying to Vancouver to be with me. I have always felt awkward about visiting people in the hospital simply because the patient, who is already uncomfortable and under stress, must entertain visitors. As a parish priest I always tried to make hospital appearances brief and to the point. For myself, I didn't want visitors at all—except for one friend who would act as a go between to relay news to my family and friends. I requested that people simply leave me to my discomfort and disarray for the few days I would be in hospital. I explained this to Devan in a phone call. He sounded unconvinced and apparently considered coming anyway, but decided to heed my wishes in the end. The thought was very sweet. I knew I would be a mess, and miserable and there was nothing that he could do to help beyond what he was doing already—sending me his love. As things played out, the surgery was routine and completely successful. I recovered very quickly scarcely believing that they had me up walking in the evening of the day of the surgery. Two months after the operation I flew to Washington to visit Devan.

For all that Devan and I felt quite certain in our feelings, we weren't sure quite how to proceed. The border between us added to the complications of either of us moving. We ran through the gamut of choices available, even considering the possibility of Devan moving to Bellingham or Seattle so we would at least be closer.

During his visit to Vancouver in February of 2004, we rented a car to go and look at some of these cross-border places. We began by driving down to Point Roberts to see what it was like as it is very close to Vancouver. Point Roberts is a bit of an anomaly. It is a small point of land that dips below the 49th parallel and although connected to

Canada, it is part of the United States. We had lunch there but found it to be rather dead at that time of year as it is essentially a summer holiday destination and retirement community. We found one restaurant open and enjoyed a nice lunch.

I was somewhat shocked when we came to the Canadian border crossing on our way back. The customs officer was perfunctory to the point of being rude. After examining our respective Canadian and American passports he asked about the purpose of our visit to Point Roberts and Devan, who was driving, told him we had gone there for lunch. The agent then asked point blank what the nature of our relationship was. I was taken aback by the question, then equally flabbergasted when Devan quite casually said, "We're lovers." The agent didn't utter another word; he simply gave back our passports and raised the barrier. As we drove off, Devan looked at me with a twinkle in his eye said, "Well, never ask a question if you don't really want to know the answer."

We went on to explore Bellingham with the thought of going on to Seattle that evening. But, as we drove around, we were both mentally assessing the possibilities. I was actually a little depressed by the situation and I felt Devan also had something on his mind. We drove in silence for a time and then stopped for a coffee and began talking. Amazingly, we were both thinking the same thing—living just across the border would be even worse than living on opposite coasts. So near and yet so far. We intuitively knew it would not be a satisfactory panacea to our dilemma. We needed to work out how we could live together and sensed somehow things would fall into place. We stayed over in Bellingham that night, and returned to Vancouver the next day with lighter hearts, despite not having solved the problem of the distance and the border.

Two years after our first 'marriage', again on a New Year's Eve, Devan and I were legally married in the presence of a small group of friends in our apartment in a beautiful, brief ceremony conducted by a marriage commissioner. In the summer of 2003, British Columbia had recognized same-sex unions and all was done according to BC law. Champagne and a buffet-style dinner followed the ceremony. It was a warm and pleasant occasion. Truth be told, Devan and I didn't see this 'legal' marriage as more important or meaningful than the private one we had shared two years before. We did, however, realize it might be helpful to have on record for purposes of immigration, the details of which we were still working through.

We had already begun the process of putting together an application so that Devan could emigrate as a "conjugal partner". Early on in our relationship, after much debate and looking at all of the factors involved, it was obvious that Devan would have fewer difficulties making the move. One of the main factors was money; I had my two pensions, one from the Church and the other from the Canadian Government, and while I would continue to receive them if I made a move to the States, their dollar amount would be lessened due to the currency exchange. To keep any possible obstacles to a minimum, Devan said he would like to move to Vancouver, if we could just figure out the best plan. It all took longer than we would have liked. However, the slow process, coupled with numerous visits, let us feel absolutely certain of our love and a commitment to a life together.

When we heard the news in early 2004 that the Canadian government would treat immigration matters for same-sex marriages the same as those of heterosexual couples, Devan and I felt a wonderful sense or relief. We would have to do much less in the way of 'proving' we truly were a couple and had a bona fide relationship. For Devan and me, this pronouncement by the Canadian government simplified our immigration application immensely. We followed the format for the immigration of a spouse with rigorous attention to the requirements. The process of getting all required data together and assembling it into the application package took about six months. We knew it would likely be another six or seven months before it would be processed.

Just before Christmas, 2004, we were delighted to be informed the application was approved, as we had plans to spend three weeks in Italy in February and March, and Devan needed time to make moving arrangements. In April of 2005 Devan finally arrived in Vancouver.

✠

As I muse on all of this drama and the way it unfolded, my mind drifts back to a summer in the 80s when I first read a hilarious book called "*Someday I'll Find You*" by Father Harry Williams of the Community of the Resurrection. It was apparently the first autobiography of a gay priest who was willing to bare his soul and share the deepest secrets concerning his sexuality. It seems he had lived a rather active sexual life when he was a chaplain and tutor at Cambridge, but later bewailed the fact that he had never found that one special person—hence, the book's title. How daring I thought, as I read his book, and how thoroughly I identified with his plight. It was fascinating and immensely liberating to read his words and to see how he had synthesized his views a propos the spirit and the flesh. He expressed precisely what my own thoughts were on so many points. I quote here just a snippet from "*Some Day I'll Find You*".

"I slept with several men, in each case fairly regularly. They were all of them friends. Cynics, of course, will smile, but I have seldom felt more like thanking God than when having sex. In bed I used to praise Him there and then for the joy I was receiving and giving."

I feel incredibly blessed, because I also had believed that I would never meet my soul mate—and now my fondest yearning has become a reality.

Friends sometimes ask Devan and me how we deal with religious views and how they bear upon our relationship. As I indicated earlier, Devan is non-religious but certainly not anti-religious. However, he does approach organized religion with some scepticism and I completely understand that. We most often find ourselves in complete agreement over ethical and spiritual matters. The simple answer I give to friends who ask about Devan's religious views is that we respect one another's perspective and have no desire to alter one another's beliefs. We think amazingly alike with regard to ethical and moral issues and find ourselves similarly dismayed by the damage religious views of all sorts seem to cause when they are taken to extremes.

A Priest's Tale

To say that meeting Devan has changed my life would be something of an understatement. I cannot think of words adequate to describe how rich and complete my life is now. My fears from so many years ago—that I would never know love; never be able to have a deep and committed relationship—have been proven quite wrong. In our meeting and the development of our relationship, I have found what I always dreamed of, but what society seemed to deny. Because we are two men, our love is no less worthwhile, moral, or true. Those who would pit God against such love, who would attempt to belittle it by arbitrarily invoking questions of what is natural or unnatural, have, in my opinion, either never known love themselves, or do not in fact know God. Perhaps because of the environment in which they grew up they have been conditioned to cringe in fear at the supposed threat homosexuality poses to masculinity. This is no longer defensible.

✠

Over the ten years since my retirement I have watched with a heavy heart as the Anglican Church, which I loved so dearly, became mired in what appears to be a dispute over homosexuality. I say *appears* because it is my opinion that this is a rather weak hook upon which to hang the present crisis. Observing the unfolding events, I have found myself turning over in my mind the multiple facets of this debate to no satisfactory conclusion. Intellectually, it seems on the surface to be a simple matter of biblical interpretation and application. However, that does not adequately explain the depth of emotion and reaction. The more I think about it, the more I rack my brain to try and grasp what is really going on. I cannot help but wonder whether the surface issues might possibly be masking deeper concerns. My mind swims with a host of knotty questions.

The complexity of the debate about sexuality and scripture make it impossible to approach it adequately in these brief pages, especially as I have chosen to use a lighter approach to the subject. I will, nonetheless, spin out a few of my prime concerns and observations, which I think are more germane to the situation.

Most Christians would allow there is a wide range of approaches to biblical interpretation—all the way from the view that scripture is God's dictated, inerrant word, to that of perceiving the bible merely as allegorical poetry. Many would undoubtedly agree that the Bible contains—at least for the most part—immense spiritual wisdom.

The very concept of the Bible as the "Word of God" has regrettably been taken and fashioned into a peculiar

A Priest's Tale

form of idolatry. It is gilt-edged paper and leather bound and is held up by televangelists as the symbol of what Christianity is all about. It is frequently the prop used to represent absolute truth and righteousness. It is treated as though it were the incontrovertible basis of everything. If one dares to question translation techniques or biblical interpretation one dares to question God Herself. Perhaps many of the current problems in the church are related to a mistaken concept of what the bible really is. Without a doubt, the bible contains, for the most part, the word of God in the sense that it represents the way in which hundreds of writers and scholars down through the ages have encountered God.

Holy Scripture contains a vast amount of spiritual material, which over time has refined and developed. Some of the earliest writings—dating from the period when Israel was a tiny tribal nation besieged by enemies on all sides—depict God as vengeful and cruel. It is from this period one encounters the endless lists of taboos and purity laws like those found in Leviticus, which separate Israel from what was perceived to be the excess and error of her neighbours. As Judaism developed and advanced in spirituality we find the beautiful, spiritual writings of people like Isaiah, Jeremiah and Hosea who saw God as the essence of justice and mercy.

As Christians we are obliged to be extremely careful how we interpret the scriptures—particularly in the way we present their contents and expectations to others. It is not acceptable to choose only the tiny bits that happen to appeal to our own needs and tastes and ride them to death. Those who focus upon the few references to homosexuality in the Holiness Code of Leviticus seem to have no problem with the plethora of other taboos—often punishable by death—such as working on the Sabbath, adultery, or violating the complex dietary laws.

With reference to the current debate about sexuality, there is a curious point that crops up from time to time in scripture, which I believe is never adequately addressed. It concerns *eunuchs* and who or what they were considered to be in biblical times. Many people perhaps think of them as men who had been emasculated (or castrated) in order that they might be harmless supervisors of the many harems that were common in the Middle East. I believe that *eunuch* was really just another word for a gay man, who would naturally be an appropriate and non-threatening person to manage a harem even if he were capable of sexual activity. Jesus on one occasion made a rather intriguing remark to the effect that some men are "born eunuchs". The particular text, found in Matthew's Gospel, 19:12, is rarely, if ever, examined or discussed. The interesting thing about this remark is that Jesus seems to be completely non-judgmental about such people. The encounter between Philip and the Ethiopian eunuch on the road to Gaza in the Acts of the Apostles is also framed as a non-judgmental relationship—in fact, an encounter of great interest to Philip, which culminates in the baptism of the man.

Another incident of a similar nature, where Jesus is welcoming and apparently quite worldly wise, is the incident which results in the healing of the Roman Centurion's slave, found in chapter 7 of Luke's Gospel. Now, although this text was often used a hundred years ago to justify slavery, there is yet another peculiar twist contained in it. The Centurion sends a messenger to Jesus asking if he will heal his 'slave'—*doulos* in the Greek. In the course of the discussion about it, the Centurion also refers to this slave as his 'boy'—*pais*. Now, pais in Greek can mean simply *son* or *boy*, but can also mean *servant* and even *male lover*, much like the term boy can be used in the same way in English. But, there is yet a further usage in this text. The Centurion refers to his boy as his *entimos pais*—precious or well-loved servant. Knowing the Roman world as well as Jesus did, he would certainly have been aware that this person was the beloved of the Centurion and Jesus accepts that, even going to the extent of stating that he *"had not found such faithfulness, not even in Israel"*.

And so we begin to see that the word of God in scripture is not just so obvious and simple—like a user's manual—as some would like it to be, but that it requires searching and language and much agonizing.

For the Church, the Word of God is Christ—the Logos—who has existed from the beginning of time—the creative Principle of the universe—the source of all Being. John's Gospel begins with a statement of this truth: "In the beginning was the Word..." John is consciously and tenaciously echoing the opening words of the beautiful creation saga in Genesis. The Christos has unfortunately been, in the minds of many people, almost eclipsed by Jesus the man and this idea is reinforced by excessive stress on the notion of having a 'personal relationship with Jesus'. The phrase is usually spoken as though it might be from scripture but it is unbiblical; neither word nor the compound phrase is found in the Bible. To have such a relationship is without a doubt a laudable thing, but if that overshadows the cosmic Christ, then it leads directly to a lopsided and egocentric faith, which is focused on *me* to the exclusion of the fullness and universality of Being.

How risky it is to stress the one over and against the other or, even thornier, to attempt to separate Christ's natures—a problem, which repeatedly plagued the Church during its first few centuries. Aside from the apparent dangers of presenting a distorted view of the Person of Christ is the danger of equating Him with a written page—Jesus the Logos is not a book—nor is He a *word* on a printed page. In John's First Epistle we find this statement: *"The Word, (Logos), who is life........has been made visible to us".*

On one occasion during a clergy gathering the subject of the centrality of scripture arose in the small discussion group I was with and in light of the issues I have just expressed I made the flippant comment, "I think the Bible is highly overrated!" That was certainly a show-stopper to put it mildly!

Fundamentalists regularly go berserk with people like me when we declare that God just might wish to draw *all* people to Himself—a very biblical sentiment—and that quite likely Hindus and Buddhists and others may at some point come to recognize that in spite of different names and ideas, that one Logos is indeed the universal Source of all things. Of course, as soon as one makes such a statement there are immediately several loud objections. One is, "Then what is the point of going to all this bother if in the long run it doesn't make any difference?" and another is the assertion—allegedly based on scripture—that at the moment of one's death everything is sealed for the rest of eternity. The first objection, of course, would be the subject matter of another book. The second objection is a notion, which evangelicals cherish and which in all probability harks back to reformation concerns about purgatory. I am fully aware that the word *purgatory* carries enormously potent negative baggage for many people—but surely the concept, when stripped away from the historic abuses, makes reasonable sense considering that millions of people have never heard of the Christ.

In the First Letter of Peter we find an interesting reference to Jesus "*preaching to those in prison*" after his death, which seems to me completely in accord with the concept of a loving Creator whose desire it is to draw all people to Himself.

✠

In discussions about same-sex attractions many Christians base their views on a scant four or five biblical quotes, some of which are not actually applicable to the question of homosexuality. Certain Christians of all traditions seem to have developed a propensity for choosing favorite issues—verses—and riding them to death. When preaching what the Bible says regarding homosexuality rarely does one ever hear mention of the beautiful saga of David and Jonathan found in chapters 18, 19 and 20 of the First Book of Samuel or the story of Ruth and Naomi to say nothing of the erotic Song of Songs. The Song of Songs—some versions call it the *Song of Solomon*—is customarily understood to be allegorical, the lover and the beloved representing the covenant relationship between God and Israel or perhaps even Christ and the Church. There is possibly some credence in adhering to the view that it is simply a love epic depicting the erotic passion between two infatuated teenage lovers. One could logically claim that this episode speaks of the Bible's attitude and teaching about sexual attraction.

Biblical commentators also tend to spiritualize the David and Jonathan story, which does make perfectly good sense because real love *is* spiritual. But to attempt to regulate how that love should manifest itself in practical terms is hugely presumptuous. The account in Samuel, which spans two full chapters, is obviously not a cavalier remark casually inserted. It, like the Song of Songs, is one of the most beautiful love stories found in any literature and can scarcely be mistaken for anything less than that.

It seems that those who are obsessed with what gay people do in their intimate moments must believe that heterosexual sex is simple, straightforward, and pleasing to God regardless of whether it is insensitive, unsatisfying or even brutal. This view of sex seems light years removed from the thinking and attitudes of Jesus and tends to reinforce my suspicion that what many Christians feel uncomfortable with is not simply homosexuality, but sexuality itself.

I am reminded of an episode in Jesus' life when someone questioned him about the Holiness Code and what it has to say concerning unclean foods. Jesus' reply was, *"It is not what enters into the mouth that defiles the man, but what proceeds out of the mouth; this defiles the man."* I am inclined to think His advice might equally apply to sexual association. It matters not so much who you love, but rather, the quality and sincerity of that love.

In spite of the fact that sex and love are so very complex and spring from the depths of desire and passion many seem to prefer to pretend that sex is always vanilla—man on top, woman on bottom and only for the purpose of having children. It reveals an astonishing naiveté about things sexual. As I pen these words an image keeps flashing through my brain. It is a scene from the 1981 movie, *Quest for Fire*, about the lives of Neanderthal cave dwellers. It was an amusing but slightly silly film dealing with early man's experimentation with language, tools, and with keeping the ever so important fire going. The scene that keeps haunting me is one in which—during a grunting and snorting sex scene employing the doggy position—the man discovers that he can also do it while facing his partner thus making it a more intimate exercise. What struck me so funny was that in the middle of the frenzied love making the actor seemed to look up at the camera with an expression of delight and astonishment at his discovery. The comic aspect of his facial expression wasn't because he believed this was a personal achievement, but rather that it was a first time ever for mankind.

People often do not allow themselves to contemplate that in sexuality there might be variety, nor what the boundaries of that variety might be. For me this raises a number of questions. What actually do heterosexual couples get up to in bed? Are they *really* always intent on conceiving children when they engage in sex? And if children are the sole goal of the act, would it not be considered sinful or inappropriate for a man to kiss or nibble a nipple? Would it be permitted that a wife might pleasure her husband by orally stimulating him? Or vice versa? Sex is surely an immensely complex and creative activity!

Statistics, produced by a 2002 *National Survey of Family Growth (NSFG)* study, revealed that from a sample of 12,000 men and women aged 15-44, 34 % of men and 30% of women reported engaging in anal sex at least once. By my rough reckoning that would seem to indicate that three or four times more straight people engage in anal sex than the total number of gay people there are in the entire population. Why are the neo-puritans not concerned about this? I have never heard mention of this trend in sermons nor read about it in church literature; perhaps this indicates that those who are so eager to point out the sins of gays have a pathetic understanding of sexuality even in the hetero world.

The obsession with sex amongst conservative Christians has actually created some extremely serious and unfortunate problems not only for homosexual but for heterosexual youth; particularly, the disapproval of—or even banning—the use of condoms. This has undoubtedly had an impact upon the spread of sexually transmitted diseases and particularly HIV and AIDS in ways the churches never envisaged. By insisting total abstinence is the only avenue for young people there has emerged a frightening complication. Obviously, no sex at all would solve the dilemmas of unwanted pregnancies and sexually transmitted diseases, but while the thought is laudable it is at the same time pathetically naive. It has proven to be a myopic approach to the issue and has failed to recognize the primeval reality of human desire. There has been such a fixation on vaginal sex and saving oneself for marriage that all other sexual activities are, by many young people, not even considered to be sex at all. This approach has in fact led to the increased incidence of oral and anal sex among young people, and, *ipso facto*, sexually transmitted diseases. This is an appallingly high price to pay for refusing to grapple with the complex questions of sexual morality and ethics.

Another critical issue with respect to attitudes about sexual morality centres on how people conceptualize the world in which we live. Christians often develop the notion that they possess a kind of direct access to God or have special insights into the Bible and therefore know what is best for everyone else. The idea of special knowledge, or *gnosis*, is not a new concept. The Church contended with it in the first centuries of its life. Those who followed this path were known as Gnostics and they followed a deviant form of Christian doctrine, which was rooted in several heretical errors. Perhaps the most insidious notion of Gnosticism is the idea that the universe has a dualistic nature—the spiritual which is good and the material which is evil.

For one who held Gnostic beliefs the object in life was to escape from the polluted, physical world and to be joined with God in pure spirit. This rejection of the physical is certainly not restricted to the Gnostics as the concept has surfaced in nearly every religion and generation. The early Church fought against the idea because it contradicted the Biblical teaching that God was Author of all creation and had declared it to be good. God has placed humans in a healthy symbiotic relationship within the created order. For followers of Christ, gnosticism was an affront to the theology of the Incarnation—that in Christ there is a union of the Divine and the human; the spirit and the flesh; Creator and created. To debase the physical world was to dishonour God's creation, and therefore to dishonour God.

One would think, considering all the atrocities in the world, the issue of homosexuality and spirituality would be a small hurdle to skip over on our way to working toward the resolution of more pressing problems. Unfortunately, it seems to have become the central focus for many Christians; a molehill that has been turned into a mountain and which I suspect is being used as a tool by certain leaders to maintain control over the minds and support of their followers.

I feel remarkably uncomfortable with people who read the Bible and consider it to be a rigid rulebook—especially one to be imposed upon others. Jesus taught that rather than being stifled by inflexible regulations imposed by a human system, one could live by the spirit or essence of the law and thus be faithful to God. Jesus' approach is naturally the one that I find enlightening.

I would find it extremely difficult to imagine God, the Creator of the galaxies and nebulae—who breathed life into the multitude of creatures on our planet—being preoccupied with the minutiae of human body parts, drives and affections. Would not God be more concerned with how we care for His Creation—the respect we give to Her world—and our concern for one another—*how* we love rather than *who* we love?

✠

Looking back on my life, I realize I have been tremendously blessed. I have had good friends; travelled more than I ever thought I would; and experienced always a rich and fulfilling communion with God. For me, the physical and the spiritual come together in everyday life; in the majesty of the world around; the wonder of existence and the profundity of an infinite universe; and in the knowledge that all we see around us is wrought by God.

The path of my life, through all its twisting and turning, has led me to a place were I am overwhelmingly happy. I have not the slightest doubt that love, whatever its manifestation, is praise to God and that God's underlying purpose in Creation is to fashion a dominion infused with love. Negativity, pessimism, hatred, destructive thinking…all are sheer darkness to God's light.

There is one final question that surely must linger in the minds of readers and which I should, in all fairness, address. "*So where does he worship now?*" The simple answer is I have tended more and more to focus spirituality on my private and personal devotion; the daily recitation of the Divine Office, which I have done continuously for 50 years, and as I am a priest, in offering almost every day, the Sacrifice of the Mass. I am discovering that I have more and more an affinity with hermits like St. Antony of Egypt and the Desert Fathers; although I am hardly any longer a hermit—but perhaps a 'catholic solitary'—focussing my attention on offering worship to God in solitude but in the company of the Communion of Saints. Being completely honest, I must confess that after many years of officiating at worship I often find it irritating and tedious to attend most church services. Perhaps it is an occupational hazard but most public worship tends to have more of a negative affect on me than a positive one because I find I am too critical and it tends to generate uncharitable feelings in me.

It may seem curious that I, as a 21st century priest, am revisiting the custom and style of those earliest days of the Church's life and offering a solitary ministry of intercessory prayer for the concerns of the Church and the world. My faith lies overwhelmingly in the love and self-giving of the Christ rather than in a vengeful God who would consign to eternal torment anyone who dares to question His infinite love.

Having come through a period of torment and confusion myself, I have now been able to set the ostensibly contradictory and bewildering pieces of life's puzzle together into a larger more comprehensive picture. This is in no way a declaration that I feel happy or satisfied with things as they are in the church or that there will ever be a time when mankind does not wrestle with the issues of the spirit over and against the flesh.

Each person needs to find, to some degree or other, his or her way through the quagmire of moral ideologies native to religion and sexuality. Such things ultimately belong to the realm of conscience and we must each accept and live with our decisions. The tension between the two will undoubtedly continue to be a perplexing challenge. Nonetheless: love, compassion and reason continue to offer hope that perhaps eventually we will all find peace—accepting our physicality and being nourished by the Spirit. I am comfortable with my universe—my integrity remains intact—and in my life and my love, I am at peace with the God of all Creation.

FIN

Made in the USA